SEVEN CHURCHES, SEVEN SEALS, ONE KING

David Perry

Bloomington, IN 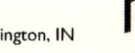 Milton Keynes, UK

AuthorHouse™
1663 Liberty Drive, Suite 200
Bloomington, IN 47403
www.authorhouse.com
Phone: 1-800-839-8640

AuthorHouse™ UK Ltd.
500 Avebury Boulevard
Central Milton Keynes, MK9 2BE
www.authorhouse.co.uk
Phone: 08001974150

© *2006 David Perry. All rights reserved.*

No part of this book may be reproduced, stored in a retrieval system, or transmitted by any means without the written permission of the author.

First published by AuthorHouse 10/16/2006

ISBN: 1-4259-4986-X (sc)

Printed in the United States of America
Bloomington, Indiana

This book is printed on acid-free paper.

Printed, Visual and Electronic Uses:
Up to 1,000 verses (inclusive) from assorted books of the New King James Version® (NKJV™) may be quoted in printed (e.g., book, brochure, magazine, newsletter, lesson outline), visual (e.g., film, videotape), and electronic forms (e.g., computer diskette, CD-ROM, on-line) without written permission, as long as the verses quoted do not amount to 50% of a complete book of the Bible and do not make up 50% or more of the total text of the work in which they are quoted.

All scripture quotations, unless otherwise indicated, are taken from the New King James Version®. Copyright © 1982 by Thomas Nelson, Inc. Used by permission. All rights reserved.

Scripture quotations taken from the HOLY BIBLE, NEW INTERNATIONAL VERSION. Copyright © 1973, 1978, 1984 by International Bible Society. Used by permission.

ACKNOWLEDGMENTS

I would like to gratefully acknowledge the encouragement of my wife Pamela in the starting and finishing of this book, without her initial endorsement I doubt if I would have carried on. This also applies to our friend Hilary Bacon, who also gave me great encouragement, as well as my pastor at the Ripley Elim Pentecostal Church, Phillip Yendle. All three read the script and gave me valuable help and advice. In this respect my wife's and Phillip's hard work was particularly appreciated. I would also like to thank my friend Quentin Dearle for the photograph on the back cover.

DEDICATION

This book is dedicated to my wife Pamela, my eldest son Matthew, to Heather my daughter and her husband Kudzie and Ashley my grandson, also to my youngest son Daniel

Table of Contents

PREFACE XIII

INTRODUCTION XV

CHAPTER 1
THE KEYS TO UNDERSTANDING REVELATION 1

CHAPTER 2
EPHESUS- THE CHURCH
IN DANGER OF REMOVAL 15

CHAPTER 3
SMYRNA – THE BITTER SWEET CHURCH 31

CHAPTER 4
PERGAMOS- CHURCH WITH AN IRON GRIP 47

CHAPTER 5
THYATIRA-CHURCH WITH A DARK SIDE 59

CHAPTER 6
SARDIS- CHURCH IN THE GRAVE 71

CHAPTER 7
PHILADELPHIA- CHURCH WITH AN OPEN DOOR 81

CHAPTER 8
LAODICEA- CHURCH WITH JESUS OUTSIDE 97

CHAPTER 9
IN THE SPIRIT IN HEAVEN 113

CHAPTER 10
THE SCROLL AND THE LITTLE LAMB 129

CHAPTER 11
THE OPENING OF THE SIX SEALS 147

CHAPTER 12
THE SEALED SERVANTS
AND THE SECURE SAINTS 157

CHAPTER 13
THE SEVENTH SEAL 169

CHAPTER 14
NO MORE DELAY 183

CHAPTER 15
THE TEMPLE AND THE TWO WITNESSES 189

CHAPTER 16
THE SEVENTH TRUMPET 199

CHAPTER 17
THE WOMAN AND THE DRAGON 205

CHAPTER 18
THE BEASTLY DUO 215

CHAPTER 19
THE SEALED SING WHILE
ANGELS PREACH AND REAP 229

CHAPTER 20
PRELUDE TO THE END 241

CHAPTER 21
THE SEVEN LAST PLAUGES 251

CHAPTER 22
MYSTERY, BABYLON THE GREAT 259

CHAPTER 23
THE FALL OF THAT GREAT CITY BABYLON.............267

CHAPTER 24
THE KING IS COMING..271

CHAPTER 25
THE DEVIL'S DOWNFALL 281

CHAPTER 26
THE FINAL JUDGMENT 289

CHAPTER 27
ALL THINGS NEW 295

CHAPTER 28
"BEHOLD I AM COMING QUICKLY 313

PREFACE

Over many years the book of Revelation has puzzled, fascinated and inspired me, as I have read it and preached from it.

It was the favorite topic of discussion in Bible studies at the church fellowship that I grew up in and over the years I have read a number of popular books based on this wonderful revelation of Jesus Christ.

So why write another book, surely all that can be written has been written? Firstly I would beg to differ and as you read this book with an open heart and mind you could see the book of Revelation in a different light or maybe see it in some light for the first time. Secondly I have had the desire in my heart to write such a book for many years, and I feel it is right to take on this task now. Thirdly as there have been a number of novels written in recent years on the end times, I think that a book based on the facts as they are recorded in this last book of the Bible is in order. I would not pretend to be a clever writer, but what I have written has been written prayerfully and with a desire to promote a knowledge of the Bible.

INTRODUCTION

My approach to this study of the Revelation is first and foremost to avoid any speculation. If those who enjoy some speculation are disappointed so be it.

It is also an approach which sees the Revelation not as being a chronological revelation of future events, but more of a revelation of Jesus Christ and the unfolding of the past, present and future as the Lamb opens the seven seals. To find out more read the book.

I shall be interpreting the text literally where appropriate and in conjunction with scripture from other books of the Bible where there is an obvious connection. Those who will want to classify this book as representing a pre or post tribulation rapture or pre or post millennial return of Jesus Christ, will have difficulties because I believe these terms are to a large extent artificial and merely serve to label different interpretations of scripture. I shall not be arguing for or against any particular interpretation but seeking only to present the plain meaning of the text.

CHAPTER 1

THE KEYS TO UNDERSTANDING REVELATION

When it comes to understanding the book of Revelation it is rather like reading a map. On a map there are symbols that represent various things such as churches, railway lines, level crossings and where battles have been fought. At the bottom of the map there will be a key showing these symbols and saying what they represent. The book of the Revelation is just like that. Many of the symbols and signs are explained in the book or in other books of the Bible. Revelation means to unveil and reveal something that was hidden, so it should be an open book. That being the case why is it that so many Christians find it to be one of the most difficult books to understand? Added to that there is the issue of how we are to interpret this most wonderful of books. Is it to be interpreted historically or is it for the most part speaking of future events? What are we to take literally and what is allegorical? In answer to these questions I would refer you to the opening five words, "THE REVELATION OF JESUS CHRIST."(all emphasis in capitals mine) This is the first of seven key statements John makes in the first three verses, which I am calling the first section of Revelation Ch.1. These statements help us to understand this book, and appreciate that from start to finish it is the final revelation of Jesus Christ.

That this is so is borne out by the words of Jesus in Ch.22v16 "I, Jesus, have sent My angel to testify to you these things in the churches. I am the Root and the Offspring of David, the Bright and Morning Star." Right to the end of the book Jesus is being revealed. There are many other characters in the book and numerous events, but none of them have any relevance other than to reveal Jesus Christ. He is the theme of the book and consequently the entire book was written as a revelation of Jesus Christ for the seven churches in Asia and for the church today. In this regard it is interesting to note that many times God the Father is revealed as the One who sits on the throne, and the Holy Spirit as seven lamps burning before the throne, or as the seven eyes and seven horns that John sees on the Lamb. This is in contrast to the detailed revelation of the character and work of Jesus.

The second of those seven statements is that Jesus sent his angel to show to his servant's THINGS THAT MUST SHORTLY, OR QUICKLEY, TAKE PLACE. Jesus sent and showed John by signs and indicators what those things were. In a similar way Jesus indicated and showed the way in which he would die, by stating that he would be "lifted up from the earth and would draw all men unto him" (John Ch.12v32)

We are all interested in the future and the people of John's day were no different. Here in this book is a revelation of things that will take place quickly. This statement in Revelation Ch.1v1 is mirrored by the words of Ch.22v6-7; then he said to me, "These words are faithful and true. And the Lord God of the holy prophets sent His angel to show His servants the things that must shortly take place. Behold, I am coming quickly! Blessed is he who keeps the words of the prophecy of this book." Only God can accurately predict the future and only God has the power to ultimately shape the future. The great overarching prediction of the Revelation is that Jesus is coming quickly to complete the work of salvation which the apostle Peter says is ready to be revealed in the last time. (1Peter Ch.1v5) All the things that are to take place in the future are working towards the twin goals of perfected and completed salvation for those whose names are written in the book of life, and most importantly the reign of the One who sits on the throne and of the Lamb forever and ever.

Thirdly John states that he bore witness to the WORD OF GOD. Because the truths of this book were revealed to John pictorially he says that he bore witness to them. He heard but he also saw, what a double impact that must have had on him. No other prophet saw the things that John saw. Isaiah saw the Lord high and lifted up and his train filled the temple. Ezekiel saw the throne of God and the wheels within wheels. Daniel saw the Ancient of Days and one like the Son of Man. But John saw the throne and the Lamb, the four living creatures, the twenty four elders, the redeemed and the millions of angels. He also saw the rise and the fall of the kingdom of Babylon and its rulers, with the ultimate demise of Satan and death and Hades in the lake of fire. This is the Word of God and a fitting end to what was begun by God in the beginning when He created the heavens and the earth.

Fourthly it is the TESTIMONY OF JESUS CHRIST. Are you a person who has the utmost respect for what Jesus Christ has to say about the future? Have you an ever growing reverence for the things that he says, do you tremble at his word? Then you will want to read the revelation of Him as it comes from his own lips and come to a greater appreciation of who He is and what He has done, is going to do and is doing. In Revelation Ch.19v9-10 John writes, "And he said to me, "These are the true sayings of God." And I fell at his feet to worship him. But he said to me, "See that you do not do that! I am your fellow servant, and of your brethren who have the testimony of Jesus. Worship God! For the testimony of Jesus is the spirit of prophecy." Prophecy throughout scripture testifies to Jesus, and especially in this book, it is the very essence of what prophecy is about.

Satan hates this testimony of Jesus. This becomes clear when we read what John saw and recorded in Ch12v17. "And the dragon was enraged with the woman, and he went to make war with the rest of her offspring, who keep the commandments of God and have the testimony of Jesus Christ." Satan hates it because it speaks of his eternal defeat in the heavens and on the earth and the only place left for him is the lake of fire. "And they will be tormented day and night forever and ever." (Revelation Ch.20v10) This book of Revelation is his death warrant written in stone and it cannot be annulled.

The remaining three statements indicate how important this book is for us because quite simply you will be BLESSED IF YOU READ IT, HEAR IT AND KEEP ITS WORDS.. The blessing of the Lord makes rich and adds no sorrow with it said the wise man Solomon. The scripture is full of promises of blessing for those who fulfill the conditions attached to the blessing, and this is but one more of them. When did you last read the Revelation of Jesus Christ all the way through? Not just the well known verses or chapters, but all of it.

Further happiness is found by those who hear the words of this prophecy. There is a deeper meaning here than just hearing audibly the words written by John although it is always good to hear the Word of God read well. For at the end of all the messages to the seven churches Jesus says "He that has an ear to hear let him hear what the Spirit says to the churches." He that has an ear to hear is also a key phrase in Matthew, Mark and Luke's gospels in connection with the parables that Jesus told. When the disciples asked Jesus, "Why do you speak to them in parables?" Jesus replied, "Because it has been given to you to know the mysteries of the kingdom of heaven, but to them it has not been given." (Matthew Ch.13v10-11) Then later in v.16 Jesus says, "But blessed are your eyes for they see, and your ears for they hear." Indeed blessed are those whose hearts are opened by the Holy Spirit to hear the message of this prophecy and discern its message.

Happiness not only comes to the one who reads and hears but also keeps those things that are written. This is emphasised again at the end of the Revelation in Ch.22v9 where the angel says to John "For I am your fellow servant, and of your brethren the prophets, and of those who keep the words of this book." Again v.7 "Blessed is he who keeps the words of the prophecy of this book." To keep these words is to observe them and obey their commands and heed their exhortations. I believe that Jesus has emphasised the importance of the whole of this prophecy for the seven churches and also its importance for the church throughout the centuries, to this present day, by restating at the end of revelation the things he says right at the very beginning.

Because this is the testimony of Jesus to the churches, and to us today, revealing His majesty and humanity in such vivid and graphic terms Satan has tried his best to keep Christians from reading and understanding this revelation of their Saviour and King. Controversy has raged and many have reached the conclusion that it is all too difficult and best left alone, or left to the theologians. But I hope that in these seven statements you will find there are seven important reasons to read and study this book and not just leave it to the professionals. My hope is that you will begin to see the wood for the trees and see Jesus everywhere as we progress through the rest of the book.

John now formally addresses himself to the seven churches in Asia, and this is the beginning of the second section of chapter one. It should always be borne in mind that John wrote initially to these seven and the message he sends and the revelations he has was for them, see Ch.22v16, where Jesus says that this testimony of Himself is for the churches. We need to fully appreciate that what John wrote is of historical significance, as with all scripture its truths are timeless. Those with spiritual antennae have always been blessed, challenged, comforted and reassured throughout the centuries by reading Revelation.

Grace and peace from the eternal God, the Holy Spirit and from Jesus Christ is the theme of the next few verses. Grace from beginning to the end is what comes from Him who is, He always was the one who is, and always will be the one who is. There is immeasurable grace expressed throughout the time that the awesome power of God is being revealed in the judgments to come. That power is displayed in a measured way, until the very end, as God even in judgment seeks to bring men to repentance. This is seen firstly in the messages to the churches as judgment must begin in the house of God, and also as

God reaches out to the world as judgment after judgment rains down in the last days. Only at the bitter end when the vials of the wrath of God are poured out does grace stand aside from an unrepentant world. But then grace is never withdrawn from those whose names are written in the lamb's book of life.

The Holy Spirit is seen by John as the seven Spirits of God before the throne. He is further described as seven lamps of fire burning before the throne. (Revelation Ch.4v5) Incidentally, the Holy Spirit is not to be confused with the seven lampstands that John saw which represent the seven churches. (Revelation Ch.1v12 and v20). A casual reading of revelation may lead one to think that the Holy Spirit does not play a very significant role in the drama, but that would be far from the truth.

It was while John was on the island of Patmos for the Word of God and the testimony of Jesus Christ, that he was in the Spirit on the Lord's day and as they say, the rest is history. The messages to the seven churches were revealed to him, giving us today a valuable insight into the prevailing condition of those churches. The churches were exhorted to hear what the Spirit was saying to them.

Again we read in Revelation Ch.4v2, "Immediately I was in the Spirit; and behold, a throne set in heaven, and One sat on the throne." Further revelations are then given to John from Heaven's perspective and it becomes clear that all authority in heaven and earth belongs to Jesus. The Holy Spirit is seen again in Revelation Ch.5v6 as John looks and sees the Lamb with seven horns and seven eyes. John is told that these too represent the Holy Spirit sent out into all the earth. More about that later!

The Holy Spirit is heard to agree with a benediction pronounced from heaven on those who die in the Lord from now on, and he adds "That they may rest from their labours, and their works follow them. (Revelation Ch.14v13)

In Revelation Ch.17v3 John is conveyed away in the Spirit to see the vision of the judgment of the great whore who sits upon many waters.

In Revelation Ch.21v10 John is again carried away in the Spirit this time to see not a whore, but a pure, holy and beautiful bride, the Lamb's wife. The Holy Spirit is active throughout, but consistent with the teaching of the rest of the New Testament He is submitted to Christ and serves to reveal Him and the truths of God's word. This is why He is not seen to be prominent in this book, as Jesus Christ is.

Grace and peace also come from the Lord Jesus Christ. It is always worth noting that God the Father, Son and Holy Spirit are always perfectly at one even though they have different functions. We can see from what John has written so far that God the Father gave the Son Jesus Christ this revelation which John sees and hears while in the Spirit.

From Revelation Ch.1v5 to the end of v6 there are seven revelations of Jesus Christ which give us further keys to understanding. The first of these is that He is the FAITHFUL WITNESS, or faithful martyr. Be faithful unto death is the exhortation to the church in Smyrna, from the one who was faithful unto death himself. Faithful to the truth of who He was, the Son of God sent from the Father, and the King whose kingdom was not of this world. Paul when writing to Timothy said "Fight the good fight of faith, lay hold on eternal life, to which you were also called and have confessed the good confession in the presence of many witnesses. I urge you in the sight of God who gives life to all things, and before Christ Jesus who witnessed the good confession before Pilate."(1Timothy Ch.6v12-13) That good confession is found in John Ch.18v36-37 and relates how Jesus faithfully witnessed to the truth in the face of an impending cruel death.

Jesus is also the FIRSTBORN FROM THE DEAD. Firstborn refers to his pre-eminent position. This is clearly demonstrated by Paul the apostle in his epistle to the Colossians Ch.1v18 where Jesus is described as the firstborn from the dead, that in all things he might have the pre-eminence. He is the prototype of those who will rise from the dead never to die again. This is the theme Paul takes up when he says "But now Christ is risen from the dead, and has become the firstfruits of those who have fallen asleep." Then he also goes on to say, "But each one in his own order: Christ the firstfruits, afterward those who are Christ's at his coming. Then comes the end, when He delivers the kingdom to God the Father."(1Corinthians Ch.15v20 & v23-24) In all things Christ has the pre-eminence.

Not only is Jesus the faithful witness, and the firstborn from the dead but also RULER OVER THE KINGS OF THE EARTH. Notice the progression, first the faithful martyr then risen glorified Lord then ruler of the kings of the earth. Jesus last words to the disciples on earth as recorded in Mathew's gospel are, "All authority has been given to Me in heaven and on earth."(Matthew Ch.28v18) Authority referring to the right to rule and exercise power and this He does over the kings of the earth. There is no doubt that this has been the case since Jesus rose from the dead and ascended to the Fathers right hand and is well portrayed in Revelation Ch.5 where He is seen as the Lamb in the midst of the throne worthy to take the scroll and open it's seals. From the opening of the first seal to the sixth seal we see the exercise of Christ's authority on earth and in heaven. When the sixth seal is opened the end of all those who oppose the rule of Christ is in view, the sky recedes as a scroll and is rolled up and men are hiding in terror from the face of Him who sits on the throne and from the Lamb. This is the first of three references in Revelation to the coming of Christ to reign and put down all other authority and power. But then when the seventh seal is opened there is silence in heaven for what seemed to John to be about half an hour. No more commands from the throne, thunder and lightning, trumpet blasts or even praise from the heavenly host. How awesome was that silence, for all things are now accomplished, the Lord God omnipotent reigns. The old order of things has passed away and all of heaven takes time to catch it's breath and take in the new reality.

Next Jesus is revealed as the one who HAS LOVED US, or better rendered as, HE WHO LOVES US. In this book of great tribulation, trials, and judgments poured out, both in the church where the apostle Peter said judgment must begin and in the world, Jesus is seen as the one who loves us. He holds the angels of the seven churches in his right hand, He is standing in the midst of the churches, He leads his flock to fountains of living water, there are so many expressions here of his love. But that love is sometimes expressed in rebuke as with the message to the church of Laodicea. Jesus also said to the church at Philadelphia that he would humble their enemies before them, that they might know that he loves them.

But the greatest proof of his love is in the shedding of his precious blood. To him who loved us and WASHED US FROM OUR SIN IN HIS OWN BLOOD. Here we see the motivation behind the giving of his life blood, he loves us. John's gospel Ch.13v1 says, "having loved His own who were in the world, He loved them to the end." Jesus was willing to serve the disciples as a slave as he washed their feet and dried them with a towel. Matthew records Jesus as saying that "The Son of Man did not come to be served but to serve and give his life as a ransom for many." (Matthew Ch.20v28)

There is further proof of his love for us; He has MADE US KINGS also. Paul wrote to the Ephesians to say that not only have we been raised to life in Christ, but also in Christ, raised to sit with him in the heavenly places. This is a theme encountered many times, that we reign with Christ now and in the future and forever. What an encouragement to the persecuted, to the faltering and erring saints of the churches John wrote to, and also to us today. To the church in Thyatira the message was "And he who overcomes, and keeps My works to the end, to him I will give power over the nations." To the Laodiceans the message was "To him who overcomes I will grant to sit with Me on My throne." Revelation Ch.22v3 says that "His servants will serve Him," and verse 5 says, "And they shall reign forever and ever."

Not only kings but also PRIESTS TO HIS GOD AND FATHER, priests who offer up to God acceptable offerings of praise and prayer and even the offering of their bodies as living sacrifices, and their lives, as they loved not their lives unto death. John himself is an example of one such priest as he is on the island of Patmos. No doubt in prayer, praise and worship on the Lord's Day the Spirit comes upon him, a man whose life is on the altar of sacrifice. Other examples are from Revelation Ch.5, the four living creatures and twenty four elders fall before the Lamb giving praise to the Lamb who has been found worthy to open the seals. They sing a song which says that he has redeemed them from all peoples and nations and made them kings and priests. Notice also that the living creatures and elders, who represent the redeemed around the throne, also have golden bowls full of incense which are the prayers of the saints being offered to God. The twenty four elders also give thanks to God, "Because You have taken Your great power and reigned." (Revelation Ch.11v17) This is the second reference to the coming of Jesus at the sounding of the seventh trumpet, "to Him be glory and dominion forever and ever. Amen."(Revelation Ch.1v6)

"Behold, He is coming with clouds."(Revelation Ch.1v7) This is the grand climax of the Revelation and from then on also for the redeemed, whose names are written in the book of life, because there are rewards to enjoy. The glorious second coming of Christ is implicit in all the messages to the churches as the pattern of every message is for Jesus to compliment his people on the things that are good in their lives, rebuke them for the things that need correcting and reveal to them the rewards that await those who are obedient. The unity of the whole of Revelation is clearly seen in this as everyone is exhorted to be an overcomer and it is overcomers that are portrayed in the chapters that follow the messages to the churches. In the messages to the churches there are struggles against Satan, against Jezebel, against false teaching, against those who say they are Jews and are not and against materialism, and these themes also are portrayed on a grander scale in the rest of the book.

Every eye shall see him, even those who pierced him, and all the tribes of the earth shall mourn because of him even so Amen. What a wonderful event this will be for the saints but how awful for those with the mark of the beast, Satan's seal. Revelation Ch.14v11 says, "And the smoke of their torment ascends forever and ever; and they have no rest day or night, who worship the beast and his image, and whoever receives the mark of his name."

John finishes this section by repeating the statement made in verse four concerning God being the beginning and the end, who is, who was and who is to come, the Almighty. Contained in these four verses are all the major themes of the rest of the book, all the major themes of the gospel are there from beginning to end, the alpha and omega of truth for time and eternity.

So far we have covered the first two sections of chapter one. From verse nine to the end is the third section which as we have come to expect gives further insight into the wonderful person of Jesus Christ, and more keys to understanding the whole book. John was on Patmos for the Word of God and the testimony of Jesus Christ, he had been faithful to the truth already revealed to him, truth clearly taught in his epistles, and is a companion in tribulation because of his courageous stand for that truth. So God gives him more revelation as he is in the Spirit on the Lord's Day. If we want more revelation on the written word we need to be faithful to what we have already received and live in the light of it. For John says he is a companion also in the kingdom and patience of Jesus Christ. Like John, let Christ rule over you and patiently live out his word that has been revealed to you.

It must have caught John by surprise to hear such a loud sound behind him, the sound as of a trumpet. But the sound was not uncertain but a voice said "I am the Alpha and Omega."(Revelation Ch.1v11) John is told to write in a book what he sees and send it to the seven churches in Asia. What he sees is primarily what he records from chapter four onwards, but before then he must see Jesus in the midst of the churches, and give each one a special message. Most of the churches would have mixed feelings about the other churches knowing how Jesus sees them. How would you or your church feel about others knowing what Jesus thinks of your life or your church? What would He have to say about your works?

When John turned around he saw seven golden lampstands, and in (v20) they are said to represent the seven churches. Matthew Ch.5v14 records Jesus as saying to his disciples, "You are the light of the world," and in v16, "Let your light so shine before men, that they may see your good works and glorify your Father in heaven." Significantly it is the works of the seven churches that come under the spotlight as to every one Jesus says, "I know your works." Jesus is in the midst of the candlesticks and is described as one like the Son of Man. Jesus is among His people, intimately involved with them and knows the secrets of their hearts and lives, He knows their works! John sees Jesus as He is going to be revealed to the churches, the majestic, powerful, glorious king of heaven, no other apostle reveals Jesus in such splendour, it must have eclipsed even the sight John saw on the mount of transfiguration. This is Jesus as He is, not as He was on earth, where human flesh veiled his glory. He had emptied himself and humbled himself but now God has highly exalted Him and His glory is no longer veiled. This is the vision of Jesus that the church needs to see today, in character He has always been the same but His role is now of One who sits at the Fathers right hand until His enemies are made His footstool. In Paul's second epistle to the Corinthians he writes that we no longer know Christ according to the flesh, as He died once for sin and having completed the work of putting away sin forever, He no longer has any use for the likeness of sinful flesh. So we need to have constantly in our minds this vision of our Almighty Saviour for this is who He is today. Not naked upon the cross but clothed down to His feet and a golden band around his chest. No more crowned with thorns with His head and hair clotted with blood, but glistening as white as snow with hair pure white. Eyes that are no longer expressing untold pain and sorrow, but now as flames of fire like all powerful laser beams. With feet not seen as weary and soiled with the dust and grime of this earth, needing to be washed, but like fine brass refined in the fire without any weakness arising from impurity, no feet of clay mixed with iron here. His voice was as the rushing sound of water over rapids, or at the meeting of two mighty rivers as the waters converge, what a contrast to the One who at His trial before Pilate was silent, not seeking to defend himself. He stood before His accusers on earth as they cried out, "Crucify Him" but one day those who pierced Him will mourn because of Him, even so Amen. His right hand is not seen here as pierced but powerful holding the seven stars, which are the seven angels or messengers to the churches. A lethal weapon, the sharp two edged sword comes from His mouth, He no more cries out in agony "Why have you forsaken me" or "I thirst." This sword He uses to fight against His enemies and will eventually strike the nations and He will then rule them with a rod of iron. With this same sword He slays the armies of the beast and false prophet who come to fight against Him. (Revelation Ch.19v15-21) Isaiah speaking of his sufferings prophesied that his face would be marred more than any mans (Isaiah Ch.52v14), yet now we see His countenance like the sun shinning in its strength. The effect of seeing this vision of Jesus was to render John lifeless as he fell at the feet of the ruler of the kings of the earth, the firstborn from the dead and the faithful witness. Revelation is not primarily about the suffering servant but about the Lamb who rules from the midst of the throne, this glorious Son of Man who is coming to earth to reign.

As with section two of this first chapter, this one also ends with "I am the first and the last." But it is important to notice that in section two the One who sits on the throne is in view, namely God the Father. However in the final section it is clear that Jesus Christ is being designated as the one who is the first and the last. Consistent with the rest of the Bible Jesus is clearly portrayed as being one with the Father in essence concerning His eternal being. The first and the last is the same one who lives, who was dead, and is alive forever more. He is Jesus who was crucified but was raised never to die again. John adds that He has the keys of Hades and of death. This clearly means that He has authority over this deadly duo, having won the victory over them, through death. We read in the epistle to the Hebrews that through death He destroyed, or annulled, him who had the power of death, that is the devil. (Hebrews Ch.2v14). In Revelation Ch.6v7 the forth seal is opened by the Lamb and after this a rider on a pale horse is commanded by one of the four living creatures to "Come." John reveals that the rider is Death and he is followed by Hades, just as a victorious Roman general would parade his captives behind him in chains. This portrays Death and Hades as under the authority of the one in the midst of the throne. Power was given to them from the one who has all power in heaven and on earth. This revelation of Jesus is not one that many in the world would be prepared to accept, or even many in the church, but let me remind you that as we saw right at the beginning this is a revelation of THE WORD OF GOD, and THE TESTIMONY OF JESUS CHRIST, and is faithful and true. We would do well to keep it and keep to it. Finally Death and Hades are cast into the lake of fire, neither of them are able to resist the power of the Lamb. (Revelation Ch.20v14)

The time that John was 'in the Spirit' must have seemed to him like an eternity, just as the times when we are lost in wonder, love and praise seem to us as if time did not exist. During that time an indelible imprint was made on John's mind and heart by the things that he saw. As we read through what he wrote it is clear that he remembers what he saw in such meticulous detail, both in the vision of Jesus and in the things that he saw when he is told to "Come up here, and I will show you things that must take place after this."(Revelation Ch.4v1) All of these things that John was told to write were for the churches in Asia, that they might be overcomers and not be ashamed at His coming, but walk with Him in white. The church of Jesus Christ today desperately needs the message of the visions John saw for as the old song says "We ain't going to heaven in a rocking chair," and there are difficult and dangerous times ahead for which the church today should be preparing themselves.

CHAPTER 2

EPHESUS- THE CHURCH IN DANGER OF REMOVAL

What could be more important for any church than to have Jesus located in their midst. To have Jesus walking with and talking with the church, guiding, correcting, feeding and communing with the church, nothing is more important. A church does not need to be wealthy, although God is not opposed to wealth, He created it and owns it all anyway. A church does not need to keep up with the latest fashions, whether scientifically, theologically or philosophically, but it does need to have agapae love toward God and be faithful to Him and to his word. A church does not need the best musicians, or have great orators as its preachers, but it does need to have ears to hear what the Spirit is saying to the churches. If Jesus is not in the central place, the place of pre-eminence in a church, the Holy Spirit will depart. He is the one who manifests the power of God in a church and serves as the agent for God's message to a church, if He is not speaking and acting then that church has become spiritually dead and has been removed from its place near to the presence of Jesus.

This was the situation facing the Ephesian church. Remember where you have fallen from and repent or be removed. Revelation Ch.2v5 says, "or else I will come to you quickly and remove your lampstand from its place, unless you repent" Jesus is revealed to the Ephesian church as the one who holds the seven stars in His right hand and walks in the midst of the seven golden lampstands, because that is the specific revelation of Him that they needed to see to help them see the danger they were in. Why was such a drastic measure needed? Why would Jesus want to remove from himself a church that had so much to commend it? It is a sobering thought that a church into which Jesus had invested so much, had fallen so far. We shall now consider some of the history of this church, as compared with the other six churches in Asia we know so much more about it.

The first mention of Ephesus in scripture is in Acts Ch18v19. It says that Paul the apostle came to Ephesus and went to the synagogue and reasoned with the Jews. This was consistent with Paul's usual practice, after all the Jews had a grounding in the scriptures, and they needed to see Jesus in the scriptures and accept Him as their Messiah, Lord and saviour. That is still the need of the church today, to see Jesus in the scriptures and acknowledge His Lordship. It is especially so in regards to the book of Revelation because it is thought of as a book full of strange beasts, difficult conundrums and impossible to understand symbols. The Jews of Ephesus asked Paul to stay, but he needed to go to Jerusalem, and promised to return.

In the meantime a Jew by the name of Apollos from Alexandria came to Ephesus. He is described as an eloquent man with a powerful ministry in teaching and preaching. He had the ability to speak with passion but also with accuracy as he expounded the scriptures, something which is not always found in preachers. However v25 of Acts Ch.18 tells us that he only knew of the baptism of John the Baptist. It should be noted that that did not stop the Holy Spirit from blessing the ministry that he had. We should not think of ourselves as being excluded from ministry because we are not fully equipped, because actually no one is fully equipped, we just need to be committed to using what God has given us. Aquila and Priscilla, who were traveling companions of Paul, heard him preaching in the synagogue, took him aside and explained to him more from the scriptures concerning Jesus. Soon after he went to Achaia to preach and there he strongly refuted the arguments of the Jews in public showing from the scriptures that Jesus is the Christ. This is the purpose of scripture, to reveal Jesus as the Christ, the Saviour of the world. No doubt Aquila and Priscilla shared with the believers there what they knew of Jesus.

Paul did return to Ephesus and finding some disciples asked them, "Did you receive the Holy Spirit when you believed?" The small band of believers at Ephesus were about to make more progress because amazingly they were unaware of the existence of the Holy Spirit! How relevant that question still is today. "Did you receive the Holy Spirit when you believed?" Upon further enquiry he found that they had been baptised with John's baptism for the repentance of sin. Paul explained to them that John was the forerunner for Jesus and his ministry was to point everyone to Jesus. They were then willing to be baptised into the name of the Lord Jesus recognising him as the Lamb of God who takes away the sins of the world and receiving Him as Lord. Paul then laid his hands on them and the Holy Spirit came upon them and they spoke with other tongues and prophesied. It is possible that these men, about twelve in number, became the nucleus if not the elders of the church at Ephesus.

For three months Paul again went to the synagogue and reasoned with the Jews from the scriptures speaking with boldness of the things concerning the kingdom of God. More of the Jews believed and joined those of the Way, this is what Christians were called at that time, but some of the Jews did not respond to the word of God and became hard and did not believe. These Jews began to malign and denigrate Paul and the disciples. When this happened Paul wisely stopped going to the synagogue and took the disciples to the school of Tyranus and taught them there. This continued for two years, and all of Asia heard the word of the Lord Jesus, both Jews and Greeks. It is highly likely that the other churches in Asia came into being at this time. Asia being what we now know as modern Turkey

God worked unusual miracles by the hand of Paul. Handkerchiefs and aprons that had been in physical contact with Paul were laid on sick folk and they were healed and delivered from demons. This in turn led to attempts by some Jewish exorcists to cast out demons with disastrous results as far as they were concerned. They were attacked by a man who was demonized and had to run for their lives battered and bruised. That the demons recognised Jesus and Paul, and their authority over them became known throughout the region and this only served to magnify the name of the Lord in the eyes of both the Jews and the Greeks. This also had the effect of convincing the believers that they should sever all their connections with magic, witchcraft and the occult. They confessed their sin and brought all the hidden things of darkness out into the open and even publicly burned all the books that they had previously treasured connected with their former evil practices. A lot of what their contemporaries would have considered to be of great value went up in smoke, Hallelujah! They burned their bridges and the Word of God grew mightily and prevailed. How wonderful it would be if that happened in the church today, fires would be alight all around the world. So they had begun fervently desiring to have a pure, holy and undefiled love for the Lord Jesus and His word and Jesus had placed their candle stick close to himself and walked among them. I wonder, what things does your church or you yourself need to burn in order for Jesus to be happy in your midst. What idols need to be reduced to ashes in order that we can have pure agapae love for the Lord?

Then came the backlash from Satan and those who were part of his kingdom of darkness. There had been a steady decline in the industry that had grown out of the worship of the goddess Diana of the Ephesians. The silversmiths who made their living from selling idols of Diana were suffering particularly badly because so many had turned from idols to serve the Living God. The church today would likewise suffer persecution at the hands of those who profit from sin and misery, if only the church were having the impact on our world that it had in Paul's day, would that it were so. Demetrius, a prominent man in the guild of silversmiths, caused an uproar in Ephesus and brought some of the leaders of the church to the public theatre in order to do them harm. Crowds gathered shouting "great is the goddess Diana of the Ephesians," and this continued for several hours, most people who were there doing the shouting actually were unaware of the purpose of the commotion. People just joined in following the crowd just doing what every one else was doing. Much like if someone was standing in the street just staring up into the sky at nothing, very soon others would come and join in not really knowing what they were looking for or looking at. It was left to the town clerk to bring some order to the situation by informing everyone that the proceedings were out of order and illegal and if the silversmiths had a proper case against the church then they should bring it to the courts for judgment, and with those words he dismissed the crowd. When things had quietened down Paul took his leave of the church and went to Macedonia.

Some time later Paul called for the elders of the church to meet with him at Miletus. He recounted to them the struggles he had endured when the church was in its infancy, especially how the Jewish opposition had plotted against him, whose hearts had become hardened towards the gospel. He said that he had kept nothing back from them that would help them, but both in public meetings and privately going from house to house he had taught them personally, preaching repentance toward God and faith towards the Lord Jesus. Paul is not afraid to share his heart with them and bare his soul when he explains that he is bound for Jerusalem where he knows that trouble is in store for him, and that they will see him no more. But he confidently asserted that he would not be held to account for neglecting to preach the whole counsel of God. He finally solemnly charges them to take heed to themselves and to the flock they had been made responsible for by the Holy Spirit. They were to be shepherds of the flock, because the flock were precious in the sight of God, for they had been purchased with the blood of Jesus. Paul is very specific in his next statement, which was a prophetic warning to them of coming dangers. He said "I know this, that savage wolves will come seeking to devour the flock of God you are responsible for." Also, the flock would not only be attacked from outside, but also from their own ranks men would rise up in order to mislead and bring confusion and division. He told them to be watchful and remember all the warnings he have given them while he was with them and that now he was warning them for the last time face to face.

Paul commends them to God and the Word of His grace, and recalls how he has been an example to them, living out the gospel he preached, summing up with the words of the Lord Jesus, "It is more blessed to give than to receive."(Acts Ch.20v35) Then they all knelt in prayer, accompanied by a great deal of weeping because they would see Paul's face no more, they then accompanied him to the ship that would take him on his way.

Some years later Paul was in prison and was inspired by the Holy Spirit to write an epistle to the Ephesian church. It is possible that the other churches in Asia also read the epistle as he addresses it to the saints in Ephesus and the faithful in Christ Jesus. There, in his epistle is the written record of all that Paul had taught them verbally while there with them for several years, as he said, the whole counsel of God. In his epistle Paul writes that God has made known to us the mystery of His will which He purposed in Himself, that finally, in the fullness of the times He might gather together all things in Christ, all things that are in heaven and earth. That is the message in a nutshell of the Revelation given to John, but here expressed by Paul. (Ephesians Ch.1v9-10) Paul has further mysteries to unveil, that Jews and Gentiles in Christ are one new man and in Christ Jesus they are reconciled to each other and to God. For now they both have access to God by one Spirit and are fellow citizens with the saints and members of God's household. They are built on the foundation of the apostles and prophets, Jesus as we would expect is the chief cornerstone. This theme is also taken up by John at the end of Revelation, and is seen as John describes the New Jerusalem coming out of heaven from God. Paul continues by writing that he preaches the gospel so that everyone might see this mystery of the church being worked out, so that the many aspects of the wisdom of God might be made known by the church to the higher unseen powers in the heavenly places. The church in Ephesus was part of this grand scheme of God which is one of His eternal purposes accomplished through Jesus Christ our Lord.

Paul's concern for the Ephesians is expressed as he exhorts them not to be children tossed about by every wind of doctrine nor to be tricked by cunning men who would seek to plot their spiritual downfall. But, instead, to speak the truth in love, agapae love, and grow up in all things into Him who is the Head even Christ. He also warns them not to let any one deceive them by empty words, because those who practice unrighteousness will not inherit the kingdom of God. Finally he exhorts them to be strong in the Lord and in the power of His might and to put on the full armour of God that they may be able to stand against the devil's schemes.

This short potted history of the church in Ephesus, and its dealings mainly with Paul, shows what a privileged beginning they had. Paul had done some planting, Appolos some watering, but God had given the increase. They were, no doubt, in the apostle's prayers continually and were carried as part of what Paul once described as the burden of all the churches. The Lord had invested so much in this church and it would be reasonable for the Lord to expect a good return, for from those who are given much, much is expected in return.

Jesus who walked among them knew their works and their labour. The implied meaning of the word labour is that of hard work, of hammering away at something, really grafting hard. They were not a church that did anything half heartedly but put their backs into all that they did. This trait is very likely to have been born in them from the example of Paul. At his last meeting with the elders of the church at Miletus Paul, at one point, said to them that he had not coveted anyone's silver or anything belonging to them, but had worked hard to meet his own needs and the needs of those who were with him in ministry. What an amazing example he set, and what an example for Christian leaders today. Not that he was not entitled to receive support from them but he lived by the message that he preached. He wanted to demonstrate to this young church that in every way that by working they should support the weak, so they became a church with a strong work ethic, believing the words of the Lord Jesus "That it is more blessed to give than to receive."(Acts Ch.20v35)

As well as this the Lord commends them not just for working hard but also for continuing to work hard. They had not given up when times were hard, they had not grown weary in well doing. They had put on the armour of God and stood their ground. The elders who taught the flock of God worked hard to equip the saints in order for them to minister according to the grace that God had given to each one. The church, as a consequence, was being built up and was growing up. They had worked hard in prayer for all the saints, and remembered their beloved Paul as he had asked them to, they had been watchful and persevered.

The Lord tells them that He is pleased that they do not tolerate those who are evil, sadly that is not something the Lord could say of every church, then or now! Right from the start they had a clear understanding of the need to depart from evil as well as to do good. How it grieves the heart of the Lord Jesus that so many of those who name His name have divorced these two things, they are keen to do some good in the world but not so keen to depart from evil. But there was no such problem in the church at Ephesus. As the Lord demonstrated His power over the powers of darkness the church came clean with regards to all those things from their past that had any association with magic, witchcraft and the occult. They gathered together all their books on magic and the like and had one great big bonfire till the whole lot were reduced to ashes. They had set their sights on the pathway of holiness and of those things that please the Lord. Their resolve is bolstered by the apostle's patience with them as he stays several years to establish them in the faith. Later as he writes to them not to grieve the Holy Spirit, by behaviour that was unbecoming to those who name the name of the Lord. "For you once were darkness," he wrote, "but now you are light in the Lord. Walk as children of light."(Ephesians Ch.5v8) For light has no fellowship with darkness. Therefore have no fellowship with the unfruitful works of darkness but rather expose them to the light, Paul commanded, and this they had done and continued to do.

The Lord commends them also for having tested those who said they were apostles and found them out to be liars. They had taken to heart the prophetic words of the Paul, when he met with the elders at Miletus. They remembered that he had said to them that grievous wolves would come, and they did. That there would be enemies from within and there were. Paul knew that he would have to put in writing the things he had taught them verbally so they could take their stand on the written word of God. All things are to be tested by the benchmark of the written word of God. It is the rule by which Christians should measure morality and spirituality, unfortunately much of what passes for these things today does not measure up to what the scriptures teach. All so called new revelations, new age teachings, old philosophies dressed up in modern clothes, all these should be tested in the test tube of scripture. Teachings that claim divine origin, or other ways to God or some promises of a better future in another life, all these need to be tested by the Word of God as we have it in the sixty six books of the Bible. John is very blunt in his assessment of those who teach contrary to the scriptures, he says that they are liars.

To emphasise the fact that they stood firm on all these things Jesus again commends them for their patience, endurance and perseverance in all these good things and for all their hard labour. So far so good, but the Lord is also deeply concerned about one major issue of their relationship with Him, so concerned that He warns them that without further notice they could be removed from their place near to himself. So all important is this one thing to Jesus that all of the things that are right and commendable in the church will not save them from being removed from him.

Jesus said to them "But nevertheless I have this against you."(Revelation Ch.2v4) Like a massive blemish that blots out all that is good, or a major gaff that undermines all that is right, is this that the Lord has against them. How pleased the Ephesians must have been when John's letter was first read to them until they heard that three letter word BUT! What could it be, Where had they slipped up? What could possibly be wrong in a church that had just been so highly commended by the Lord. It should be a sobering thought for every church today to contemplate, that even if they have reached the standards the church at Ephesus had for living a committed Christian life there could still be something so fundamentally wrong.

Jesus comes straight to the point. "You have left your first love."(Revelation Ch.2v4) On hearing this the church must have felt rather like someone at an important job interview where the panel of interviewers praise the candidate for their qualifications, experience and competence to do the job they have applied for, but then they hear that dreaded word, but, and from then on everything is downhill fast and they know they have been unsuccessful. It must have hit them hard, possibly they may have felt like Peter did when Jesus asked him three times "Simon, son of Jonah, do you love Me."(John Ch.21v16) They may have felt hurt, offended and aghast that the Lord should make such a charge against them. Left our first love, what does Jesus mean? After a feeling of hurt and a little anger, a feeling of bewilderment set in. Well what exactly did Jesus mean? Some have understood the words to mean something akin to what can happen in a relationship between two lovers. At the beginning of the relationship they could not see enough of each other, they bought each other lots of little gifts, were so besotted with each other that they decided to marry and be together for the rest of their lives. Sharing everything, enjoying the intimacies of marriage and raising a family and so on. But then over the years the passion for each other dies away, the pleasure of giving to each other has gone, the fire of love has gone out, they have left their first love. Is that the kind of thing Jesus meant, were the Ephesian Christians no longer in love with Jesus, did they feel nothing for their Lord anymore? It would seem undeniable, that on one level they still loved the Lord. After all you would not work so hard and persistently for someone and defend their cause unless you loved them, would you? It is vital for us today as it was for them then to understand exactly what Jesus meant by telling them they had left their first love, because it has a far deeper meaning than can be deduced from the illustration of a marriage where the passion has gone.

Many readers will know that there are usually three words used in the Greek language for love. Eros, meaning sexual love, phileo, meaning brotherly love and agapae meaning divine love. This divine love is described for us in the famous love chapter of the Bible 1Corinthians Ch.13. This is the God kind of love that was lived out in the life of

Jesus as he loved firstly His Heavenly Father, the disciples and the world. He said to his disciples that they should love each other as he had loved them. The Greek word for love that Jesus used in his rebuke to the church in Ephesus is the word agapae. The word first, in relation to first love means foremost or pre-eminent so what Jesus said to them was, you have departed from the foremost love, the highest love, agapae love. This was the love they had departed from, and this is why there was the possibility that Jesus would suddenly depart from them.

No doubt brotherly love continued in the church as the scriptures say it should. There is no suggestion that they were without natural affection towards each other and that there was any problem in the church because marriages were falling apart due to couples falling out of love. But agapae love is on an altogether higher level, and it was from this high level that they had fallen. Jesus had a remedy for the situation and speaks to them in love as he rebukes them. "My son, do not despise the chastening of the Lord, nor be discouraged when you are rebuked by Him; For whom the Lord loves He chastens, and scourges every son whom He receives," said the Lord to the Hebrew Christians and Jesus had an unbounded love for this church, as for all his people. Nothing quite compares to the loving, yet firm way that Jesus brings his people to book, when they have gone wrong.

The first thing they are told to do is remember There are three "R"s in God's school of discipline just as we used to talk about the three "R"s when we were being educated. The first is REMEMBER, the second is REPENT and the third is REMOVE.

Remember how things were at the beginning, how the love of God was foremost in your lives. All other kinds of love are limited compared to agapae love. Erotic love is, according to the scriptures, to be between a husband and wife. The writer to the Hebrews writes that "Marriage is honourable among all, and the bed undefiled; but fornicators and adulterers God will judge."(Hebrews Ch.13v4) Brotherly love is expressed between friends and is a wonderful expression of love. Jesus felt this love for his disciples, he said I no longer regard you as servants but as friends. The affection between

David and Jonathon is another example of this kind of bond of brotherly love. But we all know that we choose our friends and that some people we forge these bonds of friendship with and others we don't. Gods love is an all inclusive love. With it we are to love our husband or wife, our children, relatives, friends and enemies. With Gods love we are to love our neighbour as Jesus said, the one we have never seen or met before who comes across our path and is in need. Most importantly with this high standard of love we are to love God. This is the first and great commandment and the Ephesian church had fallen short of it and needed to return to it. They had departed from the longsuffering love that shows kindness to those they found it hard to get on with. With brotherly love it is no problem getting on with those who love you, and are easy to get on with, but they were called to a higher love. Agapae love is that pure love born of the Holy Spirit in the heart, so although they continued to work hard and had made their stand for all the right doctrines Jesus could see into their hearts and discerned envy, pride and selfishness. Paul had written to them to be imitators of God as dear children and walk in love as Christ Jesus had also loved them, but in their hearts they had left that love. They were still giving and still caring but the element of sacrifice had gone. King David had said on one occasion that he would not give anything to the Lord that cost him nothing. But their motivation for giving had become self interest and convenience, and it fell far short of the high standard they had followed in the early days of the church. A judgmental attitude had come into the church and that determined how they behaved towards others, especially towards those who were unbelievers. Jesus said, "Give to those who ask of you, go the extra mile love your enemies, for if you only love those who love you how are you any different to the unbelievers? Paul had written to them to walk worthy of their calling in all lowliness and gentleness with longsuffering, bearing with one another in love. In fact Paul had written more about agapae love to the Ephesian church than to any other church, yet this is the very thing that they were failing in. It is a human weakness common to us all that the very things we have heard most of and been taught in, both by word and by example, are the very things we fail most spectacularly in. It seems that knowing something somehow in our minds equates to doing that thing, but we need to examine ourselves to see if we are in the faith we say we believe in. If any one thinks he stands he should take heed in case he falls.

Next Jesus commands them to repent. Turn around and walk in the way of God's love. They had the way mapped out in the scriptures they had received, they knew the way they now had to walk in it. Jesus is giving them a chance to change, for with the command to repent comes the grace to change. The change that Jesus is looking for would be evidenced in their lives by doing what Jesus called the "first works." The word first here is the same as in "first love" and refers to the works that are of primary importance. These works would, of course, coincide with the works they had done when the church was in its infancy, where the elements of Godly love were clearly seen in them and the Lord was pleased to be near them.

Some things that we have to do as Christians are more important than others. The most important work for a Christian is that which is connected with his relationship and fellowship with God. To love God is the primary function of a Christian. Worship, praise, prayer seeking to know God through His word, serving Him and serving others, believers and unbelievers, these are the first works, when they are performed motivated by, and displaying Gods love.. Our primary task is to be rooted and grounded in love, comprehending with all the saints what is the width, length, depth and height of that love, that we may know the love of Christ being filled up unto all the fullness of God. Many of us, if not all, may feel this is an impossible task, but Paul continues, "Now to Him who is able to do exceedingly abundantly above all that we ask or think according to the power that works in us, to Him be glory in the church by Christ Jesus to all generations, forever and ever, Amen."(Ephesians Ch.3v20-21) Grace and strength is available from the Holy Spirit who works in believers to bring them to repentance and do the first works.

Jesus said to them right at the beginning of his message that he knew their works. He had called for a fundamental change of heart and behaviour or the result would be removal from his presence. How important was the presence of the Lord to them only time would tell. How important is the presence of Jesus in our churches today? That question can only be answered by the commitment we have to living out the love of God.

Having spoken to them the truth in love Jesus further commends them for hating something that he hates. Having God's love does not preclude us from hating certain things, the things that Jesus Himself hates. They hated the deeds of the Nicolaitans which Jesus also hated. The Nicolaitans were very likely those in the church who had begun to form a hierarchy, putting themselves above those they considered were merely the laity in the church. Instead of functioning as Paul had taught in his epistle, some other church leaders did not train the flock to do the work of the ministry, but initiated a priesthood that excluded the church from the ministry. This eventually developed into what was the situation in the church during the dark ages when the ordinary church member only knew what the so called priests wanted them to know. This in reality meant that the people were led astray by any number of false teachings and practices contrary to the scriptures and the presence of Jesus departed from the church directed from Rome. Imperfect though it was thank God for the protestant reformation which took place through Zwingle, Luther, Wycliffe and countless others who sacrificed their very lives in taking a stand for the truths of the priesthood of all believers and justification by faith only.

He that has an ear let him hear what the Spirit says to the churches. This was not just a message for the church at Ephesus but for the churches, all seven of them and for the churches of Jesus Christ today. Would the church at Ephesus hear the testimony of Jesus in the rest of what John wrote to them, would they have ears to hear its message and see its relevance to them in their day? A key verse in Chapter 22 is verse 16 where Jesus says "I Jesus have sent my angel to testify these things in the churches." What things were these? The answer is in Ch.22v9, the things written in this book. The messages to the churches is vitally linked to the whole of the book of Revelation which is why I have entitled this book, Seven churches, seven seals one King.

Those who remember and repent and do the first works are the overcomers, and for them there is a reward. Overcomers will be able to eat of the tree of life which is in the middle of the paradise of God. The tree of life was barred to Adam and Eve in the garden of Eden so that they would not live forever in a state of spiritual death. In Christ Jesus the tree of life again becomes available to those who overcome. The tree of life is mentioned again in Ch.22 where John sees that it is planted by the river of life that flows from the throne of God. It is unusually fruitful as it produces fruit every month of a different variety. Overcomers will enjoy all the fullness of the fruit of the life of God that flows from his throne, enjoying that everlasting life that has begun here and now, but will find its perfection in the paradise of God.

CHAPTER 3

SMYRNA – THE BITTER SWEET CHURCH

Nothing is known about the beginning of the church at Smyrna from the scriptures, but as I suggested in the previous chapter, it may have come into existence because of the Word of the Lord going throughout Asia during the time Paul and his fellow workers were at Ephesus.

In modern times the city of Smyrna has become known as Izmiur and is on the western coast of Turkey. Smyrna had been in existence from ancient times and was important both to the Greeks and to the Romans. The Romans chose Smyrna, before the other eligible cities of the region in which to build a temple to the emperor Tiberius. It was a very beautiful city, some say the most beautiful city in Asia with a pleasing climate, cool breezes coming from the sea to ease the harshness of the summer sun. One of the streets of the city was known as the Street of Gold, being the shape of a semi circle, with a temple at each end of the street. The goddess of the city was Nemesis, the goddess of retribution. It had always been an important city for trade, the study of the sciences and for the production of medicines.

The name Smyrna means myrrh, which is the resin obtained from a shrub which grows wild in the Middle East, west as far as India and to the south in parts of East Africa. Myrrh is mentioned a number of times in the Old Testament. It was, and still is, a substance of some value as it was used for a number of different purposes. It was traded by the Ishmaelites who took Joseph down to Egypt and sold him as a slave. It was the predominant ingredient in the recipe that God gave to Moses for the production of the holy anointing oil. Before Esther was presented to king Ahasuerus, as a potential queen, she was beautified with myrrh for six months before having further beauty treatments with other ointments and perfumes. Most of the references to myrrh in the Bible come from the Song of Solomon where it is referring to perfumes. It was one of the gifts that the Magi brought to the young child Jesus in Bethlehem, as they came to worship the one born the King of the Jews. At the time of his crucifixion Jesus was given wine mixed with myrrh to drink, which he refused. The myrrh would have alleviated the pain to some extent. Myrrh was one of the ingredients of the embalming substance that Nicodemas used when preparing the body of Jesus for the tomb. The taste of myrrh is bitter, but as can be inferred from its uses as a perfume it has a pleasant smell. The root of the word myrrh is a Semitic word that means bitter.

In the Scriptures sometimes names are of significance. When you read the message that Jesus sends to the angel of the church at Smyrna, there are distinct parallels between the contrasting properties of myrrh, the bitter taste and sweet smell, and the high regard the Lord has for His people and the suffering inflicted on them by their enemies. They were going through some bitter experiences but they were as a sweet aroma to the Lord.

Jesus specifically reveals Himself to these persecuted Christians as the First and the Last. This is the way that Jesus is revealed to John when he first hears the voice behind him, the voice as of a trumpet. John needs to hear this revelation of Jesus too, as he is among those suffering for Jesus' sake. This is the message of the trumpet of God as it sounds throughout time, "I am the First and the Last, I am the Beginning and the End" says the Lord. "Who is, who was and is to come, the Alpha and Omega". This is repeated again as John falls at the feet of the Almighty Son of God. It bears repeating again in Rev. Ch.22v13, because He is the same yesterday and today and forever. I AM is such a significant statement, as it says that Jesus is, always was and always will be the first, the foremost, the pre-eminent One from before time in eternity, from the beginning of the creation of time to the end of time and into eternity. Jesus is the first in everything, in time and in status. In creation for everything was made through Him and for Him. In that He holds the creation together by His all powerful word. In being the One through whom The Father works out all of His eternal purposes. Purposes that involve those who have their names written in the book of life and those who will have their part in the lake of fire. He is the only one through whom the Father could bring about His plan of redemption and is Himself the firstborn from the dead, having died for the sins of many and has been raised from the dead and now lives by the power of an endless life. In time, creation and redemption He is the beginning and the end. The most important reason for the revelation that John received of Jesus, was that God's people then and now might know the end of their salvation. God will bring His plans to a successful conclusion in Jesus and this is just what the saints in Smyrna needed to know. Would all the suffering be worth it in the end? Would there be a reward for their labours or would they die in vain?

Christians at Smyrna needed to see Jesus as the great overarching figure of all time, as the colossus of time standing astride time from the beginning to the end. The reality on the ground for them was that in their city, as in most of the known world, Rome ruled. But as they were to read further into the revelation of Jesus that had been written to them they would understand that all the kingdoms of the world, even Rome, would fall before the Lamb who is in the midst of the throne. What a comfort this revelation would be and has been down through time and still is for suffering Christians today, that Jesus is King and will take His rightful place on the throne. They would be further comforted by visions of saints, who were once persecuted on the earth, now at rest with the Lord. For example when John sees the Lamb open the fifth seal he sees the souls of those who had been slain for the Word of God and the testimony of Jesus. They are under the altar in heaven and are told to rest a little while until everyone who in the future would be killed as they were would come and join them. There are further revelations concerning those who have come through the great tribulation, but are now crying out with loud cries in heaven "Salvation belongs to our God who sits on the throne, and to the Lamb!" (Rev Ch.7v10). They are now before the throne of God and serve Him day and night in His temple, all their sufferings are now left behind. The Lamb shepherds them and leads them to fountains of living waters. God will ensure that they will weep no more.

Not only were they comforted regarding their future but also in regards to the present. As they read what John saw in heaven of the throne of God in Ch.4 and then saw the Lamb and the Holy Spirit as seven horns and seven eyes on the Lamb, in the midst of the throne in Ch.5, they would know that their God reigned. That there and then God was ruling over the kingdoms of this world. In Ch.5 the four living creatures and twenty four elders sing a song of redemption, which speaks of the redeemed being kings and priests to God and that they shall reign on the earth. Peter also wrote to the pilgrims who were scattered abroad, which included those of Asia. In his first letter to them in Ch.2v9 he speaks of them as being a chosen generation, a royal priesthood, a holy nation, His own special people, that they may proclaim the praises of Him who called them out of darkness into his marvellous light. These believers at Smyrna may have been despised by the world they lived in but were chosen and special to God.

They were kings and priests in the sight of God, not nothings to be downtrodden and ill-treated. In what sense were they kings? They were poor and powerless as far as any earthly authority was concerned. Paul when writing to the church at Rome gives us a clue. In Ch.5v17 he tells the saints at Rome that as death had reigned by one man's disobedience, so now through the abundance of grace and the gift of righteousness given to them, they now reign in life though the one man Jesus Christ. Paul emphasises how much greater the reign of life is in Christ, than the reign of death was through the sin of Adam. The saints at Smyrna were reigning in life, for the Lamb in the midst of the throne was the same one who reigned in their hearts, and they were seated with Him in the heavenly places. They were reigning now on the earth as they would in the future on the new earth. Chapters 21 and 22 of Revelation describe the new heaven and earth, along with the Bride of Christ, which is said to be the New Jerusalem. Now the dwelling of God is with men and He will be with them and be their God. The beauty of the Bride is described as a fantastically beautiful city. No temple is there for God and the Lamb are the temple and in the midst of the street is the river of life with the tree for the healing of the nations. John says there will be no more night, but also no more day as we know it for there will be no sun to shine by day. Then he says, and they, the saints shall reign forever and ever as Kings and priests, when all earthly kingdoms have gone and been forgotten forever. No wonder this book of The Revelation is described as the testimony of Jesus from the very beginning to the very end. They needed to see the big picture then as we do today.

Peter speaks of the pilgrims in Asia and elsewhere reigning on the earth then, as now, in order to serve God as priests, proclaiming praises and offering sacrifices of praise. Persecuted Christians have always known how to praise God, when maybe others who are having an easy time become easy prey to a spirit of complaining and unthankfulness.

Jesus, the eternal One, assures them that He knows their works, that they are not forgotten in their time of trouble. The words of Jesus to His disciples in John's gospel were so relevant to their situation, when He said, "If the world hates you, you know that it hated Me before it hated you. If you were of the world, the world would love its own. Yet because you are not of the world, but I chose you out of the world, therefore the world hates you. Remember the word that I said to you, 'A servant is not greater than his master,' if they persecuted Me, they will also persecute you. If they kept My word they would keep yours also." (John Ch.15v18-20). Also John Ch.16v1-2 would be meaningful for the church in Smyrna when Jesus said, "These things I have spoken to you, that you should not be made to stumble. They will put you out of the synagogues; yes, the time is coming that whoever kills you will think that he offers God service." But finally

Jesus said to the disciples in the last verse of chapter 16, "These things I have spoken to you, that in Me you may have peace. In the world you will have tribulation; but be of good cheer, I have overcome the world." Hardship, hatred and all kinds of persecution has been, and still is the lot of God's children, as Jesus warned the disciples, and warned the church at Smyrna, so He warns to us today. If the church is functioning as it should then the world will hate the church.. It was only the five churches in Asia that were compromising with the world that were not suffering persecution, but the Lord was not pleased with them as He was with the church at Smyrna.

Along with persecution often comes poverty. The church at Smryna would have suffered deprivation, as do churches in our day where Christians are hated and put to death for Jesus' sake. Christians then as now would have been discriminated against and not been able to work to earn money and provide adequately for their needs. Or else they would have to be content with the lowest paid jobs, the kind that nobody else would want to do. If they did have wealth or money it would be stolen from them, such would have been the plight of the Christians at Smyrna. No doubt they faced a similar situation to the Christians the writer to the Hebrews is referring to when he writes "But recall the former days in which, after you were illuminated, you endured a great struggle with sufferings: partly while you were made a spectacle both by reproaches and tribulations, and partly while you became companions of those who were so treated; for you had compassion on me in my chains, and joyfully accepted the plundering of your goods, knowing that you have a better and more enduring possession for yourselves in heaven."(Hebrews Ch.10v32-34) But Jesus knew their poverty and said to them that in reality they were rich. It is often the case that Christians who are poor in this world, and despised, are rich toward God. Jesus had a great deal to say about the importance of laying up treasure in heaven and not on the earth, as does John in the visions he sees and records later in Revelation. Jesus said that those who accumulate for themselves treasure on earth and are not rich toward God are fools. Jesus said this while recalling the life of a rich farmer who owned land that was very fertile indeed. He was so blessed by God with the land that he owned and so blessed with a good supply of sun and rain to make his crops grow, that he had to pull down his old barns and build new ones, far bigger ones, to store all his harvest. He did not acknowledge God's goodness to him or the fact that fundamentally all he did was to plant the seed and then harvest the grain. But he said to himself, soul you have a lot of wealth stored up for many years ahead, you have no worries about having more than enough for the future, relax and take it easy, eat drink and be merry. Little did he realise that on the very day he presumed that everything was going to be hunky dory for the foreseeable future, that God would say to him, this very night your soul will be required of you. Jesus said he was a fool, along with all those who think that the only wealth there is, is on this earth. This truth is stated again for us in James Ch.4v13, where we read, "Come now, you who say, "Today or tomorrow we will go to such and such a city, spend a year there, buy and sell, and make a profit"; whereas you do not know what will happen tomorrow. For what is your life? It is even a vapour that appears for a little time and then vanishes away." Yet despite this most people, in the comparatively wealthy western world, dream of living the millionaire lifestyle, and play the lottery, do the pools and do what they can to escape what they consider to be the drudgery of ordinary life. But who would choose to be poor and persecuted in order to be rich toward God?

Jesus not only points out the foolishness of thinking as the rich farmer did, considering the fact that at any moment God may require our presence before His judgment seat. "And as it is appointed for men to die once, but after this the judgment." (Hebrews Ch.9v27.) But He taught His disciples that they should NOT lay up for themselves treasures on earth, where they would decay and be stolen, but that they should lay up for themselves treasures in heaven, where nothing decays, is stolen or can be spoilt in any way. For where your treasure is your heart will be there also. This was part of the teaching of Jesus in what we have come to know as the Sermon on the Mount recorded in Matthew Ch.6. Jesus was pleased with the Christians at Smyrna because they had set their affections on things in heaven and not on things on the earth. They were serving God not mammon.

In the same teaching from the Sermon on the Mount Jesus promised that God would look after his children. He said to His disciples, "Do not worry about your life what you will eat or what you will drink." (Matthew Ch.6v25) Look at the birds, how your Heavenly Father feeds them. Do not worry about clothing what you are going to wear, see for yourself how God clothes the lilies. Jesus said that His disciples should leave all the worrying to those who seek after the wealth of this world, and that they should seek the kingdom of God and His righteousness first, and all the things they needed would be given to them by God. Jesus set the example Himself. He once said that "Foxes have holes and birds of the air have nests, but the Son of Man has nowhere to lay His head." (Matthew Ch.8v20) Yet God still provided for His necessities.

God will at last bring all the wealth of this world to ashes, and those who have lived for it, been seduced by it and made wealth their god, will come to experience the outpouring of the wrath of God without mixture. For John sees in Revelation Ch.18 the downfall of Babylon the Great. World leaders today are moving towards more and more of what has come to be known as globalisation. Blocks of trading nations are forming all around the world in order to facilitate global trade and multinational companies. The wealth of the world will eventually come under the control of a very few people who will give their allegiance to the god of this world, the devil. This will become what John saw as Babylon the Great and is described as a great city filled with merchandise, riches of all kinds and traders from around the world accumulating wealth. In Ch.18v4 the people of God are called to come out of Babylon. God's call to the church down through the centuries, and at this time still, is not to stay in the Babylonian system of this world, not to be involved in living to make wealth to consume on yourself. This will still be the call to God's people, if they will hear it, right up to the last moment before judgment falls on Babylon and its smoke rises up for ever and ever. Do not share in her sins, or you will share in her punishment, unless you repent. Ominously among all the long list of things that Babylon traded in John heard it said that it traded in the souls of men. Men who thought they could use the system to gain wealth ended up by being abused by the system. That is exactly what we are seeing today, men giving their lives for what they cannot keep, instead of giving their lives for treasure in heaven that they cannot lose. For the saints in Smyrna, as they were to read this revelation, it would reassure them that they were far better off being poor in this world but rich toward God. Where are your riches? Where is your heart?

If the church at Smyrna was not rich in wealth, what were they rich in? What does Jesus consider to be the true riches? The message to the angel of the church does not specify what they were rich in but there are plenty of scriptures to look at in order to see what God considers to be of value. No doubt the Christians there were rich in these things. When Paul wrote to Timothy he tells him to run away from certain things like the love of money which is a root of all kinds of evil and also to run after other things that are of value. Firstly he tells Timothy to pursue righteousness. I believe the saints at Smyrna were rich in righteousness. Firstly because they had received the righteousness that comes to all believers by faith only, and not by any works that they had done. They had been justified by faith, and this had been made possible because the Lamb had shed his blood as a propitiation for their sins. Secondly they were rich in righteousness because of the righteous way that they lived, they were living uprightly before God. They were obeying the Holy Spirit and submitting themselves to His leading, and putting to death the deeds of the flesh. For, as Paul wrote in Romans Ch.8v8, "So then those who are in the flesh cannot please God." These Smyrna saints would eventually be among those who John sees who were clothed in fine linen, clean and white, which are the righteous acts of the saints. (Revelation Ch.19v8.)

Paul also tells Timothy to run after Godliness, or Godlikeness, for Godliness is great gain. As God looked on this suffering church He saw, imperfect as it was, a reflection of Himself. This is not surprising, when all the suffering they were going through, is taken into consideration. God had a purpose in allowing them to go through tribulation, and primarily it was that His image would come to maturity in them. Paul in Romans Ch.5v3-4 wrote, "knowing that tribulation produces perseverance; and perseverance, character;

and character, hope." Peter in his first epistle Ch4, in several verses expresses the same thought as Paul when he wrote in v.1, "Therefore, since Christ suffered for us in the flesh, arm yourselves also with the same mind, for he who has suffered in the flesh has ceased from sin." In v.12 he says, "Beloved, do not think it strange concerning the fiery trial which is to try you, as though some strange thing happened to you." Also in v.14 he says, "If you are reproached for the name of Christ, blessed are you, for the Spirit of glory and of God rests upon you." Finally v19 which says, "Therefore let those who suffer according to the will of God commit their souls to Him in doing good, as to a faithful Creator." Jesus Himself, who is the express image of the Father, was their example and as they were following in His footsteps in suffering for righteousness sake they were becoming like him in character, and would share in His glory and victory.

The church at Smyrna would also have been rich in faith, as this was the next thing Paul listed for Timothy to pursue. God was pleased with them, and without faith it is impossible to please God. They were rich in the faith of God, for faith without works is dead, and Jesus has nothing to say as He did to other churches in Asia, that was anything but complimentary about their works. No doubt they actually grew in faith because of the harsh conditions they were in, they learned to trust God or fall by the wayside. They were doers of the word and not hearers only. Their faith was a sacrificial faith, as is often the case with those who have little and are Godly, they are prepared to give generously. They did not neglect the orphans or widows in the church, and did not hold the faith of the Lord Jesus, the Lord of Glory, with partiality. For when a rich man came into the church meeting they did not pamper him or give him any more preferential treatment, than they did to the poor in the fellowship The poor were not despised, by the poor, in this church and the Lord certainly did not despise them for their lack of wealth. They would not have been able to finance any great projects, or support evangelists or missionaries, out of great financial resources, but Jesus said they were rich. They could be compared to the churches of Macedonia that Paul wrote of, in 2Corinthians Ch.8v1-4, "Moreover, brethren, we make known to you the grace of God bestowed on the churches of

Macedonia: that in a great trial of affliction the abundance of their joy and their deep poverty abounded in the riches of their liberality. For I bear witness that according to their ability, yes, and beyond their ability, they were freely willing, imploring us with much urgency that we would receive the gift and the fellowship of the ministering to the saints." No wonder James wrote that God has chosen the poor of this world to be rich in faith and heirs of the kingdom which He promised to those who love Him. When we today, in our wealthy churches, read of the sacrificial giving and faith in action of these saints, do we not feel at all ashamed? Would not most of the other churches in Asia have felt ashamed, as they read of how the Lord in the midst of the candlesticks saw this poor church, as compared to how others saw them?

They would also have been rich in love, unlike the Ephesian church. Love for God and love for each other. The love that grows as the fruit of the Spirit. Love was the central core strength of their richness in God, for God is love. It shone through in their upright living, in their Godly character and the faith that works by love that they lived by.

This love manifested itself in patience, as they endured persecution, imprisonment and the slander of those who hated them. They never turned back from following Jesus. If they had known the hymn, 'I have decided to follow Jesus, no turning back, no turning back,' it would have been a firm favourite. They allowed God to mould them in their sufferings committing themselves to God. This is what Peter encouraged the saints to do by writing, "But when you do good and suffer, if you take it patiently, this is commendable before God. For to this you were called, because Christ also suffered for us, leaving us an example, that you should follow His steps."(1Peter Ch.2v20-21)

Love also expressed itself in gentleness among them. How remarkable it is that those who suffer cruelty also have gentleness produced in their lives. This can only come about because of the work of the Holy Spirit in the heart of a believer. Peter speaking of Jesus said, "Who, when He was reviled, did not revile in return; when He suffered, He did not threaten, but committed Himself to Him who judges righteously."(1Peter Ch.2v23) Jesus who could have called ten thousand angels to destroy His enemies, instead allowed Himself to be lead as a lamb to the slaughter.

The riches of this church were I am sure not just confined to righteousness, Godliness, faith, love, patience and gentleness, but the whole array of the fruit of the Spirit would have been seen among the members of this truly rich church. They are certainly an example for churches today to seek to emulate, as more than any of the other churches in Asia John wrote to they were pleasing to the Lord who walked among them.

Jesus was also aware of the slanderous things being said about them, by those who claimed to be Jews, but were frauds. They were, what Jesus described as, a synagogue of Satan. There is no information to hand as to the nature of the slanderous things being said about the saints at Smyrna, but there is no doubt at all about the origin of the lies that were circulating about these poor folk. The, so called Jews, were a synagogue of Satan, and Satan was the inspiration behind all the gossip. Satan was obviously so agitated by this poor little church that he orchestrated a campaign of slander against them. He recognised the potential danger to his kingdom because these Christians were rich toward God, and fully committed to serving God. Revelation Ch.12v9 reveals something of the character of Satan, where he is called the serpent of old, the devil, which means slanderous accuser and Satan, the adversary. He is the accuser of the brethren, who accuses them before God day and night. That the adversaries of the Christians in Smyrna are called a synagogue of Satan, who say they are Jews and are not is of considerable interest, as are all the many references to Jews and things Jewish in the whole of the book of Revelation. Jesus is not saying that these Jews are not real descendents of Abraham, as far as natural descent is concerned. What He is saying is that if they were truly Jews then they would not be slandering His people. In Romans Ch.2 Paul refers to those who are called Jews and rely on the law and make their boast in God. He writes that, they consider themselves to be in a position to instruct others, but asks them, do you not teach yourselves? Paul goes on to conclude that if you are a teacher of the law, but do not keep the law yourself, you make the circumcision in which you boast, into uncircumcision, taking away the very essence of what it is to be Jewish. For circumcision was meant to be the outward sign of the faith of God in the heart of a man.

Paul, inspired by the Holy Spirit, argues "For he is not a Jew who is one outwardly, nor is circumcision that which is outward in the flesh; but he is a Jew who is one inwardly; and circumcision is that of the heart, in the Spirit not in the letter, whose praise is not from men but from God." (Romans Ch.2v28-29) Clearly those of the synagogue of Satan in Smyrna were those who had an exterior only form of false religion that was controlled by Satan. Further revelations come in Revelation Ch.17 where the same work of Satan has matured from a synagogue of Satan to a worldwide movement of powerful proportions, a false church inspired by the evil one. This false church is described as a harlot, who sits on many waters, which is the typical description in the scriptures for those who pretend to worship God, but are unfaithful to Him. The harlot is called "MYSTERY, BABYLON THE GREAT, THE MOTHER OF HARLOTS AND OF THE ABOMINATIONS OF THE EARTH."(Revelation Ch.17v5) Sickeningly she was drunk with the blood of the saints and martyrs of Jesus. The church at Smyrna was suffering at the hands of Imperial Rome, and also because of the evil speaking of the spiritual power of darkness that was the embryonic Mystery Babylon.

But Jesus, who is the First and the Last, says to them do not fear any of those things you are about to suffer. Jesus was right there with them, and so was the Holy Spirit the Comforter, the powerful all seeing one. Jesus was not expecting them to overcome their fears in their own strength, but with the exhortation to, fear not, would be given the supernatural ability to do just that. Jesus knew how to bring comfort and strength in difficult situations. Before His departure, to go to the cross and after the resurrection to go back to the Father, Jesus said to the disciples "Peace I leave with you, My peace I give to you; not as the world gives do I give to you. Let not your heart be troubled, neither let it be afraid."(John Ch.14v27)

"The devil is about to throw some of you into prison that you may be tested, and you will have tribulation ten days." That was the stark warning that came from the lips of Jesus. They would have understood that ten days did not refer to a literal ten day period, but a set time and predetermined period in which God would test the faith of His people. Notice this testing was only for some of the saints, as God knows what each one of us can endure, for our good and his glory, so He does not go beyond what we can bear. Although Satan is the instigator of the imprisonment of some, God is clearly in charge of the situation. This has always been the case, and is illustrated most clearly by the story of Job, in the Old Testament. God gives Satan permission to try Job and always gives him strict limits in which he can operate. Satan has to keep to these limits and when God decided that Job's trials should come to an end they did. God rewarded Job for his patience in the trial by giving him back twice as much as he had before and blessing him with sons and daughters. Satan had lost out in every way, he lost the argument, he lost credibility in the heavenly places as his predictions as to what Job would do in the face of his onslaught did not come to pass. Sometimes we suffer because of our own fault, but when we suffer for Jesus' sake God will make sure that good will come through the trial. This truth is famously expressed in Paul's letter to the Romans Ch.8v28, "And we know that all things work together for the good to those who love God, to those who are the called according to His purpose." In the next verse Paul explains why this is so. It is because God has predestined us to become like His Son Jesus Christ, and becoming like Jesus equates to being fruitful as a Christian. The church at Smyrna, although poor, was spiritually very fruitful. Jesus explained to his disciples that He was the vine, His Father God was the gardener, and they were the branches.(John Ch.15) He further explains that every branch in Him that bears fruit is pruned, or purified, that it might bear even more fruit to the glory of God. Branches that are unfruitful would be taken away, the Ephesian church was in danger of this very thing. The trials that God was allowing the church at Smyrna to go through were part of the pruning process.

Be faithful unto death, and I will give you the crown of life, Jesus promised. This was a warning as well as a promise, that some Christians would pay the ultimate price, but would win the ultimate prize, the crown of life. James writes that the crown of life is for those who love the Lord, those willing to lay down their lives for the Lord could not express that love in any greater way. This crown is an imperishable crown, a victors crown an over comers crown. Not a crown of laurel leaves, as was awarded to Olympian athletes in John's day, or even a royal crown that could only be worn on a temporary basis, but a crown that did not perish and would be worn forever. Paul was looking forward to wearing such a crown when he wrote to Timothy and said, "I have fought the good fight, I have finished the race, I have kept the faith. Finally, there is laid up for me the crown of righteousness, which the Lord, the righteous Judge, will give me on that Day, and not to me only but to all who have loved His appearing."(2Timothy Ch. 4v7-8)

The message to the angel of the church at Smyrna ends in the same way as the message to all the other churches from the Lord Jesus, "He who has an ear, let him hear what the Spirit says to the churches."(Revelation Ch.2v11) There are things for the Christians at Smyrna to overcome, such as the fear of persecution, imprisonment, slander, and for a few death itself. John will yet see visions of multitudes of those who have overcome all these fears, and are now enjoying freedom from all the temporary troubles that they experienced on earth, because they are now with the Lord forever. In our day thousands upon thousands have made the same stand for the Lord and have suffered all these trials and have overcome and now rejoice in the life they now have with the Lord. We salute those who suffered under communist regimes in what was the Soviet Union, those who are currently suffering in China, and other far eastern countries. Many have faced and suffered death and the threat of death, the loss of all that they posses for the sake of their faith in Jesus, in some African countries, principally those who have Muslim governments. Who is to say that we in the democratised wealthy western countries, will not at sometime in the future, have to take our stand for Jesus and suffer for His sake, as some of our faithful forbears did. Those with spiritual perception and ears to hear what the Spirit is saying to the churches in our day would not rule out the possibility. The Heavenly Gardener who tends the vine, in seeking to gather more fruit from the so called rich and pampered western churches, may decide that the best way to do this would be with a severe pruning in order to produce in them the true riches that were in the church at Smyrna.

The reward for those who overcome is that they will not be hurt by the second death. Revelation Ch.20v14 says, that the meaning of the second death is to be cast into the lake of fire. This is the fate of the devil and his angels along with all those whose names are not in the book of life. What a wonderful thought it is that in exchange for what Paul once described as "these light afflictions" we who patiently endure have an eternal weight of glory, untouched by the second death, we will be enjoying eternal life.

CHAPTER 4

PERGAMOS- CHURCH WITH AN IRON GRIP

Pergamos, or Pergamon was an important city in the time of John the apostle and was situated north of Smyrna about fifteen miles inland from the coast of what is now western Turkey. It was strongly influenced by Greek culture and the worship of Greek gods. After the emergence of Rome as the dominant world power it also became a centre for emperor worship. The dominant Greek god at Pergamos was the greatest and most powerful of all the gods, Zeus. According to Greek mythology Zeus was the god of the sky who ruled in the firmament controlling thunder, lightening and rain. Athena, who was the offspring of Zeus, was also worshiped there. One of the things that dominated the city was a huge altar to the god Zeus. Dionysis and Askleios, who was supposedly a god who brought healing to people, had their followers at Pergamos. Jesus describes Pergamos as the place where Satan's throne is, with such a concentration of idolatry it would seem an apt description.

To the church at Pergamos, the specific revelation of Jesus is, the one who has the sharp two edged sword. When John first saw Jesus this sword comes out of His mouth. This is an obvious reference to the sword of the Spirit, which is the word of God. Hebrews Ch.4v12 says, "For the word of God is living and powerful, and sharper than any two-edged sword, piercing even to the division of soul and spirit, and of joints and marrow, and is a discerner of the thoughts and intents of the heart." Some of those at the church at Pergamos needed to know that Jesus had this formidable weapon, with which He would come and fight against them if they did not repent of holding on to false doctrine. Like a surgeon, cutting out a cancer, Jesus would use the sword to cut His enemies off from His church.

But firstly, as with the other churches where there is sin to be dealt with, Jesus speaks to those He is pleased with. This not only serves to emphasise the gravity of the things that need to be cut out, but also accentuates the positive aspects of the church. He knows their works and where they live, where Satan's throne is. None of the other churches are so surrounded by such a concentration of evil influences and spiritual forces of darkness. This is the seat of Satan's operations in the region, a place filled with different 'spiritual' attractions and distractions from the worship of the one true God, the creator of the heavens and the earth, the only living God.

Ever since Satan succeeded in deceiving Eve, and through Eve causing Adam to disobey God's command not to eat the fruit of the tree of the knowledge of good and evil, Satan has succeeded in seducing men and women of all nations to worship him by proxy, as they worship a multitude of different gods. An idol itself is nothing but wood or stone or some other material, today they are made of glass and steel and plastic and can be anything that is worshipped, and put before God who is the only one who should be worshipped. But the systems associated with idol worship, then as now, are demonically inspired to lead people as far away from the worship of God as possible, to the worship of Satan. To have the worship of men, this has always been Satan's goal, as he has from the time of his fall wanted to be God. He has appealed to every aspect of man's fallen and corrupted nature in order to achieve his goal. Idolatry was the foremost and most persistent sin of the children of Israel, as is recorded in the Old Testament. No wonder the very last words of John's first epistle are, "Little children, keep yourselves from idols." The Gentile nations were, more or less, totally dominated by idolatry before the dawning of the New Testament church age. The Holy Spirit sent, in particular Paul as the apostle to the Gentiles, to preach the gospel far and wide as far as Rome, so that they would turn from idols to serve the living and true God

Inspired by Satan men had changed the glory of the immortal God into images made like mortal man and birds and all kinds of animals and insects. They worshipped and served the creature rather than the creator. They worshipped the sun and moon and the multitude of stars and mother earth. Therefore God gave them over to all kinds of unclean and vile practices, in which they dishonoured their own bodies. They chose not to retain God in their knowledge, and without the knowledge of God man became full of unrighteousness, sexual immorality, wickedness, covetousness, maliciousness, envy, murder, strife and deceitfulness, having evil minds. Men apart from God became whisperers of evil things behind closed doors, backbiters, boasters, inventers of evil things, disobedient to parents, undiscerning, untrustworthy, unloving, unforgiving, and unmerciful. Paul wrote this comprehensive list in Romans Ch.1, cataloguing the whole gambit of the works of fallen man, in the context of idolatry, and through idolatry, the worship of Satan. It should surprise no one that men have become like the one they have really been worshipping, the god of this world, who has deceived the sons of disobedience.

The later chapters of Revelation show how idolatry will reach its zenith. Ch.13 describes John seeing a beast rise out of the sea and it is given great power by the dragon, who is the devil. John saw that all the world marveled and wondered at this beast and followed him. Revelation Ch.13v4 says that they worshipped the dragon who gave authority to the beast, and they worshipped the beast saying, "Who is like the beast? Who is able to make war with him?" In the same chapter in v11 John records that he saw another beast arise out of the earth, who had equal authority with the first beast. The role of the second beast is to cause the people of the world to worship the first beast. He is given the power to perform signs, one of which is to give life to an image of the first beast, so that it becomes a speaking image. He then demands that everyone worships the image of the beast, the refusal to do so resulting in death. So the satanic trio are given their little time of world domination, and then Jesus comes to deal with them once and for all, and they get their just deserts in the lake of fire.

Despite living where Satan's throne is, there are dogged saints in Pergamos who hold fast to Jesus and His name. They are saints with an iron grip that will not let go. Like a man clinging with all his might to a tree, growing from a cliff face, to stop himself from plunging to his death, or like a dog holding on to a bone with its teeth, these saints had held fast to the name of Jesus. They had held on, strengthened by the Lord in their midst, they held on and prevailed against all the odds. Jesus said that they had held fast to his name. The question is sometimes asked, "What is in a name?" Do names matter, or are names just random labels given to things to identify them? So does the name of the god that we worship matter, or are they all the same anyway? For the majority of worshipers at Pergamos, the worship of one god as opposed to another would have been a matter of tradition or preference, or maybe the deciding factor would be which god most satisfied their sensual desires. Satan has always tried to deceive men into believing that God is just one among many gods and that it does not really matter who you worship. This thinking has come to the fore in recent years in the guise of the new age movement, eastern mysticism and the emergence of Hinduism in the western world. Christians have always been under pressure from the world to renounce the name of the one true God and His Son Jesus Christ. Over the centuries many have been faced with the choice of denying the Lord who saved them, or forfeiting their lives. Unbelievers have never been able to stomach the idea that there is only one God, revealed in the scriptures, and manifested in the person of His Son, Jesus Christ. They say you can be just as good a person as a Jew, Muslim, Hindu, Siek, or Buddhist, surely it is wrong to put the Christian religion above all the others, and insist that Jesus is the only way to God. But Jesus firstly compliments this church on the fact that they have held fast to HIS NAME! He is the Alpha and Omega, the Beginning and the Ending, the First and the Last, His name is King of Kings and Lord of Lords, his name is the Word of God. No other person, god or thing that is worshipped has names that compare to His names. Christians are, absolutely and without reservation or qualification, right to tenaciously hold on to the name of the one who, as God the Son, became the Son of Man in order to save us from our sins.

Furthermore they did not deny the faith, which Jesus described as My faith. My name, My faith, Jesus regards these things as issues of personal allegiance to Him. The faith, as is contained in Christianity, is not just another among many moral teachings, it is an allegiance to Jesus Himself, His name and His faith. The faith of Jesus is contained in the gospel, but it is more than the gospel, it is also the outworking of the salvation that comes through the gospel. Paul, writing to the Philippians in Ch.2v12-13 said to them, that they should work out, or outwork, their salvation with fear and trembling, for it was God who worked in them both to will and to do of His good pleasure. But although it is more than the written word, the faith never deviates from the written word of God contained in the Bible. The faith of Jesus is pure and never tolerates evil. Jude, writing to saints everywhere, said that the faith we should contend for, which was ONCE FOR ALL delivered to the saints, does not include turning the grace of God into lewdness, or a license to commit sin, and denying the only Lord God and our Lord Jesus Christ. Near to the end of his letter he says, "But you beloved building yourselves up on your MOST HOLY FAITH," (Jude v20) The faith is holy because it is His faith, and not to be confused with or compared with any other faith. For by definition all things that are holy are holy because they are separated to God and for God, from other unholy things that do not belong to God.

There were those in this church who had not let go of His name and His faith, Jesus said, even in the days when Antipas was my faithful martyr, who was killed among you where Satan dwells. These faithful ones were a tremendous example to the other churches in Asia. Antipas had become part of the ever growing number of those who had given their lives for Jesus sake. I have referred previously to the visions John sees of those under the altar in heaven, and before the throne of God, who have shed their blood as martyrs. This book of Revelation, was written in part, to bring comfort to suffering, persecuted Christians, and to encourage and strengthen the resolve of those who would give their lives for His name and His faith, for it gives an insight into the glory that follows the valley of the shadow of death.

It is worthy of note that Jesus calls Antipas, My faithful martyr. Jesus takes ownership of the name above all other names, and the most holy faith, and also those who die for His name and His faith. Jesus takes the death of martyrs for His cause, in a personal way, and says they are mine. They are My witnesses, for that is the meaning of the word martyr, and their blood speaks louder and more eloquently than their words ever could. The pagan, idolatrous world disowns them and kills them, but the Lord of glory owns them, and says they are like jewels in my crown. Would John have to face a martyr's death? If so Jesus had shown him, and all the churches, how richly they would be rewarded in heaven. They had held tenaciously onto these things and Jesus would not let them go, even though their bodies were destroyed, He would bring them safely into His presence.

But, despite there being the example of faithful ones in the church, there were those who tenaciously held onto things that were evil. So Jesus puts the sword that is in His mouth to good use and decisively cuts to the chase, exposing false doctrine. "But I have a few things against you, because you have there those who hold the doctrine of Balaam," Jesus said. (Revelation Ch.2v14) Out had come the sword from His mouth, and it had cut right to the heart of the problem. This doctrine was and still is an age old scourge that arises, from time to time in different guises, Satan presenting it as something new and a good idea. At this point, we may be inclined to think that Jesus is being rather harsh and hard on this church, which has really not had an easy time of it, and if they have strayed a little in doctrine is that so bad after all? Is doctrine all that important? Is it not far more important that we just love each other and get along with each other? This I am sure, would be the typical response today of many, if Jesus were to speak to some churches today about wrong doctrine. But Jesus loves them so much, and for the sake of those who have been faithful, He must deal with the issue of the doctrine of Balaam in the Pergamos church. God hates wrong doctrine, for it leads to wrong teaching, which leads to evil practices. This is the inevitable effect of wrong doctrine. The doctrine of Balaam is the idea that you can 'run with the fox and hunt with the hounds,' or adapting the saying to this context, that you can worship and serve God and idols at the same time. To trace the history of this doctrine we need to go back to the book of Numbers, in the Old Testament, and briefly recount the time when the children of Israel are beginning to take possession of the land God had promised them. Balaam was a Midianite prophet, who was summoned by Balak, a Moabite king, to curse the Israelites so that He would be able to defeat them in battle, as he was very afraid they would over run his land, which thing they did. On the first occasion that Balak sent men to Balaam the Lord gave him specific instructions not to have anything to do with them or go with them. However that was not what was in Balaam's heart, for he was a greedy man, and the Lord could see his heart. On the second occasion Balak sent even more prestigious men to Balaam, the Lord said to Balaam, go with them, but, say only the things I tell you to say. On the way to meet with Balak, the scriptures record the famous incident of Balaam's donkey speaking to him. This arose because the Lord wanted Balaam to be in no doubt that although He had told him to go, it was not His real intention and He knew what was in Balaam's heart. When Balak showed Balaam the multitude of the Israelites, and asked Balaam to curse them, all Balaam was able to do was bless them. This happened on three separate occasions, until Balak's patience was exhausted. Balaam returned to his home having blessed Israel three times and without any reward from Balak. But it had not been Balaam's intention to bless Israel, but he rather hoped that God would change His mind and allow him to curse them so that he could profit by it. On one occasion while pronouncing blessing he said, "God is not a man, that He should lie, nor a son of man, that He should repent. Has He said, and will not do? Or has He spoken, and will He not make it good?"(Numbers Ch.23v19) God had determined to bless Israel and would not change His mind. Having failed to get Balaam to curse Israel it would appear that, prompted by Balaam, Balak changed his strategy and instead of trying to defeat them in battle, tried to assimilate them into Moabite culture and the worship of idols. Moabite women were introduced into the camp of Israel and soon the Israelites were entering into relationships with the women and worshiping Baal. In consequence, God sent a plague among the people, which resulted in death for those involved. One notable case was of an Israelite man, who brought a Moabite woman into the camp in sight of Moses and those who were weeping before God for the situation they were in. Phinehas took prompt action and went into the tent where they were and killed them both with a javelin. This action stopped the plague in the camp, because he had been zealous for the Lord. This incident with Balaam shows that he himself, on the one hand spoke the word of the Lord concerning Israel, yet still hoped to profit by pleasing Balak, which is why he tried tree times to curse Israel but God would not allow him to. Then the people of Israel themselves became involved in idolatry, thinking they could worship the Lord and Baal at the same time.

Jesus said to the church at Pergmos, there are those among you that hold the doctrine of Balaam. This resulted in some in the church teaching that it was alright to mix it with the pagans around them, and to commit sexually immoral acts in connection with idolatry. Some in the church became involved in voluntarily eating food offered to idols. Paul, once explained to the Corinthian church, that if they ate food offered to idols that they had brought from the market place without knowing it had been offered to idols that was alright, when they gave thanks to the Lord for it. But to become knowingly involved was a different matter, as this would involve them in the worship of demons. These teachings had caused some in the church to stumble and the Lord was no more pleased with this situation than he was with Israel in Balaam's time. Why were some tenaciously holding on to this doctrine and not willing to let go of it? The answer may be, that like Balaam there was either the prospect of some profit in it for them, or there was some actual gain in connection with the heathen temples. Peter wrote of such people that, "They have forsaken the right way and gone astray, following the way of Balaam the son of Beor, who loved the wages of unrighteousness." (2Peter Ch.2v15) Jude v11 says they, "have run greedily in the error of Balaam for profit." It was clearly because Satan had been unsuccessful in destroying the church through the threat of martyrdom, and actual martyrdom, and not been able to crush this church even though it was where his throne was, that he tried the more indirect, subtle approach in order to try and defeat them. He tried the approach of assimilation, which was Balak's strategy against Israel, and it would appear from the message to them from Jesus that he had succeeded to some extent. The doctrine of Balaam, unfortunately, is still hampering the church today. All who would be zealous for the Lord, as Phinehas was, will have nothing to do with it, but rather seek to cut it out of the church, and have no association with those who hold such doctrine. They are those who teach that all roads lead to God. Gone are the days when some so called church leaders advocated that the church should be an amalgamation of all 'so called Christian' denominations. Today there are distinct moves by some who want all religions to join together, under the banner of what is the lowest common denominator, we all believe in some god or other. The prospective, although thankfully not the current governor of the Church of England, has said that he wants, not to be defender of THE FAITH, but defender of faiths. The religious media, in recent times has published and broadcast the fact that leaders of different faiths in Britain have been coming together to explore common ground, but the outcome of such meetings, and the coming together in so called worship of God by such groups, usually results in the casting aside of the Lord Jesus Christ, so as not to cause offence to those who adhere to other faiths. My reaction to this kind of thing is, "Let God arise, His enemies be scattered." Oh Lord arise in your church and weald the two edged sword that comes out of your mouth, and fight against those who hold the doctrine of Balaam.

Unfortunately Satan was also attacking the church with those who were holding on to the doctrine of the Nicolaitans, which Jesus says that he hates. In the special message to the Ephesian church we are told about the deeds of these people, and what they did is discussed at length in the second chapter. Again we notice that doctrines lead inevitably to deeds, which is why Jesus is so concerned that His church holds tightly on to sound doctrine.

So here is a church that has, as its main characteristic, tenacity and an unshakable spirit, the church with an iron grip. Some are holding on to what is right, and what pleases the Lord. Others are holding on, but to entirely the wrong things, teachings that have their origin with Satan. Jesus has now, to come and fight for His faith, His name and vindicate His martyrs, by using the mighty sword that comes out from His mouth, unless they repent. But the sword that comes out of the mouth of Jesus, is not just words that convey a convincing argument against all wrong doctrines, although I am sure that is the case. For this sword is not just for defending His faith, it is not just a sword that is able to cut to the heart of a situation and expose its true nature, as with the words Jesus speaks to this church. But it is a weapon that has devastating power, as is clearly demonstrated by what John sees in Revelation Ch.19v14&15 where we read, "And the armies in heaven, clothed in fine linen, white and clean followed Him on white horses. Now out of His mouth goes a sharp sword, that with it He should strike the nations. And He Himself will rule them with a rod of iron." With the word of His mouth He created the heavens and the earth, and by the power of His word they will disintegrate in a cosmic conflagration as Peter wrote, with a great noise, they will melt away with fervent heat. By the power of His word He will bring the nations into submission to His rule and rule them with a rod of iron. Just imagine as the church at Pergamos read Ch.19 and realised the power of the sword in the mouth of Jesus, they would know that to make themselves enemies of the Son of God would end in death as a judgment on them, for v21 says, and the rest were killed by the sword of Him who sat on the horse. Repent or be guilty of the sin unto death, that was the choice some faced then and I believe some still face today.

He who has an ear to hear let him hear what the Spirit says to the churches. What the Spirit is saying to any one who will hear, is the same message that Malachi brought to Israel, the last message to Israel before the coming of Jesus the Messiah. Part of that message was, "But who can endure the day of His coming?" "And who can stand when He appears?"(Malachi Ch.3v2) Jesus said He would come quickly to the church at Pergamos and fight against those who continued to hold on to wrong doctrines, and who would be able to stand against the sword of His mouth? To Israel through Malachi

God had said, "For He is like a refiners fire and like launderer's soap, He will sit as a refiner and a purifier of silver; He will purify the sons of Levi, and purge them as gold and silver, that they may offer to the Lord an offering in righteousness."(Malachi Ch.3v2-3) In a similar vein, John the Baptist, who Malachi predicted would come, said of Jesus, "His winnowing fan is in His hand, and He will thoroughly clean out His threshing floor, and gather His wheat into the barn; but He will burn up the chaff with unquenchable fire."(Matthew Ch.3v12) Would not Jesus do a similar work in the church at Pergamos, unless they repented, and will not Jesus continue to do so today, unless those who profess to be Christian stop associating with the things that Jesus hates?

To those who overcome, and hold on to His faith, His name and even give their lives in defence of these things, Jesus promises hidden manna to eat. This is the true bread of heaven, that which sustains the life of God in a believer, the source of which is hidden to those who do not overcome. Significantly, to those who hold fast to His name Jesus promises a name, a new secret name, just as He has. Jesus promises to initiate over comers into a select group who share the rewards that others cannot receive because their works do not merit these rewards. For all believers Jesus knows their works and they will be rewarded according to their works. Revelation Ch.14v13 says, "Blessed are the dead who die in the Lord from now on." "Yes," says the Spirit, "that they may rest from their labours and their works follow them."

CHAPTER 5

THYATIRA-CHURCH WITH A DARK SIDE

Thyatira was a city to the south east of Pergamos and the two cities, had over many years had a close association, being linked together by a road. There would probably have been an exchange of fellowship between the two churches, which may explain, to some degree, why similar problems existed in both churches. Thyatira had a protecting god called Pythian Apollo who was associated with the sun god. It was a strategic city both for trade and also the militarily, especially during Roman times. There were more trade guilds at Thyatira than at any other city in Asia, so it was a city bustling with all kinds of craftsmen and traders from far and wide. Craftsmen such as those who worked with wool, made linen, manufactured garments, leather workers, bronze metal workers, as well as dyers and tanners. Acts chapter sixteen records the meeting that Paul and his helpers had with a lady called Lydia. She was a seller of purple cloth and was from Thyatira, who along with some others met to pray at a riverside near Philippi. When Paul joined with them and told them the good news of Jesus the Messiah, she accepted the Lord into her heart and became one of the founder members of the church there.

The special message to the church at Thyatira reveals Jesus as the one who has eyes as a flame of fire and feet as fine brass. As always the particular way that Jesus is revealed is relevant to the need in the church. It is worth noting that whatever need that exists in any church, Jesus has the answer and is the answer, whether the need is for comfort or correction. Jesus is seen here as having a piercing and penetrating gaze that searches hearts and minds. Flaming eyes not only search out sin and darkness, but also speak of judgment as is illustrated by what John records in Revelation Ch.19v11&12 "Now I saw heaven opened, and behold, a white horse. And He who sat on him was called Faithful and True, and in righteousness He judges and makes war. His eyes were like a flame of fire, and on His head were many crowns." This is how John sees Jesus when He comes to earth at His second coming, in flaming fire to take vengeance on His enemies. He strikes the nations with a rod of iron and the beast and the false prophet are cast into the lake of fire. Finally the rest of the men who followed them and had come to fight against the Lord are killed. The feet of Jesus, as fine brass that have passed through a furnace, speak of judgment and justice having a firm foundation as He comes to execute judgment and justice in the world.

With penetrating insight Jesus is able to see and know all that is going on in the church at Thyatira, so He says to them as He does to all the other churches, "I know your works." Firstly Jesus commends them for their love, the Greek word for love here being the God kind of love, agapae, which was explored in some detail in chapter two. They did not just love in word only but also in deeds. Their love was a practical love that fed the hungry and clothed the naked. They also had love for those who were outside of their own church fellowship, even extending to those who hated them. Allied to this Jesus said, I also know your works of service. This word service is translated from the Greek word diakonia from which we get the word deacon, one who serves in the church. We first read of deacons in the church in Acts Ch.6. There were many poor widows in the church, both Jews and Greeks, and the apostles had taken it on board to minister to their needs by daily serving them with meals. Unfortunately the Greek widows were being neglected, which prompted complaints on their behalf, so the apostles decided that it was necessary to appoint seven men, who met their criteria, to do the job so they could concentrate on prayer and the ministry of the word of God. The result was that every one was cared for and the word of The Lord increased and the church was built up. These men who served, made all the difference, showing just how important works of service are to the growth of the church. They were men of high calibre who were full of wisdom and the Holy Spirit, Stephen being the most well known.

When Paul wrote to Timothy, he stressed the high standard of behaviour required, in order for someone to be eligible to serve as a deacon. He said that deacons must be reverent, not double tongued not given to much wine, not greedy for money, holding the mystery of the faith with a pure conscience. But let them also first be tested, and then let them serve as deacons, being found blameless. I am not suggesting that every one who was commended for their service by the Lord was officially recognised as a deacon, but these scriptures from Timothy serve to highlight the importance of serving in the church and as they were commended by the Lord for their service, they must have reached an acceptable standard of godliness and maturity.

Connected to the loving way some in the church served, was the fact that they served faithfully. Jesus acknowledges their faith, the trust and reliance they have in Him that enables them to serve faithfully and be steadfast. Paul when writing to the Corinthian church, in the last verse of 1Corinthians Ch.15 said, "Be steadfast, immovable, always abounding in the work of the Lord, knowing that your labour is not in vain in the Lord." Those who are in the Lord's service have a stewardship committed to them. A steward's role is purely to serve his master and look after his interests. Paul also wrote to the Corinthians that it is a requirement for a steward to be found faithful regarding the tasks he has been set. Jesus when telling the parable of the talents, related how two of the three servants who were given talents traded with them and doubled their money. When their Lord returned he was able to say to each of them, "Well done, good and faithful servant; you were faithful over a few things, I will make you ruler over many things. Enter into the joy of your Lord."(Matthew

Ch.25v21) So the Lord Himself will be pleased with all who take their service to him seriously and use the gifts He has given in His service. To those who are faithful and overcome at Thyatira Jesus promises, "I will give power over the nations, He shall rule them with a rod of iron; they shall be dashed to pieces like the potters vessels." (Revelation Ch2v26&27)

The companion of faith is patience, as in scripture the two are almost inseparable. Where the faith of God is there is always patience. The saints at Thyatira patiently endured hardships, due to practicing sacrificial love. They patiently waited for the Lord to bless their labours, and were quite willing to wait for the rewards that they could expect for the work that they did. This is Godliness in action, as God is patient, like a farmer is content to wait for the seed he has sown to mature, before he harvests it. In fact we may never enjoy the rewards of our labours in this life, but as we are constantly reminded in the messages to the churches, there are rewards in heaven that are eternal. Many are applauded by men, for charitable works done in the public eye in the here and now, but Jesus said that to be rewarded by our Heavenly Father we need to do our good works in secret, and then He will reward us openly whether in this life or the next..

Jesus further commends them for the fact that their works had been more of late than they had been at the beginning. They had not been content just to do the minimum, but had excelled, I believe both in quantity and quality. Have you slowed down as time has gone on and done less and less? Or could Jesus praise you for a greater effort in His service now than there used to be?

No church is perfect, even those two churches who the Lord had nothing against, but there were very serious charges that the Lord had to bring against the church at Thyatira which merited severe judgment. Jesus had seen a number of excellent things, how gracious the Lord is to say that He had just a few things against them.

The first thing is that the leadership, who are responsible to the Lord for the care of the church, had allowed a woman called Jezebel to teach and seduce the Lord's servants to commit sexual immorality and idolatry. This was a serious lapse in leadership, which considering the quality of what was good in the church is quite amazing! Some clue as to why this situation existed may lie in the suggestion in most Bibles, that this woman Jezebel was the wife of the leader. How often have good people turned a blind eye to things that are evil, because the source of that evil is someone close to them, or dear to them. Remember Eli's sons, as recorded in the first book of Samuel, that they were priests in the tabernacle at Shiloh, and committed immoral sexual acts with the women who came there in full sight of the Lord's people. They also took by force, the best of the offerings that the people brought to the Lord, because of their greed. The Lord had to speak to young Samuel of the judgment to come, not only on Eli's sons, but on Eli himself because he had done nothing to stop this gross sin.

The second problem, regarding this situation, was that this woman was allowed to teach as a self appointed prophetess. It was bad enough that there was someone in the church who held views that were totally unscriptural, but to allow her to teach those things claiming that she was something she was not, was inexcusable. Who said she was not a prophet, well Jesus did, and He is the one who gives authority and power by the Holy Spirit to teach or prophesy or to do anything else in the church. After all Jesus is the head and everything flows down from the Head, so if He does not acknowledge someone, then they have no authority. Furthermore the situation of this woman was untenable as far as scripture is concerned. Paul when writing to Timothy in 1Timothy Ch.2 set out for us the order of things as they should be in the church. He wrote in v11-12, "Let a woman learn in silence with all submission. And I do not permit a woman to teach or to have authority over a man, but to be in silence." The reason being that the man was first formed, then Eve, it was not Adam who was deceived, but the woman being deceived was guilty of transgression. There are of course those who would point out that there are women teaching in the church, and some of them doing a good job. But the point Paul is making is that a woman should not be allowed to teach in the church unless she is under the authority of the men who are responsible for leadership. Elders in the church are responsible before the Lord for what is taught in the church, and the Lord is holding the leader of the church in Thyatira to account in this instance. The church needs to always beware of those who claim a position, or status with a title, such as apostle, prophet, and teacher and so on, whether they be men or women. Paul never called himself the apostle Paul, neither did any of the other apostles claim any title, or status, above other believers. In fact Paul on one occasion said, "To me, who am less than the least of all the saints." (Ephesians Ch.3v8) But Paul did on a number of occasions defend his calling and ministry, against those who sought to discredit him in the sight of the churches he had established. He did this because he loved those churches and did not want false apostles seeking to take advantage of the churches. Paul could show proofs of his apostleship, he could write to the church at Rome, in Ch.15v18&19 of his epistle to them, "For I will not dare to speak of any of those things which Christ has not accomplished through me, in word and in deed, to make the Gentiles obedient-in mighty signs and wonders, by the power of the Spirit of God, so that from Jerusalem and round about to Il-lyrcum I have fully preached the gospel of Christ." He could also write to the Corinthian church in 2Corinthians Ch.3v1-3 and say, "Do we begin again to commend ourselves? Or do we need, as some others, epistles of commendation to you or letters of commendation from you? You are our epistle written in our hearts, known and read by all men; clearly you are an epistle of Christ, ministered by us, written not with ink but by the Spirit of the Living God, not on tablets of stone but on tablets of flesh, that is of the heart." No one needs titles in the church in order to gain respect, or a position of authority, but if they have a ministry to the body of Christ, it will be because Christ has gifted them and that gifting will become self evident.

That Jezebel was allowed to teach and seduce the Lord's servants was the crux of the complaint the Lord had against the leader in particular. With her teaching she had seduced and led astray those who belonged to the Lord, to commit with her acts of sexual immorality, and to eat things sacrificed to idols. Jesus is justifiably aggrieved with the leader in particular, as there can be no excuse for this kind of thing happening in the church of God, and it was not happening in secret either, but quite openly. It is remarkable, that despite the weakness and vulnerability of those who have been seduced, Jesus still calls them His servants, and owns them.

Some teachers, and teachings, are very seductive and we all need the help of the Holy Spirit, and the Word of God, to discern good from evil. The Israelites were seduced by the Moabite women, in Balaam's time, to commit acts of sexual immorality and idolatry. Satan is very adept in devising ways to lead God's people astray, and this is especially true when he, or his servants, appear as angels of light. Jezebel came as a 'prophetess' claiming divine authority for what she taught, and some in the church believed her teaching and fell into Satan's trap. Many still come today, with the trappings of ecclesiastical authority claiming to be something, or someone really important with a fresh message from the Lord, but their teachings are to be tested by the Word and the Spirit of God. The truth of God's word is timeless, and it is the truth because truth never changes, it has no reason to change, as the psalmist wrote, "Forever, O Lord your word is settled in heaven."(Psalm 119v89) We are given a clue as to why the teachings of Jezebel were so seductive from what is written in Revelation Ch.2v24 which says, "Now to you I say, and to the rest in Thyatira, as many as do not have this doctrine, who have not known the depths of Satan, as they say, I will put on you no other burden." This verse speaks of what Jezebel, and her followers called, 'the depths of Satan,' other Bible versions have something similar to 'the deep secrets of Satan.' In other words Jezebel is claiming that she and her followers have experienced the deep secret things of Satan and that they have the edge over others in the church because of this. There are today, corruptions of the truth that teach that God and Satan are like the two sides of a coin. That light and darkness are two facets of the same thing. Ying and yang, and the teachings of the free masons, who believe that it does not matter which god you believe in, as long as you believe in a god, are manifestations of this teaching. It would appear that the doctrine that Jezebel was teaching was something of this ilk. She was claiming that she and her followers had acquired knowledge, and a knowing through experience, that others did not have and that made them superior. This knowledge, she claimed, could be acquired through sexual relations with her, and through eating things sacrificed to idols. This not only appealed to the sensual, fleshly desires of the men who followed her, but also to their pride in acquiring knowledge that was hidden from others. This is the essence of occult teaching, as occult means things that are hidden. Our sinful natures do have a definite propensity to be inquisitive, and want to discover things that are hidden, and forbidden. Satan knows this and has used it against us ever since Adam sinned.

It is interesting to note that Satan used this form of seduction to introduce sin into the human race. When Eve sought to resist Satan's advances, she told him that God had said that they were not to eat the fruit of the tree of the knowledge of good and evil. Satan in reply claimed that, in fact, God was trying to withhold knowledge from them that would give them an equal standing with Himself. "For God knows that in the day you eat of it your eyes will be opened, and you will be like God, knowing good and evil," Satan lied.(Genesis Ch.3v5) Even though, at this point Eve had not sinned, she begins to be interested in what the serpent is saying to her. "Your eyes will be opened", he said, to see things that have been secret and hidden, you will know things that God has been hiding from you. All this, along with the lie that there would be no consequences for sin and disobedience, was too much for Eve, so seeing the fruit was good to eat and good to look at as well, she gave in. Adam was with her and did nothing to prevent her from taking the fruit. That sounds like a familiar story, doesn't it, when we read of what was going on at Thyatira, and still goes on in the church today! Having introduced sin into the human race, Satan now finds it all the easier to seduce even the Lord's servants into sin with the allurement of hidden knowledge and so called enlightenment. You will be as God, he said to Eve, and that is still the lie of Satan today, as he seeks to appeal to the prideful, fallen nature of men and women in the church. Self appointed prophets, men or women, only seek to usurp the place of Christ in the church, as they resist any rightful authority. We today need to be on our guard against the occult, in all its various forms, as those who practice it are heading for judgment, in the lake of fire, and exclusion from the holy city the New Jerusalem. John writes in Revelation Ch.22v15, "But outside are dogs and sorcerers and sexually immoral and murderers and idolaters, and whoever loves and practices a lie."

The character of this woman is exposed in Revelation Ch.2v21. Jesus said, "I gave her time to repent of her sexual immorality, and she did not repent." This implies that in some way the Lord had previously sent other warnings to this woman regarding her sinful behaviour. The patience and kindness of the Lord are here contrasted with the stubbornness of this woman. She was very much someone who was not going to humble herself and turn to the Lord, but was rather like the characters that Paul refers to in 1Timothy Ch.6v3 where he said, "If anyone teaches otherwise and does not consent to wholesome words, even the words of our Lord Jesus Christ, and to the doctrine that accords with godliness, he, or she, is proud, knowing nothing, but is obsessed with disputes and arguments over words, from which come envy, strife" and so on. In riding rough shod over the leadership in the church, and most importantly resisting the grace of God, Jezebel was heading for trouble, and trouble she would get.

Because the leader of the church, much like Adam with Eve, would do nothing to stop her, Jesus Himself would have to act. I will cast her into a sickbed Jesus said. She had prided herself, in seducing the Lords servants into bed with her to commit acts of sexual immorality, so now it is quite appropriate that the Lord should cast her into a sick bed. Those who committed adultery with her would be heading for great tribulation also, unless they repented. It seems that the Lord knowing, that she as the instigator of all this trouble in the church had been given time to repent and she spurned the opportunity, is now giving those she seduced an opportunity to turn away from her teachings and her ways. In Revelation Ch.9v20-21 we read of others who refuse to repent. It says, "But the rest of mankind, who were not killed by these plagues, did not repent of the works of their hands, that they should not worship demons, and idols of gold, silver, brass, stone, and wood, which can neither see nor hear nor walk. And they did not repent of their murders or their sorceries or their sexual immorality or their thefts." For those who refuse to repent there is no hope, but only a certain looking forward to judgment and the lake of fire which burns for ever and ever.

God the Father and Jesus Christ the Son always work in perfect harmony. There is no conflict between them, either in character or actions. Jesus said to the church at Thyatira that He will lay Jezebel low in a sick bed and bring her followers into great tribulation, unless they repent. Furthermore Jesus said I will kill her children with death. This revelation of Jesus has never been popular, both within the church and outside of it. Many people cannot conceive of Jesus punishing sin with sickness, tribulation or death. Some in the church would argue that God never uses sickness as a means of disciplining His children, although this is not the only scripture to indicate that He does. Paul warned the Corinthians that if they did not discern the Lord's body aright they would come under the judgment of God, and that was why some were weak and sick among them, and even why some had died. Those outside the church also find it impossible to come to terms with a Jesus who does such things, because they have a Jesus in their minds that they have conceived from their own imaginations, and do not have an understanding of Jesus as He is revealed to us in the Bible. This is one of the reasons why the book of Revelation is neglected by Christians and ridiculed by the world. They want to have Jesus as someone who is tender, and as they think loving, and kind, who will accept any kind of behaviour from anyone. A soft, sugary kind of daddy, who will just pat them on the back, and say never mind, try to do better in the future. Revelation blows this kind of thinking about Jesus right out of the water, as He is seen as the mighty coming king who is coming to execute righteous judgment on the earth, and before He does that He will put His own house in order first.

Jesus is concerned not just for the welfare of His servants who have fallen into sin at Thyatira, but also for the whole church in this region of Asia. The reason for His concern is obvious. If the other churches see what Jezebel is doing, and seeming to get away with it, some may be tempted to fall into the same kind of sin. But when they hear of the judgment of God on those guilty of sin, they will all know that Jesus in their midst is the One who has eyes of flaming fire and feet of burnished bronze. They will all take note that He is the one who searches, and examines closely, the minds and hearts of His people. He is the one who searches out pride, contempt for the grace and patience of God and the stubbornness and rebellion, that comes dressed up as sound doctrine in order to deceive. No seemingly clever arguments, or persuasive words, or seductive reasonings can count for anything before His fiery gaze. Sin is sin, and He is the one who defines what sin is. Satan, the serpent said, "Has God said," when he was tempting Eve. So for us today there can be no question as to what God has said, it is clearly written in the Bible. It was also very clear to Jezebel and her group, that Jesus defined what they were doing as sin, for He had already called on them to repent of it. To the rest of the churches, and also to the church today, the gospel, which is the same in both testaments, lays down the standard of righteousness that God requires. It is contained in the Law of Moses, which God gave to him, and has never been annulled. The letter to the Romans makes it clear that the Christian gospel does not annul the law but establishes it. Paul goes on to argue that neither does the grace of God in the gospel, give anyone the license to sin. But rather through the Holy Spirit's work in us, although we are not sinless, we can delight to do the will of God and fulfill the spirit of the law.

So Jesus will give to every one according to their works. To those who claim to represent Jesus in the church, but lead others astray, there is severe judgment. Those who knowingly and continually commit sin in the church, have only one thing facing them, a great deal of trouble. The Lord is patient, but those who walk in disobedience cannot continue to presume that they will never be punished, for they will.

Jesus speaks more personally to the leader of this church than to any other leader, because of the gravity of his failure. Jesus said, "Now to you I say, and to the rest at Thyatira, as many as do not have this doctrine."(Revelation Ch.2v24) It can never be repeated too many times that wrong doctrine leads to gross sin in the church. Jesus is passionate about correct doctrine, and its importance in the church can never be overemphasised. Yet to hear some in the church today speaking about doctrine, you would think that it was the least of all of God's priorities. I would argue that God has taken so much trouble to give us His written word, that sound doctrine is a number one priority with God. Yet the argument goes that doctrine divides, and that love unites, so let there be love, and not worry about the doctrine. That doctrine divides is not a problem to God, for He would have His people separated from false doctrine. Jesus himself said, I have not come to bring peace but a sword. I have come to divide men and women between those who receive my words and those who don't. Paul encouraged the Corinthians to examine themselves, to see if they were in the faith. To do that they would need some criteria to examine themselves by, and that criteria is the Word of God as we have it in the Bible from Genesis to Revelation.

To those who remained faithful to the Lord, Jesus said He would impose no other burden on them. But that they were to hold fast to what they had till he came. This could refer to His coming in judgment to deal with the sin in the church, or it could refer to His second coming for His people. He who overcomes, and is not seduced by Satan or his servant, Jesus said, "I will give power over the nations. He shall rule them with a rod of iron."(Revelation Ch.2v26-27) God's faithful children are destined to rule on the earth over the nations. More than that, Jesus said, "I will give him the morning star." In Revelation Ch.22v16 Jesus says that He is the bright and the Morning Star. Those who overcome will receive the Lord Himself as their reward, and what greater reward could there be? Why does Jesus call Himself the Morning Star? The answer may be that as the morning star is the precursor to the dawning of the day, so Jesus, when He comes for His people, will signal to the world that is now, that the long night of Satan's power and influence is about to end. After this there will be for God's people eternal day, as there will be for the new heavens and earth also.

CHAPTER 6

SARDIS- CHURCH IN THE GRAVE

Sardis was a very ancient city, which was the capital city of the kingdom of Lydia. It was ideal as a fortress city. It was a rich city enjoying all the advantages of commerce and trade. It was conquered by Cyrus, the Persian king, and later by Antiochus the Great. The patron deity of Sardis was Cybele, to which was attributed the supposed ability to give life to the dead. However the city in Roman times declined in importance, although the Romans did reconstruct the city after a devastating earthquake. But its reputation, for greatness remained, even though the reality was somewhat different. It may have been entirely coincidental, that the church at Sardis was in the same position, having a name but not living up to it. Today it no longer exists as a city that is inhabited, but is an important archaeological site.

To the church in Sardis Jesus is the One who has the Seven Spirits of God, and holds the seven stars in His right hand. As a reminder of how the Holy Spirit is pictured in Ch.4, John sees Him as seven lamps of fire burning before the throne of God. In Ch.5 the Holy Spirit is seen by John as the seven horns and seven eyes of the Lamb in the midst of the throne. Burning fire, horns speaking of power and authority, and all seeing eyes, this is the Holy Spirit of God; this is just what the church in Sardis needed to see. They were dead and needed the fire of God to burn away their complacency, the power of God to reenergize them, and the insight of God to show them the way out of their terrible condition. They also needed to know that Jesus held the seven stars in His right hand. These were the angels, or messengers, of the seven churches who have a singular responsibility to convey to their particular church, the message written by John that came from Jesus. It is the message also from the Holy Spirit that those with ears to hear needed to hear. These messengers were personally in the right hand of Jesus Himself, they were to come to the churches with their prophetic message that should be heeded by the churches, or ignored by them at their peril. It was vital then, as it is now, that those with a prophetic message for a church, or for the church generally are heard. We are not to despise prophecy, but to test it. The Lord then was giving a special message, by special messengers to seven particular churches, that is now part of the cannon of scripture, messages for the church for all time. Now, His prophetic message comes to us firmly based and rooted in the written word of God, from Genesis to Revelation. There are no authentic scriptures outside of these sixty six books; in them we have the fullness of divine revelation.

The prophetic message to Sardis is different from those that have preceded it. In this message Jesus comes straight to the point, in much the same way that Paul does when he writes to the Galatians, after the most cursory of introductions, Paul says "I marvel that you are turning away so soon from Him who called you in the Grace of Christ, to a different gospel."(Galatians Ch.1v6) So in that verse Paul sums up what he intends to write to them about. In the same way Jesus says to the church at Sardis, "I know your works, that you have a name that you are alive, but you are dead."(Revelation Ch.3v1) Even the church at Ephesus, that Jesus threatened He would remove from Him if they did not repent, had some commendation before Jesus said, "Nevertheless I have this against you."(Revelation Ch.2v4) But the stench of death is so pervasive in this church that Jesus has no good thing to say about them first, before He lets them know exactly what He has against them. Reputation was one thing, reality was quite another. This church had a reputation for being spiritually vibrant and active in the community that it was in, but it was in a deep sleep, it was in rest mode, and as far as Jesus was concerned, the grave yard was not outside the church, but inside. For most people in the church, rigor mortis was well advanced, so the ever living one who has the life giving Spirit, now comes to wake the dead.

How many churches have a reputation that cannot be backed up by anything substantial? How many are living in the past, basking in the afterglow of bygone years when the church was really alive? From what Jesus says about the church in Sardis, it would be reasonable to deduce that there was a time when there was life in the church, for reputations are usually built on reality. Compared to the other churches in Asia Minor the church at Sardis had been a hive of activity, excelling the best of the others. They had been more zealous in looking after widows and orphans, had worked harder to spread the gospel of the grace of God, and the forgiveness of sins through faith in Jesus, than the others. They also had made sure that those who received Jesus as saviour were taught the faith and became disciples. They met together regularly to praise and worship the Lord, they shared meals together and enjoyed fellowship and recreation together. They looked out for each others interests. They were well known for all these things, so that when others wanted to site a good example of a living, vibrant church, they would talk about Sardis. Theirs was a reputation like Rolls Royce, for being the best, but as ever, Jesus is only concerned with the reality of the situation. In reality they were not a Rolls Royce but a clapped out old fashioned Skoda, ready for the scrap heap. You remember the jokes that used to be told about Skodas.

Jesus warns them that they need to be watchful, and WAKE UP! This was not the time for sleeping. It was not the time for sleeping, for as Paul wrote to the Thessalonians, you are sons of light and sons of the day. Jesus never intended that they should be sons of the night, or of the darkness, therefore they should not have been asleep, but alert and watching. Satan was highly delighted at the condition of this church, for he loves to see Christians inactive and irrelevant. He had managed to lull them to sleep, and they were snug and comfortable in their complacency, especially because to them reputation was everything, along with image and façade. Jesus once said "I must work the works of Him who sent Me while it is day; the night is coming when no one can work." (John Ch.9v4)

"Be watchful, and strengthen the things which remain," Jesus said to them. (Revelation Ch.3v2) All was not lost; there was a glimmer of hope, for there were some things that remained of their former walk with the Lord that needed to be salvaged. The heartbeat of this church still beat slowly through those who had remained faithful to the Lord. The word strengthen, in this context means to make firm and fix down. They needed to firm up on their service to the Lord, and establish those things that remained, that were about to disappear. There are things in the church that need to be affirmed and established in every generation, things that become the fixtures and fittings of the life of the church. The church after the Day of Pentecost had the essentials of a living, active church, that was fully alive and awake, for they had established practices that they continued steadfastly in, and this should be the aim of every church. They continued steadfastly in the apostles' doctrine and fellowship. They did not neglect to meet together to be taught the word of God, and then to go out into the world and practice what they were taught. They were not hearers only, but doers of the word. This is what it means to continue steadfastly in the apostles' doctrine, because continuing in a doctrine is, not just continuing to hear it taught, or continuing to agree with it, but continuing to practice it. We have seen in previous chapters of this book, that doctrine and practice are indivisible from each other; our lifestyle is determined by the doctrines we believe in. Fellowship, being together, sharing the good times and the bad times, ministering to each others needs, is essential for the church. Christian fellowship is only possible when certain things exist in a church. We can read about them in Philippians Ch.2v2-3, they are having a mind like Christ's, having the same kind of love that Christ had for us, and being one in spirit and purpose as Christ was one with the Father. Also doing nothing out of selfish ambition or vain conceit, but humbly considering others better than yourself. Lastly not just looking out for number one, but equally looking out for the interests of others also. These things make for wonderful Christian fellowship, and were also the things that characterised the attitude of Jesus, when He came to be a servant and give His life, so that fellowship could be restored between God and man. The church in Acts Ch.2 had these things well and truly fixed and fitted into the framework of their existence, the church at Sardis needed to re-establish them.

Acts chapter two also tells us that they continued steadfastly in the breaking of bread and prayers. They broke bread from house to house; they ate their food with gladness and simplicity of heart. What a wonderful picture of unity and openness! Simplicity of heart speaks of an integrity, without any ulterior motive or duplicity, a purity of heart. This should be the norm in the church, but is often sadly lacking. They went to each others homes to share in fellowship and meals and pray together, without evil intent of any kind. No one had anything to hide, no one was afraid of anyone else. So they were all together and shared what they had with each other, the rich meeting the needs of the poor, so that there was an equality among them.

We do not know how many of these essentials to life in the church remained at Sardis, but we do know that what did remain was ready to die. They were like a young man with his life ahead of him with so much more left to achieve, in hospital in an intensive care ward and on a life support machine because virtually all the vital signs of life have gone. Jesus says to them, "I have not found your works perfect before God."(Revelation Ch.3v2) "I know your works," Jesus said, and not one of them has been completed. We usually think of the word perfect, as meaning without any fault, but in the scriptures it usually means complete, or mature. God once told Abraham that he should walk before Him and be perfect. God was not expecting sinless perfection from Abraham, but maturity of faith. Jesus is saying to them, not one of your works have reached maturity, not one thing has been completed. They had made a start, but good starts are not as important as a strong finish. Their works were just like buildings that are half finished that used to be called follies. They are reminiscent of the Galatian church, who had begun to run well but had been hindered along the way by some people who had persuaded them that it was alright to begin in the Spirit, but they could only come to maturity through keeping the law. How many churches could have this kind of indictment leveled against them? How many of us, as individuals are guilty of similar shortcomings? Maybe you can remember old school reports that said something like, you have made a good start, but you need to keep up the effort, to reach the required standard. If Jesus were the school teacher of the church at Sardis, in the end of term report He would write, this pupil is popular and well liked in the class, and his fellow pupils think very highly of his work, but his exam results are poor and he needs to do a lot better. Jesus said He had examined their works and found them sadly lacking in content in every department, they had to wake up and do a lot better.

Having said that they were dead, and then what they needed to start to do to revive their spiritual fortunes, Jesus then goes on to say what they needed to do to return to their former glory, when they resembled the church in Acts Ch. 2.

The first thing they had to do was remember! How easy it is to forget. One of the complaints God had against Israel was that they had forgotten Him days without number. How could they forget, when God had done such great things for them? But they did. "Bless the Lord, O my soul," wrote the psalmist, "and forget not all His benefits." (Psalm 103v2) Scripture is full of exhortations for the people of God not to forget, but remember. Peter, writing to the church in general in 2Peter Ch1v12-15, three times speaks of his responsibility to remind the church of the things he has written to them, because he will not always be there to remind them in person. Peter knew how easy it was to forget, even important things.

The church at Sardis had forgotten how things had been at the beginning of their walk with the Lord. Remember how you have received and heard, Jesus urges them. Remember how enthusiastic you were about the things of God. How keen you were to know the Lord better, to serve Him zealously, and love one another out of a pure heart fervently. Remember how you could not wait for the next meeting time, to hear the word of God taught, how you received that word, not as the word of men, but as the word of God. Your ears were open to hear what the Spirit was saying. Remember how you received brothers and sisters from other churches, and ministered to them with hospitality. Call to mind when you did run well, when the life of the Spirit pulsated through the church. When the heart of the church beat strongly, and all the members functioned according to the direction of Jesus the Head of the church.

Having told them to remember, Jesus then calls on them to hold fast and repent. Turn again and find the former path that you used to walk on. Again Jesus urges them to be watchful, and keep the things you remember you used to do. Wake up to the way you remember you used to be, and keep hold of those things. Turn away from the way you have been going, this is the divine remedy for their plight. Repentance is always the way forward for God's people, and all through scripture God calls on His people to repent. This patient was not dead yet, and if they received the treatment that Jesus is prescribing, they will make a full recovery.

How relevant this message of Jesus to Sardis is, for churches and individuals today. What remains of your spiritual life, establish and fix it, don't let everything go. Then go on and remember how you were when you first received Jesus as your Saviour and Lord, and re-establish the things you have let go, through acts of repentance. Jesus warns that if they did not wake up, and follow all His instructions, He would come upon them as a thief, and they would not know when He was coming. Like a thief in the night, is a phrase that is usually associated with the second coming of Jesus. It is a phrase that is used in Revelation Ch16v15, "Behold I am coming as a thief. Blessed is he who watches, and keeps his garments, lest he walk naked and they see his shame." These are the words of Jesus to those who are on the earth just before His coming in judgment to the earth. He will come suddenly, and quickly upon an unsuspecting world, at a time when through deception and force, Satan will have the world believing that he is in control, and that he will be victorious in his warfare against God. Indeed, the Lord will ensure that they believe this lie, because they would not receive the love of the truth. Jesus had taught His disciples this very same truth. Matthew Ch.24v42-44 says, "Watch therefore, for you do not know what hour your Lord is coming. But know this, that if the master of the house had known what hour the thief would come, he would have watched and not allowed his house to be broken into. Therefore you also be ready, for the Son of Man is coming at an hour you do not expect." It is important to notice that the Lord's second coming is likened to a thief coming in the night, not in the manner of His coming, which will be spectacular and glorious, but in the timing of His coming. The message is clear, just as the thief does not announce to the householder what time he is going to break into his house, for obvious reasons, so Jesus is not going to announce the timing of His coming. Both Paul and Peter testify to the same truth, that the Day of the Lord will so come as a thief in the night. Paul, in his letter to the Thessalonians, speaks of the sudden destruction that will come on an unsuspecting world, and they will not escape the judgment of the Lord as He comes in flaming fire to take vengeance on His enemies. Peter also speaks of the Day of the Lord coming like a thief, in the which, the heavens and earth that now are will be burnt up, and melt with a fervent heat. Just previous to this, he says that in these unbelieving days, there will be scoffers saying, "Where is the promise of His coming? For since the fathers fell asleep, all things continue as they were from the beginning of creation."(2Peter Ch.3v4)

The church at Sardis was all but dead and Jesus warns them that if they do not wake up He will come to them, and if they refuse to listen, He will come and find them not ready for His coming. Not ready, unprepared for the coming of the King of Kings, nothing could be more reprehensible. This could refer to His coming to discipline them for their laziness and wickedness, but it could equally refer to the second coming of the Lord, which many in the time of the very early church were expecting. Like the seven foolish virgins, who had been asleep, but with no oil in their lamps, they could find themselves out in the cold, when the Lord came. Ever since the Lord returned to heaven, the church has needed to be ready for His coming.

What Jesus says next really emphasises how serious a condition the church at Sardis was in. Jesus says, "You have a few names even in Sardis who have not defiled their garments."(Revelation Ch.3v4)

"Even in Sardis," Jesus says, as if it were the very last church on earth that one would expect to find saints with pure garments. But there were the faithful few, and the rest had filthy, soiled and defiled garments in the sight of the Lord. This explains why they had begun well, but had not been able to continue, and have a sustained effort in the work of the Lord. Why nothing that they started for the Lord came to fruition. No church, or individual Christian, should be in any doubt whatsoever, that indulging in sin, and those worldly things that are defiling, is the greatest hindrance to fulfilling the work God gives us to do. The sad fact is that multitudes of men and women, through the centuries of church history, both well known and obscure, have lost the plot as far as God's work is concerned, because of something they have allowed into their lives that has been defiling. Whole churches have been sullied because of false teaching and the work of God, as a result, has been curtailed. For it is not only evil deeds that defile, but as we have seen from the messages to the churches, false doctrines also make us unclean in the sight of God. James, in the last verse of the first chapter of his epistle says, "Pure and undefiled religion before God and the Father is this: to visit orphans and widows in their trouble, and to keep oneself unspotted from the world." The church in Sardis had not kept themselves unspotted from the world, consequently neither had they continued to look after the orphans and the widows. Paul wrote to the Corinthians in 2Corinthians Ch.6v16-18, "For you are the temple of the Living God. As God has said: "I will dwell in them and walk among them. I will be their God, and they shall be my people." Therefore "Come out from among them and be separate," says the Lord. "Do not touch what is unclean, and I will receive you." "I will be a Father to you, and you shall be My sons and daughters, says the Lord Almighty." Then in Ch.7v1 Paul continues, "Therefore, having these promises, beloved, let us cleanse ourselves from all filthiness of the flesh and spirit, perfecting holiness in the fear of God." There can be no question, that God's will for His church, is that once having been cleansed we keep ourselves clean.

For those who had kept their garments clean, and their lives unspotted from the world, Jesus promises, they shall walk with Him in white for they are worthy. This refers to when these faithful few are in heaven, and white garments will be given to them. These white garments, we are told, are the righteous acts of the saints. They will be given them because they are worthy. Would you walk with Jesus in white? Then overcome the world as He overcame the world, and you will have that reward. It will be worth the struggle, and the fight against the world, the flesh and the devil, to be able in that day to wear white with Jesus, to be like Him. Everyone who is pictured in heaven near to Jesus and the throne of God is wearing white garments. The twenty four elders are clothed in white robes, so are the saints who are under the altar. The great multitude, from every tongue, tribe and nation, who had come through the great tribulation are dressed in white too. The bride of the Lamb is dressed in white, fine linen, clean and bright, and the armies of heaven that accompany Jesus at His second coming, are also dressed in white.

The reassurance from Jesus that overcomers, and all true believers are overcomers, will not have their names blotted out of the book of life, but rather their names will be confessed before His Father is further reward for those who overcome and keep themselves clean. In 1John Ch.3v6 he writes, "Whoever abides in Him does not sin. Whoever sins has neither seen Him nor known Him" This means that those who continue in sin and practice sin have never come to know God, but those who practice righteousness and keep themselves clean by confessing their sin do know God, and their salvation is assured. Would the church at Sardis repent, and exchange their filthy garments for ones that are white and clean? We have no information in scripture, as to the outcome of this message from Jesus. But if anyone reading this, needs to wake up and repent and hear what the Holy Spirit is saying, may the incentives of these heavenly rewards spur you on to do what Jesus tells this church to do, so that you can walk with Him in white and be assured that your name is in the book of life.

CHAPTER 7

PHILADELPHIA- CHURCH WITH AN OPEN DOOR

Philadephia was about thirty miles south east of Sardis, in an area ideal for vine growing. It was founded by Attalus the Second. In AD17 it was devastated by a severe earthquake, and was more or less wiped out as a city. But the Romans considered it important enough to revive, and Tiberius re-named it Neo-Cesarea, and honoured it with the Neocorate, which was the wardenship of the temple for emperor worship. Modern day Philadelphia is named Alashehir, where a sizable proportion of the population claim Christianity as their religion.

To the church in Philadelphia, Jesus is He who is Holy, and He who is True. Holiness is something that can only be attributed to God, in that He sets the standard for holiness, and no one can possibly attain, in themselves, to that standard. God's standard of holiness is absolute, just as He is Light, and in Him is no darkness at all. No man can claim holiness, or lay claim to any title, such as his holiness. Any such claim or title is blasphemous. All the children of God, who have been washed in the blood of Jesus and set apart for

God through the sanctifying work of the Holy Spirit, are holy in the sight of God. No one can claim any innate holiness of his own. Jesus was never made holy, for as God the Son, He is holy. All that is said concerning Jesus in Revelation Ch.3v7 speaks of His divinity. Jesus is the only man who has ever walked this earth that can justifiably claim the title of His Holiness. For this church, that has a little strength, it is a comfort to know that the one who is in their midst is God himself. In Ch. 4 we read of the four living creatures, who are constantly worshipping God and saying, "Holy, holy, holy, Lord God Almighty, Who was and is and is to come." They are surely calling the Father, Son and Holy Spirit, holy in their worship. In Ch.15v3-4 those who have won the victory over the beast, and are now in heaven are standing on the sea of glass and singing the song of Moses and of the Lamb. The words of this song are, "Great and marvellous are your works, Lord God Almighty! Just and true are your ways, O King of the saints! Who shall not fear You, O Lord, and glorify your name? For You alone are holy. For all nations shall come and worship before You, For your judgments have been manifested." In every revelation of Jesus in this book holiness shines out, He is the Holy One in the midst of His people.

Jesus is also, He who is true. Jesus is for real, there is nothing false in Him. There is no duplicity in Jesus, He is full of veracity. Only God is that true, that it is impossible for Him to lie. In His dealings with His people Jesus has always been straightforward and honest. He has given His word and He will always be as good as His word. As this weak church, has persevered in keeping His word, Jesus reassures them that it has all been worth while, for He is the one who is True. In His dealings with the world Jesus is no less scrupulous. John sees the Lord Jesus descending from heaven, riding on a white horse, and He is called Faithful and True, and in righteousness He judges and makes war. Jesus now comes to destroy His enemies, and because there is no injustice found in Him, no darkness or underhandedness, His enemies cannot claim that they are being treated unfairly when He comes to deal with them. They have had chance after chance to repent and turn to Him, and they have spurned every attempt by Jesus to bring them to their senses, through measured judgments, but like the Egyptians of old they will not acknowledge Him, so there is only one recourse, and that is destruction.

Jesus is the one who has the key of David. This is a rather unusual phrase, but the mention of it here in the book of Revelation is not the first time it occurs in the Bible. It is always interesting, and enlightening, to look at the first occurrence of a verse or phrase in the scriptures. So much of the New Testament, is taken from the Old Testament, which is not surprising seeing that God is the same God, He has not changed, and neither has His word. This phrase, the key of David, occurs for the first time in Isaiah Ch. 22v22. The chapter is about the Lord demoting a man called Shebna, who was over the royal household, and giving his job to another man called Eliakim. God said, in Isaiah Ch.22v20-23 "Then it shall be in that day, that I will call My servant Eliakim the son of Hilkiah; I will clothe him with your robe and strengthen him with your belt; I will commit your responsibility into his hand. He shall be a father to the inhabitants of Jerusalem and to the house of Judah. The key of the house of David I will lay on his shoulder; so he shall open, and no one shall shut; and he will shut, and no one shall open. I will fasten him as a peg in a secure place and he will become a glorious throne to his father's house." So Eliakim, by Divine appointment, became head over the royal household, and at a time when Judah was under threat from the king of Assyria. He was sent by Hezekiah the king, to speak with the representatives of Sennacherib, the Assyrian king. It was a time when Judah was under severe pressure, and most of the land was under the domination of the Assyrians, but Jerusalem still held out against them. When the threats of the Assyrians to Jerusalem became clear to Hezekiah, his response was to go into the house of the Lord and spread the words of the Assyrian king out before the Lord. He then sent Hilkiah to Isaiah, to hear what the Lord had to say. The message from Isaiah was one of deliverance for Jerusalem. For the Lord, through the offices of Hilkiah, was shutting the door to the conquest of Jerusalem, and also opening a door of deliverance. Like the church at Philadelphia, Jerusalem at this time had only a little strength against such a mighty enemy as Assyria, but when God shuts a door it stays shut, until He opens it. 2Kings Ch.19v32-34 record these comforting words to the king in Jerusalem. "Therefore thus says the Lord concerning the king of Assyria: "He shall not come into this city, nor shoot an arrow there, nor come before it with shield, nor build a siege mound against it. By the way that he came, by the same shall he return; and he shall not come into this city," says the Lord. "For I will defend this city, to save it for My own sake and for My servant David's sake." We do not need to ask any questions here about why God should do anything for His own sake, but why also for His servant David's sake? I believe the answer to this lies in the fact that God made a covenant with David, with regard to the throne and the kingdom of Israel.

After the failure of Saul to be obedient to the word of the Lord, God sent Samuel to the house of Jessie in Bethlehem to anoint one of his sons to be king in the place of Saul. After all the sons of Jessie who were in the house, had passed before Samuel and the Lord had not chosen any of them Samuel asked if there were any more sons. The reply was that there was one more, and he was looking after the sheep. When David was brought before Samuel God said to him, "Arise, anoint him; for this is the one!"(1Samuel Ch.16v12) Sometime after this David killed Goliath the giant, and from then on gained the favour of Saul, who sent him out to fight against the enemies of Israel. Soon the women in Israel were singing a popular song and the lyrics were, "Saul has slain his thousands, and David his ten thousands."(1Samuel Ch.18v7) From that time on Saul eyed David jealously, and eventually this turned to hatred, and a desire to murder David. So began David's time of exile and being in hiding from Saul, until eventually Saul along with Jonathan, David's friend, were killed by the Philistines in battle. Then, firstly the men of Judah, then all the tribes of Israel came to David at Hebron, and he became king, and reigned over all Israel for thirty three years.

In 2Samuel Ch.7 it is recorded that David, having defeated all his enemies and built himself a house, desired to build a house for the Lord. But the Lord told Nathan the prophet, to tell David that this would be something that his son would do, after he had gone. In the word of the Lord to David concerning this, part of what the Lord said was, "He shall build a house for My name, and I will establish the throne of his kingdom forever. I will be his Father, and he shall be My son. If he commits iniquity, I will chasten him with the rod of men and with the blows of the sons of men. But My mercy shall not depart from him, as I took it from Saul, whom I removed from before you. And your house and your kingdom shall be established forever before you. Your throne shall be established forever."(2Samuel Ch.7v13-16) The Lord was saying to David that his throne and his royal line would never end. Also it was the reign of David, that laid the foundation for the powerful reign of Solomon, his son. All the wealth and prestige, and land that Israel ruled over during the reign of Solomon, was due to the fact that God gave David success in everything that he did. David defeated his enemies all around, he was the foreshadowing of the King of Kings who was great David's greater Son, who shall establish a kingdom that shall fill the whole earth. The key of David is the key to success and victory, and the one who has the key of David wealds great power and authority, just as David did in establishing the kingdom of Israel.

At this critical time in Israel's history, the Lord laid the Keys of David on Hilkiah's shoulders, and the Assyrian army was unable to conquer Jerusalem. The first deliverance came, because of a rumour that the Assyrian king heard, and he withdrew from Jerusalem to fight against the Lybians. The second and final deliverance came, when the angel of the Lord went out and killed, in one night one hundred and eighty thousand troops of the Assyrian army that was camped outside Jerusalem in order to besiege it. Sennacherib then returned home, and sometime later was killed by two of his sons. In the special message to the church at Philadephia, Jesus is the one who has the key of David. He is the rightful, and final owner of the keys of the house of David. For God promised David that his throne would last forever, and in Jesus it does. When Gabriel was sent to Nazareth to announce to Mary that she would become pregnant by the Holy Spirit, he said of Jesus that, "He will be great, and will be called the Son of the Highest; and the Lord God will give Him the throne of His father David. (Luke Ch.1v32) In Acts Ch.2 Peter quoted from Psalm 110v1-2 where David inspired by the Holy Spirit writes, "The Lord said to my Lord, "sit at My right hand, till I make Your enemies Your footstall. The Lord shall send the rod of Your strength out of Zion, rule in the midst of Your enemies." Or as Peter puts it, "Therefore let all the house of Israel know assuredly that God has made this Jesus, whom you crucified, both Lord and Christ."(Acts Ch.2v36) Jesus reigns in heaven OK! Speaking of the throne and reign of Jesus, the writer to the Hebrews in Ch1v8-9 says, "But to the Son He says; "Your throne, O God is forever and ever; a sceptre of righteousness is the sceptre of your kingdom. You have loved righteousness and hated lawlessness; therefore God, Your God, has anointed You with the oil of gladness more than your companions." This is the message, conveyed by the phrase the keys of David, and as the saints at Philadelphia read the rest of what John is going to see, they will be in no doubt as to who the King is. It is the glorious Jesus in their midst.

Having the key of David, means that Jesus can open any door He wants to, and close any door also, He has the power and authority to do just that. For God has laid the key on His shoulder just as Isaiah in Ch.9v6 prophesied, "And the government will be upon His shoulder," Jesus as the Lamb in the midst of the throne, is and always will be, in charge of events on the earth. Raising up a door of power and opportunity to whoever He chooses. If He raises up His enemies, it is only, that they may fall under His hand of righteous judgment. History is littered with the debris of thrones and kingdoms that have come and gone at His behest, as He works His purposes out, for His glory and the good of His people. Pharaoh is a good example, as Paul writes in Romans Ch.9v17, 'For the scripture says to the Pharaoh, "For this very purpose I have raised you up, that I may show My power in you, and that My name may be declared in all the earth." The four riders of Revelation chapter six, go out at His command, the beast, the false prophet, the kings of the earth who are seduced by them, and even Satan himself, have their moment of power. But He has the key that enables Him to overrule all other principalities and powers, seen and unseen, for He is the one who shuts and no one opens and opens and no one shuts.

What strength it gives to this church, that is in need of some strengthening, to come to know Jesus as the one who is in their midst and can do such mighty things for them. What encouragement to the messenger of this church to know that he is in the right hand of such an all powerful one. It gets even better for them, because Jesus says to them, "I know your works. See, I have set before you an open door, and no one can shut it."(Revelation Ch.3v8) How wonderful when the Lord opens a way for His people, that no one else can block. It is a good thing, and a right thing for God's people to take opportunities as God presents them, and not to try and create situations, or try to open doors that are shut. If doors are shut, and locked, it could well be that God has shut those doors and it would be foolish and fruitless for us to try and open them. There is and old chorus I used to sing and the words are, 'The Lord knows the way through the wilderness, all I have to do is follow.' Let the pillar of cloud by day and the pillar of fire by night, the presence of the Lord, be our guide. The children of Israel did not have to open up the way through the Red Sea, the Lord opened the door. They did not have to find their own way to the land flowing with milk and honey, the Lord led them. They did not have to try and cross the Jordan river, the Lord opened the door. They did not have to besiege Jericho, the Lord opened the door, by destroying the walls. It should be our desire to live our lives, going through the doors that the Lord opens up for us. They will be doors of blessing and fruitfulness, and most importantly they will be doors of fulfilling His purpose.

We are not told what the open door, for the church at Philadelphia, refers to specifically and it would be wrong to speculate. But it would be good for us to look at the open doors that are mentioned in the scriptures. Firstly there is the open door referred to in Revelation Ch.4v1, "After these things I looked, and behold, a door standing open in heaven." What a wonderful sight, the door into heaven is open. John saw it open and was called up into heaven, to see things that were to take place after this. But in a general sense what a wonderful thing it is that we, through the things John saw and wrote down, are able to see into heaven, even the Heaven of Heavens where the throne of God and the Lamb is and to see in detail all the wonders of the Holy of Holies where our great high priest intercedes for us. But more than this, those who are in Christ Jesus are seated with Him in the heavenly places. Through Jesus there is a door opened for us into heaven, and these saints at Philadelphia would be making full use of the opportunity to go through that door, in order to receive grace and strength to help in their time of need. This was a door that Jesus had opened, and no one could shut it, or prevent them coming to the throne of grace. This is of course true for all the saints of God, whether they are weak or strong, old or young, rich or poor, all can come through the open door into heaven. The writer to the Hebrews explains how Jesus has been able to open this door into the presence of the Father. In Ch.10v19-22 he writes, 'Therefore, brethren, having boldness to enter the Holiest by the blood of Jesus, by a new and living way which He consecrated for us, through the veil, that is, His flesh, and having a High Priest over the house of God, let us draw near with a true heart in full assurance of faith, having our hearts sprinkled from an evil conscience and our bodies washed with pure water." Thank God for the gift of His Son, who shed His blood, in order to open the door to heaven for us to come with boldness before the Father.

Paul speaks about an open door in 1Corinthians Ch.16v8-9. He writes, "But I will tarry in Ephesus until Pentecost. For a great and effective door has opened to me, and there are many adversaries." We have already looked in some detail at that open door in chapter two of this book. Paul is clearly speaking about the way the Lord opened the way for his extended stay at Ephesus, and the establishing of the church there. Doors of opportunity for the gospel were opened in Asia Minor, at this time, no wonder Paul said it was great and effective, for the gospel spread throughout Asia. Another door that opened to Paul for the preaching of the gospel, was at Troas, and the region of Macedonia, which led to the church at Philippi being established. This was the door that the Lord opened through a vision that Paul had of a man of Macedonia calling to him, and saying, "come over to Macedonia and help us."(Acts Ch.16v9) The Lord is constantly opening doors of witness for his people, both as individuals and churches, let us recognise and grasp these opportunities.

We need to ask the question, why did the Lord set before this particular church an open door? Surely there were other churches that were better placed to take advantage of an open door. What about Ephesus, with its record of hard work and persistence, or Thyatira, where they were doing more for the Lord than they used to, or how about Laodicea, where there was plenty of money for spreading the gospel with no shortage of resources, these would appear to be better candidates for big opportunities. The answer lies in the fact that this church had been faithful to the Lord in ways that are important to Him. The church at Smyrna, had also been faithful, but the Lord had different plans for them, they were to go through a time of testing, and some of them would be imprisoned, or even lose their lives. God does not have the same plan for every church, but the important thing is to be in His plan! The church at Philadelphia, had been faithful in keeping the Lord's word, and in not denying His name. These are the things that are dear to the heart of the Lord, and these are the reasons that He rates them so highly. How different this is from the ways of this world. It is as if Jesus, as chief executive of the universal church, decides to make a major investment in this small church that does not have very much going for it. To any one with a keen business eye, it would seem a crazy thing to do. But it is in the character of God to do things which seem foolish and strange to the natural mind. So Jesus chooses this church, small, despised, and weak, yes He actually chooses this church. It is not as if He had no other choice, but as always He does not look at the outward appearance of things, but at the heart of things, and people. Paul wrote, "For you see your calling, brethren, that not many wise according to the flesh, not many mighty, not many noble, are called. But God has chosen the foolish things of the world to put to shame the wise, and God has chosen the weak things of the world to put to shame the things which are mighty; and the base things of the world and the things which are despised God has chosen, and the things which are not, to bring to nothing the things that are, that no flesh should glory in His presence."(1Corinthians Ch.1v26-29) The things that this world rates highly, God despises. This church at Philadelphia had what Jesus was looking for, in a people that He could give great opportunities to, and make a major investment in.

They had kept His word. They had treasured His word. The Psalmist, in that wonderful Psalm 119v11 says "Your word I have hidden in my heart, that I might not sin against you." These saints had recognised the value of the word of God, and treasured it, and not let it slip away. Now they had even more to treasure. The words of Jesus to them, "I have set before you an open door, and no one can shut it."(Revelation Ch.3v8) How precious those words would be to them, and no doubt they would take full advantage of this open door. The words of the Lord were sweet to these folk, sweeter than honey, and they loved the commandments of the Lord more than gold, they considered all the precepts of the Lord to be right in every way. Do you treasure the word of the Lord, is it precious to you? If it is, the Lord will open doors for you, and you will have wonderful visions of what is possible in the purposes of God. Anyone who was anyone, in the sight of God, has been someone who has kept His word, and highly esteemed it. It was written of the virgin Mary, that when the shepherds came and reported all that they had seen and heard from the angel of the Lord, that Mary kept all these things and pondered them in her heart. In these days, when in the so called church in general, as also in the world, where the word of the Lord is despised and lightly esteemed, how important is it for the true church to hold up the Word of the Lord and proclaim it without fear or favour. There is a lot of picking and choosing going on today, by church leaders and others alike, as far as what they want to believe and not want to believe. The word of God in the Bible, is like a chain, and take away any of it and it is no longer the revelation God has given, add to it and it is polluted. As for me, I choose to keep His word, that is once and for all settled in heaven.

Also they did not deny His name. This is remarkable, when we consider the context of their lives. They lived in a city where emperor worship was practiced, and it was dangerous to call Jesus Lord. You will be familiar with the chant of the Jewish leaders at the mock trial of Jesus in John Ch.19v15, "Away with Him, away with Him! Crucify Him!" Pilate said to them, "Shall I crucify your King?" The chief priests answered, "We have no king but Caesar!" The confession of the saints at Philadelphia, was not that Caesar was Lord, but that

Jesus is Lord. For His name is, King of Kings and Lord of Lords, and how this book of Revelation trumpets out this wonderful truth. In the conflict between emperor worship and the worship of Jesus the Son of God, the saints at Philadelphia did not compromise, or give way under this pressure. Much of the so called church of Jesus Christ in Britain today, has buckled under the pressure of multiculturalism and secularism, and is denying the precious name of the One who has called them out of darkness into light, by fraternising with other religions, and acknowledging them as having an equality with the faith once and for all delivered to the saints. Jesus is looking for more churches like the church at Philadelphia, who will not deny His name.

How interesting it is to note, that the two churches that the Lord has nothing against, are both opposed by those the Lord describes as a synagogue of Satan. These are people who lie about their allegiance to God. They pretend to belong to God, but they have another agenda, that they like to keep hidden. They have all the appearance of worshippers of God, but they do not keep His word and they deny His name. Jesus says to the faithful, don't be worried about them, because I will come and make them worship before your feet. The word worship literally means to kiss the hand, and is a sign of submission and reverence. It is a sign that the one whose hand is being kissed is lord over the other. The kissing of a person's hand, in these days usually occurs, when a man kisses the hand of a woman, and has lost all of its former significance. Jesus is saying to this church, that those who think they are something in this world, I will make them come and acknowledge that I have loved you, and you are the ones who are really significant. In acknowledging the saints, and coming to worship at their feet, the synagogue of Satan people would really be acknowledging that Jesus is Lord. They will come and submit to you because I have set before you an open door, and although you only have a little strength now that will not always be the situation. For God gives grace to the humble, and exalts them, but the proud will be humbled, and God knows them from a great distance. The Lord will raise up the church at Philadelphia, and humble the synagogue of Satan. The rest of the things that John sees, confirms that all those who are of the same ilk, will be brought down, and acknowledge that Jesus Christ is Lord. For after seeing the things that concern the seven churches in Asia, John sees the things that will concern the church universal and also, the wider world. Part of what John sees that are the things to come, is the rise of the two beasts who are allowed to make war with the saints and kill them, but in the end when the Lord returns with His saints, the situation will be reversed. The seeming victories of Satan are only temporary, as the Lord will demonstrate very clearly that He loves His children. This is just another example of things that will happen on a global scale, that are foreshadowed in embryo, in the messages to the churches.

The Lord had already spoken to this church and commanded them to persevere, and they had been obedient. In persevering, they had kept the word of His patience. The word of the Lord comes to His people that they might persevere in it, and stick to it. Jesus said to them that there is an hour of trial that is coming upon the whole world. But as they had kept His word He would keep them from that hour. He did not say He was taking them out of the world, but simply, that He would keep them separate from what the rest of the world would go through. Nothing is said about what is involved in this hour of trial, but there can be no doubt as to its purpose. It will be a testing time for the world, a proving time. Things and people are tested, as the old saying goes, in order to test their metal. This saying comes from the practice of testing metal components to their breaking point, in order to see if they will stand up to the stresses and strains that they will normally have to endure. The first transatlantic jet service was initiated by B.O.A.C. and very proud they were of it, because they had just piped the Americans to the post by a few weeks with the comet jet airliner. But triumph soon turned to tragedy, when some months later one of their comets plunged mysteriously into the sea, killing all on board. After extensive examination of the wreckage that was recovered, they found that the metal of the fuselage was not able to withstand the constant pressurisation and decompression that took place with an aircraft that flew higher than any other airliner had flown before. This caused cracks to appear in the metal, until it finally broke up in mid air, and resulted in the fatal crash. In other words, the metal was tested, after the plane came into service, when it should have been extensively tested beforehand. This awful incident occurred, because the British were in far too much of a hurry to beat the Americans, in the race to cross the Atlantic by jet, and the metal was not tested properly.

God is in the business of testing the metal of this world, and test it He will to breaking point, and beyond. He will test the world that rejects Him totally, and test it to destruction. God has always tested men and tried their hearts, to see what they made of, and also so they will know the state of their hearts too. Jeremiah Ch.17v9-10 says, "The heart is deceitful above all things, and desperately wicked; who can know it?" After the question comes the answer as to who can know the heart of man, v10 says, "I the Lord search the heart, I test the mind, even to give to every man according to his ways, according to the fruit of his doings." Even though God knows what is in the heart of man, He still gives man a chance to prove his metal, to see if there is anyone that is truly righteous. God did this even with such a wicked place as Sodom and Gomorrah. God said, I will go down and see if what I have heard is really so. The Lord sent two angels to Sodom and they came into the house of Lot, Abraham's nephew. After they had eaten, the homosexual men of Sodom surrounded the house, and called on Lot to bring the men out to them, so that they could have forced sexual intercourse with them. Lot went out to try and reason with them, even offering to bring out his two daughters for them to abuse, but the angels had to rescue him, striking those vile men with blindness. Now the Lord certainly knew, that indeed they were every bit as depraved as He knew them to be, and they had amply demonstrated it. They proved themselves worthy of the destruction that came upon them. God has always given men a chance to repent, or has proved that when He poured out His judgment, it was because there was no other action He could take. Jesus came to His own, and His own people rejected Him, and cried out for Him to be crucified and to be done away with, and they proved themselves worthy of the destruction that came on Jerusalem in AD70, because they did not recognise the things that belong to their peace. Jesus wept over

Jerusalem because of their stubbornness, He knew what was coming because they had rejected their Messiah. The destruction of Sodom and Gomorrah, and the destruction of Jerusalem by the Romans, will be as nothing compared to the total destruction of the earth, at the Lord's coming. Even the destruction that occurred at the time of the universal flood, when Noah and his family were saved in the ark, will not compare with the total destruction of the old order of things that will come about before Christ, and His church, reign on the new earth. The only ark of salvation then will be Jesus, and anyone not in the ark, will face the lake of fire forever.

The church at Philadelphia had already passed the test that the Lord had set them, they had persevered and kept the faith. In a similar way God tested Abraham, when He told him to sacrifice his son, his only son, Isaac. Abraham obeyed God fully and was just about to slay Isaac, when the angel of the Lord intervened and said, "for now I know that you fear God, since you have not withheld your son, your only son, from Me."(Genesis Ch.22v12) God had tested Abraham, and he had passed the test, God had proved Abraham would obey Him. Will you and I pass the tests that God sets us? Will we be kept from the tests that are still to come on the earth from God? There are many Christians who have been taught that they will escape the trials that are to come, but those who are living carelessly, selfishly, and sinfully will not escape. But, as Lot was rescued from Sodom, and Noah from the flood, so the Lord knows how to keep His own from the things that are coming on the earth.

For, behold, the Lord is coming quickly, as the lightening strikes, and there will be no time to change when he comes. The Lord is specifically talking about His second coming, which at first sight may seem strange, as this was written nearly two thousand years ago to the church at Philadelphia. Why would the Lord say He is coming quickly, when it is quite reasonable to say that the Lord knew He would not be coming any time soon? Quickly refers to the speed of His coming when He comes, not to the timing of His coming, but also it needs to be borne in mind that the Lord is dictating to John scripture and truths that will be needed for the church universal, until He does come. Jesus has always wanted the church to live in the light of His coming, because everyone who has this hope in him, purifies himself.

Hold fast what you have, let no one take your crown. The same sentiments were expressed by Paul when He wrote to the Philippian church. In Ch.3v12 he wrote, "Not that I have already attained, or am already perfected; but I press on, that I may lay hold of that for which Christ Jesus has also laid hold of me." In v14-15 he writes, "I press toward the goal for the prize of the upward call of God in Christ Jesus. Therefore let us, as many as are mature, have this mind; and if in anything you think otherwise, God will reveal even this to you." Whatever you have attained to walk by it, don't let it go, but go on and build on it, and never let go what you have received from God, for in the end there is the prize, the crown, the reward for faithfulness.

He who overcomes and perseveres, I will make him a pillar in the temple of My God, and he shall go out no more. In Solomon's temple, there were two enormous bronze pillars, and Solomon gave them names. One pillar he called Jachin, which means He shall establish. The other pillar he called Boaz, which means, in it is strength. Jesus is not promising that over comers will be literal pillars in a temple, but that He will establish them forever in His presence, and make them eternally strong. "I will write on him the name of My God, and the name of the city of My God, the New Jerusalem, which comes down out of heaven from My God. And I will write on him My new name."(Revelation Ch.3v12) The Lord is laying claim to His people and owning them. In John Ch.17 Jesus when praying to His Father said, "All Mine are Yours, and all Yours are Mine, and I am glorified in them."(John Ch.17v10) Overcomers belong to the Father, and to the Son as His bride. The bride of Christ is seen coming out from heaven, and is pictured as the New Jerusalem, that fantastically beautiful city. The glory of that city, is the glory of the church, the bride of Christ. One of the angels who had the seven last plagues said to John, "Come I will show you the bride, the Lamb's wife." In Revelation Ch.21v10 we read, "And he carried me away in the Spirit to a great and high mountain, and showed me the great city, the holy Jerusalem, descending out of heaven from God."

I wonder if the other churches were listening to the message that came to Philadelphia. For he that has ears to hear him let hear. This small, feeble, seemingly insignificant church comes highly recommended, by none other than the Head of the church, Jesus Christ. They are fruitful branches on the vine, they have endured testing and opposition, and now have the chance to blossom, and bud, as they are presented with an open door of opportunity. The church today needs to take careful notice of the message to this church, and remember the things that please the Lord. We should not judge our successes, or failures by worldly standards, but listen to what the Holy Spirit is saying to the churches.

CHAPTER 8

LAODICEA- CHURCH WITH JESUS OUTSIDE

Laodicea was founded by Antiochus the Second around about the third century B.C. It was nearby to Colosse, both cities being in the Lycus valley. The shape of the city was nearly a square, and it was very well fortified. For its water supply the city depended on an aqueduct that was fed by hot springs. These springs were six miles from the city, which resulted in the water that reached the city being lukewarm, which was incidentally the major characteristic of the church at Laodicea. Under Roman rule the city became particularly prosperous. Its industries included the manufacture of clothes made from soft, glossy black wool. It was also famous for the manufacturing of medicines, and its medical school. Among the medicines made at Laodicea were ointments for the ears made from spike nard, and a powder that was used on the eyes, produced by crushing the Phrygian stone. Paul wrote to both the Laodicean and Colossian churches, and told the churches to make sure that they read each others letters from him. Like Philadelphia, Laodicea was also destroyed by an earthquake, but at the later date of A.D.60. In the present day Laodicea is called Eski Hissar, and is found in eastern Turkey.

Jesus addresses Himself to the church at Laodicea, as the Amen, the Faithful and True Witness, the Beginning of the creation of God. The Amen is a most interesting name for the Lord Jesus to call Himself. Its meaning is explained by the name that follows, which is Faithful and True Witness. Faithfulness and truth are at the root of the meaning of the word amen. So as Jesus is the Amen, He is also automatically the Faithful and True Witness. In John's gospel Jesus is recorded as often using the phrase, verily verily, or truly truly, when what He actually said was amen amen. Amen amen I say to you, Jesus often said when He was revealing the truth of God. God has said amen amen to all of His word because it shall surely stand and abide forever. It is a faithful word, a dependable word that we can stake our lives on. Not one part of it shall pass away until it is all fulfilled. It is the truth, as well as stating what is true, that is why it will never change, nor ever need to change. Philosophies of men change, science textbooks need to be revised very often, opinions change frequently, and of course politicians are always changing their minds, but the truth of God never changes because the truth is always the truth no matter what the circumstances are or whatever may happen. That is why it is always appropriate to say amen, to preaching or to prayers that are in line with the Word of God. John in his gospel, in the very first verse calls Jesus, The Word, and says that the Word became flesh and lived among us. That is why it is absolutely right for Jesus to call Himself the Amen

Jesus is also the Beginning of the creation of God, or as Paul wrote to the Colossians in Ch.1v15-16, "He is the image of the invisible God, the firstborn (the premier) over all creation. For by Him all things were created." Then in v17, "And He is before all things." Jesus is head over all things to the church which is His body. There is absolutely no one who is higher in rank or name than Jesus. He is God, as the Father is God.

This great and almighty Amen creator, now assesses the works of the Laodicean church. In doing so, He has absolutely nothing to say about any specific works of any kind. No comment about anything that they have done, or are doing. There is also silence in respect of the spiritual environment that they are in, or anything that they may be doing that is wrong. All Jesus is concerned about, in His special message to them, is their relationship to Him. So in the specific way that Jesus reveals Himself to this church, He impresses upon them His greatness, because they do not seem to have grasped exactly who Jesus is.

In His comment on their works all Jesus says is, that they are neither hot nor cold. They are lukewarm in their relationship to Him, and consequently this affects all that they do. They were a middle of the road church, that did or said nothing that would be deemed controversial, by the non Christian world around them. They would have fitted very nicely into the kind of society that values political correctness. On all important issues they were neutral, and sat on the fence. They were a church the world could live with, because they were so accommodating towards everyone. Compromise was their watchword, finding the third way was their ambition. But they had, as far as Jesus was concerned become a nauseating taste in His mouth, and as far as the world was concerned, an irrelevance because they did not challenge anything that was evil and sin in the sight of God. They were like a car with the engine running, but in neutral gear going nowhere.

Jesus said to them, I could wish you were either hot or cold. Extremism is something that today's politically correct set frown on, but Jesus is calling on them to be in one extreme or the other, and not somewhere in between. The Greek word, in this context, is zestos which is fervent or boiling hot. I could wish that you were either boiling hot, at the one extreme, or cold, Jesus said. But because their works and their lives were lukewarm, they had become insipid. Paul agreed with Jesus, as all Christians should, when he wrote to the Roman church and said, that they should not be lagging in diligence, but be fervent, or white hot in spirit, serving the Lord. There was nothing middle of the road about Paul, in his attitude towards the Lord or his service for the Lord. He was at boiling point, giving one hundred percent, and that is what he exhorts the Roman church to be like. To the Colossians he wrote, "And whatever you do, do it heartily, as to the Lord, and not to men."(Colossians Ch.3v23) Paul was primarily concerned about what Jesus thought about his works, the opinions of men were very much of secondary importance. 2Samuel Ch.6 records a very important event in the life of King David. When the Ark of God was brought to the city of David, David was so overjoyed and exhilarated, that he danced before the Lord with all his might, and the Lord was pleased with the fervency of this act of praise and worship. But his politically correct wife thought it was most unseemly, the way the king of Israel had debased himself, in front of all his people, and she told him so. As a result the Lord caused her to be childless for the rest of her life. David's response to her was, you think I behaved myself in an unseemly way, well I will be more undignified than this if I so choose, for I will praise God for His goodness with all my heart and all my strength and all my might. There was nothing lukewarm about David's service to God, and God loved that about him.

So then, because you are lukewarm and neither hot nor cold, I will vomit you out of my mouth, Jesus said. Jesus could not have chosen a more graphic way to describe how He felt about their lukewarm attitude towards Him. We all know what a horrible feeling it is to need to vomit, so Jesus is telling these Christians in no uncertain terms how they make Him feel. Jesus is saying to them that He finds them disgusting to the taste, as they lack any convictions and try to be men pleasers. He feels like utterly rejecting them, as the stomach rejects food that it cannot digest. I reject your spirit of compromise and worldliness, either serve me with all your heart, or don't serve me at all. Give me your best efforts, or just don't bother, is the essence of what Jesus is saying. That is exactly what Jesus says to the church today, as many who attend a church do so half heartedly and in a spirit of compromise towards a sinful world. In some ways the conditions that prevailed in this church, were similar to those that existed in Israel, at the time that Malachi prophesied to them. In Ch.1v6 God says to Israel, "A son honours his father, and a servant his master. If then I am the Father where is my honour? And if I am a Master, where is My reverence?" Israel had the attitude that any old thing would do for God, just like the half hearted ways of the Laodiceans. They were offering to God for sacrifice animals that were blind and blemished, when God had demanded only the best from them and God questioned them and said, "Is it not evil?" God asks them again another question. "Offer it then to your governor! Would he be pleased with you?"(Malachi Ch.1v8) Anyone who holds down a regular job will know that earthly employers expect their employees to give of their best, and anything less would be displeasing. God goes on to say that His name will be great among the nations, yet Israel has despised His name. The church at Laodicea also despised Jesus, even though He is God, by not acknowledging in their service to Him, how great he is and Jesus finds this very distasteful. The people of Israel were also saying many things that displeased the Lord, and grieved Him, just as the Laodiceans were. Firstly they were questioning God's love for them by saying, "In what way have you loved us?"(Malachi Ch.1v2) Israel was also saying that the table of the Lord was contemptible, and they despised it. They said, "Oh, what a weariness,"(Malachi Ch.1v13) and they sneered at it. Another thing they were saying was, "Everyone who does evil is good in the sight of the Lord, and He delights in them." or, "Where is the God of justice?"(Malachi Ch.2v17) The Lord said to them that their words had been harsh against Him, yet they said, "What have we spoken against You?" And yet they had said, "It is useless to serve God; What profit is it that we have kept His ordinance, and that we have walked as mourners before the Lord of hosts?"(Malachi Ch.3v13-14) Although the church at Laodicea were not saying the same things as Israel, yet in principle they were guilty of the same kind of sin, in that they were saying things that could not be justified before the Lord.

Jesus says to them, "I will vomit you out of My mouth." Because you say, "I am rich, have become wealthy."(Revelation Ch.3v16-17) Not only does their lukewarm attitude make Jesus feel sick, but their opinions of themselves also make Him want to vomit them out of His mouth. It would be reasonable to suggest that some of the richest people in the city had become Christians, and consequently the church was not short of finance. The inference, from the words of Jesus, was that they considered that money and material wealth, were the only riches worth having. They were also saying that because of their wealth, they had need of nothing. What a thing to say of yourself, that you are totally self sufficient! The fact is, only God can truthfully make such a claim. As they considered that they already had everything that they could possibly need, it would be fair to say that they had a very short sighted view of what their needs were. While the Bible extols the virtue of being content, there is a world of difference between being content with your lot, and being complacent about your needs. Their whole attitude was one of complacency. They were neither hot nor cold, they were in a very comfortable position, thank you very much, and they did not intend to rock the boat by becoming extreme in their views or actions. They had no pressures, no concerns, and they were not being persecuted like some of their brothers and sisters in other churches, and neither would they do anything that might invite that sort of thing. They had comfortable homes with all the latest mod cons. They were well respected in their community. They were probably involved in the civic life of their city, and some of them may have been members of various committees. They were morally upright, pillars of the community. There is nothing wrong with that of course, but according to Jesus they were ignorant of their true condition.

So Jesus goes on to tell them things that they seem blissfully unaware of. You think you are rich but, the way I see it you are wretched, miserable, poor, blind and naked! How could there be such a difference in how they saw themselves and how Jesus saw them. The problem lay in their value system, in what they considered to be riches and wealth. Money, possessions, prosperity and the luxuries of this life meant everything to them. They were not serving God, but mammon. Their goal had been to become rich, in terms of worldly wealth, and they had achieved their goals. No wonder they were lukewarm towards God, for Jesus said, "You cannot serve God and mammon."(Matthew Ch.6v24) Having hit their financial targets, they were now in spiritual complacency, sitting back cloaked in self satisfaction. Of course they did not know their true condition, because their riches had blinded them, and they were dazzled by their wealth. God said to Israel through the prophet Malachi, that they were under a curse because they had been robbing God, in that they had been withholding their tithes and offerings. So with the Laodiceans, they were under a curse of spiritual poverty, because they had withheld from God their service of fervent devotion, and probably their wealth as well.

Jesus first described them as wretched and distressed, like a ship floundering in a storm, battling against giant waves. Their spiritual state was highly precarious, and they were in danger of being totally swamped by their riches and the pleasures of this life. They were typical of the kind of ground that Jesus described in the parable of the sower, where the seed fell among thorns. Jesus, when interpreting the parable to the disciples said, that the seed that was sown among the thorns, was unfruitful because the thorns choked the seed as it tried to grow. This is like those who heard the Word of God, but then the cares of this life and the deceitfulness of riches choked the word, and no fruit was the result. This is exactly what had happened in the Laodicean church, riches had chocked spiritual growth and they were completely deceived by their riches into thinking they were rich and in need of nothing.

In this state of wretched distress, they were to be pitied. They were just like a few struggling ears of corn in God's field, fighting for survival, against a mass of weeds. The irony was that the things that they valued, were the very things that were choking the spiritual life out of them, and they did not know it. They had no time to read and study the word of God that they had received, contained in the letters from Paul. There was no time to pray together very often and they neglected to fellowship together as often as they should. They were too busy making money. Too busy aiming at the next sales target. Too busy traveling from city to city trading their goods. Too busy networking to make sure they had the right business connections, altogether too busy to nurture the spiritual life that the Holy Spirit had birthed in them. The situation reminds me of a hymn I used to sing in Sunday school. The words from one of the verses are;

> Room for pleasure room for business
> But for Christ the crucified
> Not a place that He can enter
> In the life for whom He died.

The opening line of the first verse posed the question, Have you any room for Jesus? Sadly as far as the Laodicean church was concerned the answer was a very definite no! How incomprehensible, how utterly amazing that a Christian church had no room for Jesus Christ. But in fact it is typical of many churches today. They do and say the Christian things, but Jesus Himself is ignored His word is belittled or not believed and Jesus is regarded as merely a historical figure who was a good example.

Jesus said they were poor, but why would He say that of a wealthy church? Firstly because they were full of themselves. We are rich, they said, we have increased in wealth, we have arrived, we have reached a pinnacle in life, we have need of nothing. Jesus said, in His sermon on the mount, "Blessed are the poor in spirit, for theirs is the Kingdom of Heaven."(Matthew Ch.5v3) The Kingdom of Heaven is where the true riches are, and in this heavenly kingdom the Laodicean church was definitely bankrupt. They were bankrupt because all their deposits were in earthly banks, and they had neglected to bank anything in heaven. In the same sermon Jesus said, "Do not lay up for yourselves treasures on earth, where moth and rust destroy, and where thieves break in and steal; but lay up for yourselves treasures in heaven, where neither moth nor rust destroy, and where thieves do not break in and steal. For where your treasure is there will your heart be also."(Matthew Ch.6v19-21) When Jesus looked at their account in heaven He could see that the people of this church were paupers, and that was the reality of their situation. A person's true state of wealth or poverty is whether or not they are rich toward God.

They were also blind, unable to see their true condition. They did not seem to realise that God had different values from them. They had wrongly assumed that their riches were a blessing from God. Wrongly assumed that God approved of what they were saying about themselves. Some Christians today think that godliness is a means of gaining riches and wealth, when the Bible expressly says that we are not to seek after riches, and the love of money is the root of all kinds of evil. But like any blind man, without any reliable guide, they were forced into making assumptions that were not according to reality. They were also oblivious of the fact that Jesus was not in their church,

He was on the outside, wanting to come in. The fact is they did not take the time to get to know Jesus so they did not even miss Him. Jesus was a stranger to these people, as He is to many today even in the professing church. If Jesus were to come into many churches, He just would not be recognised for who He is. So too the church at Laodicea was ignorant and blind, as to who Jesus is, otherwise He would not have been outside, and they would have realised their desperate need of Him.

They were also naked in the sight of God. They were still as they were when they were first born into the kingdom of God. As babies are born naked, so these Christians were still naked, when God's desire was that they should be clothed with Christian character. Paul had written to this church, when he wrote to their next door neighbours at Colosse. In the letter to the Colossians Paul said that as the elect of God they should put on certain things just as we put on clothes when we get dressed. He said they should put on tender mercies, kindness, humility, meekness, longsuffering, that they should bear with one another and forgive each other. But above everything else they should put on love. In heeding these basic instructions they had manifestly failed, for Jesus said they were still naked. What a rude awakening this was for them. What a shock it must have been for these self confident, self satisfied and self sufficient people, to learn that in fact they were blind beggars sitting in the gutter naked. Instead of sitting in splendour, they were sitting in shame! Instead of being the bees knees, they were the spiritual untouchables of the churches in Asia. How ashamed they must have felt knowing that the other churches would know what Jesus thought of them, as opposed to what they thought of themselves and how they must have assumed other people saw them.

But all was not lost. That is why Jesus speaks to them in this way. Jesus as head of the church knows how to discipline His children, so He not only tells them very frankly what He thinks of them, but also has sound advice for their full recovery. Jesus advises them to come and buy from Him various items that will enrich them with riches worth having. It is most interesting that Jesus tells them to buy from Him. They are rich, so they say, so let them come and buy. But they will soon learn, if it were not already obvious to them, that the currency they value is of no worth at all in buying what they need from Jesus. What does Jesus infer when He says come and buy from Him? Christians are not used to getting things from Jesus that they need to pay for. Salvation, as regards the forgiveness of sins, the gift of eternal life, justification, that is the pronouncement by God that we are no longer guilty of our sins but are righteous in His sight, these things and others are free gifts, because Jesus paid the price for them when He died for us on the cross. But for the development of Christian character, growth in grace, and for becoming like Jesus in the way we live, there is a price to pay. Jesus has called His people to become His disciples, and to follow Him, and there is a price to pay for following Him. Jesus said, "If anyone desires to come after Me, let Him deny himself, and take up his cross, and follow Me," (Matthew Ch16v24) and be prepared to be rejected possibly by family and friends alike. To these people who have such a high opinion of themselves Jesus is saying, come on get real about being Christians, come out of your complacency, lethargy and self deception, and pay the price for the riches that I have to offer you.

Buy from me gold refined in the fire, Jesus said. What is it that Jesus wants them to buy when He talks of gold refined in the fire? Gold is something that is very precious, and highly prized. Something that men have risked their lives to obtain, and some have laboured endlessly to get, sometimes without any success. But also something that is very pure, when refined in the fire. I believe Jesus is referring to His Word, what we know today as the Bible when He speaks of gold refined in the fire. Psalm 12v6 says, "The words of the Lord are pure words, like silver tried in a furnace of earth, purified seven times." The Lord wants this church to think the same way as the psalmist when he wrote in Psalm 119v14, "I have rejoiced in the way of your testimonies, as much as in all riches." Likewise in v72 of the same psalm, "The law of Your mouth is better to me than thousands of coins of gold or silver." In v140 he writes, "Your word is very pure; therefore your servant loves it," Jesus wants the saints at Laodicea to love His word, and pay the price to make it their own. Jesus wants them to rejoice over His word as one who finds great treasure, as the psalmist wrote in v162. Buy the gold of My word, the pure, refined word of God, and as Solomon wrote in Proverbs Ch23v23, "Buy the truth and do not sell it." Buying the truth of God's word implies that they will make it their own. How many people listen to sermons, read their Bible, listen to audio tapes and cds, and yet never make the word of God their own. They never own the word and take it into their heart. They never make the effort to feed themselves from God's word and let the Holy Spirit reveal the truths that are there to them. The Word of God is a gold mine, and Jesus wants His people to make the effort to go and dig out the nuggets that are there, and work at understanding His word. Nothing that is worthwhile is ever achieved without a great deal of effort, and a price being paid which is in some way comparable to the value of what is being bought. As we should seek to know Christ through His word, is there any price too high to pay to achieve such a goal? As we should seek to know God's ways and His will, should we not pay the price to obtain such treasures? These are the true riches that we can obtain from God's pure word, which will enrich us for eternity, which is why Jesus said to the Laodicean church, and to His church today, buy from Me gold refined in the fire that you might be rich.

Buy from me as well, white garments that you may be clothed. Not just any old garments, but white garments, pure and clean. White garments that are garments of righteousness. Following on from buying the pure word, Jesus now urges them to clothe themselves, by making the effort to obey the word and live righteously. Titus was told by Paul, to tell servants in the way that they served their masters, to adorn the doctrine of God our Saviour. In other words, make sure that in the way you work you beautify and present the gospel you believe in the best light, so that others will see how wonderful it is. In their living, Christians should always have their very best clothes on, clothing themselves with love. Love will be seen by actions, which is why Jesus said, "Let your light so shine before men, that they may see your good works and glorify your Father in heaven."(Matthew Ch.5v16) "For we are His workmanship, created in Christ Jesus for good works, which God prepared beforehand that we should walk in them." (Ephesians Ch.2v10) Jesus does not want His church to be naked, but clothed with righteousness, which is not only the gift He gives us but also the righteous acts that we do in His name and for His sake. Make the effort to clothe yourself, in love and good works, Jesus is saying to them, for it is a shameful thing for a Christian to be naked and devoid of these things. It is a shame both before God and men.

For their blindness Jesus counsels them that they buy from Him eye salve. Maybe some in the church had become wealthy through the sale of the eye salve that Laodicea was famous for. In any case, this church needed the eyes of their heart opened and their spiritual perception healed, that they might see their true condition. As a medicine the eye salve needed to be applied, otherwise it would do the eyes no good. That is a very obvious thing to say, and yet it is not always obvious to us that it is not only necessary to hear the word, but also to apply it. The entrance of the Word of God into our lives brings the light that dispels our blindness, but the word only enters when we apply it and start to obey it. As the Laodicean Christians would start to buy the word and obey it, then they would begin to see exactly where they were and what condition they were in. They would only have to begin to read and understand and believe the letters Paul wrote to them to begin to see how pitiful they were. They would only have to take to heart what Jesus is saying to them, in this message from John, and it would make all the difference. They would be able to rise up and begin to sit with the rich folk in the heavenly places in Christ Jesus, dressed in white, seeing the glory of God and of Christ Jesus their saviour.

Jesus reassures them of His love for them. If they had ever doubted it, Jesus says to them, "As many as I love, I rebuke and chasten."(Revelation Ch.3v19) Jesus is treating them as sons of God, for the writer to the Hebrews says, that every son that God receives is chastised, so that the fruit of righteousness is borne in the life of every one. Despite all that Jesus has said to them, never once does He infer that they are not children of God. But in fact He speaks to them in this way precisely because they are sons of God. Jesus loves these poor, miserable spiritual beggars so much that He is determined that He will spur them on to love and good works, to rise up and become rich toward God. Therefore be zealous and repent, Jesus urges them. Jesus has held up the mirror of His Word so they can see themselves as He sees them. This is their big chance to change, turn things around and repent. Jesus is extending, through this message to them His grace and mercy, they will never have a better chance to change. There are times and seasons in our lives when Jesus reaches out to us, in order to effect the changes that He sees as desirable, and it is at those times that we need to take advantage of the grace that He extends to us. For if we only want to have dealings with the Lord on our terms and in our time, we may well find that Jesus is unresponsive. We might think that Jesus has been harsh in the things He has said to these people, but Jesus has been as gentle as He can, in order to bring about the result that He is looking for, which is to awaken this church out of their complete apathy. Jesus will always be fair with us and only apply the rod of correction as necessary.

Up until now Jesus, through the messenger to this church, has been addressing the church as a whole. But now Jesus appeals to each one as an individual, by saying, "Behold, I stand at the door and knock."(Revelation Ch.3v20) Jesus is on the outside trying to come in. Paul in his letter to the Colossians, which they were also to read writes, "For in Him dwells all the fullness of the Godhead bodily."(Colossians Ch.2v9) With this in mind, if Jesus was outside the church, how could it be anything other than wretched, miserable, poor, blind and naked. That is the condition of every person's life, in the sight of God, when Jesus is on the outside of that person's life wanting to come in. In all that Jesus has said so far He is knocking very loudly indeed. Jesus is looking for anyone in this church who will hear His voice and open the door of their life to Him. He is not looking for the richest, the cleverest, the most influential or those who are leaders, but He says if anyone hears my voice, and opens the door I will come in.

If, and it is a little word with a big meaning, if anyone does choose to respond to my word and open the door I, the Amen, The beginning of the creation of God, The Alpha and Omega, The King of Kings and Lord of Lords, will come in. Amazing! Fantastic! Jesus will come in and have a meal with anyone who opens up to Him. If you are hearing His Word, you are hearing His knocking, asking for entrance into your life. He wants to have fellowship with you, talk to you and share His life with you. When Paul wrote to the Corinthian church in 1Corinthians Ch.1v9 he said, "God is faithful, by whom you were called into the fellowship of His Son, Jesus Christ our Lord." The church at Laodicea was among those also who had been called into the fellowship of God's Son, but up until now they were not fulfilling their calling. Are you fulfilling your calling, and having fellowship with Jesus? What good times are to be had by those who share a table with the Son of God. If we are in good health, we enjoy eating, and it is one of the God given pleasures of life. The smell of good food, followed by the taste of good food, and the satisfaction of a full stomach that follows the meal. The fun of lively conversation around the table, the bonding and friendships that are forged around a meal table, these are important things in our lives. Jesus said to them, "I will come in to him and dine with him, and he with Me."(Revelation Ch.3v20) When did you last get together with Jesus and share a meal, feeding on His word, and enjoying conversation with Him in prayer? It should also be borne in mind the importance that eastern culture places on hospitality. The writer to the Hebrews talks of those who have entertained angels without being aware of it, But how much more wonderful to entertain Jesus in the inner sanctuary of our lives, where we can share so many wholesome and nourishing things that will bless us and make us strong and healthy Christians. So far from wanting to vomit this church out of His mouth, Jesus wants to sit down with them and have a continual feast with them. But He will not compromise on what it will cost them, to turn around from being rejected by Him because of their wretchedness, to being in full fellowship with Him. He will not take second, or any other place, to riches or wealth or anything else. Why should He? He is the King. If they refused to let Him in they would remain in poverty, He would not loose out they would.

"To him who overcomes, I will grant to sit with Me on My throne, as I also overcame and sat down with My Father on His throne."(Revelation Ch3v21) The invitation is a simple one. If you repent and overcome the deceitfulness of riches, you will rule with me. Jesus overcame all the temptations to wealth and riches and worldly power, not only in the wilderness when tempted by Satan himself, but throughout His life on the earth, and then went on to humble himself to the death of the cross. Therefore God has highly exalted Him and given Him a name above all names. Those who humble themselves and hear His voice and obey Him, He also will exalt to His throne.

The church, then and now needs to have ears to hear what the Spirit is saying to the churches. Worldly riches count for nothing in God's economy, and they are not what He is looking for in His church. Remember the words of Jesus to the church at Smyrna. "I know your works, tribulation, and poverty, but you are rich!"(Revelation Ch.2v9) Does the church, particularly in the rich western world, need to assess what true riches are? Is Jesus outside the church knocking, waiting to be invited in? Is He about to vomit us out of His mouth?

CHAPTER 9

IN THE SPIRIT IN HEAVEN

At this point we come to chapter four of Revelation and it needs to be borne in mind that John is still writing to the seven churches in Asia. We could easily think, that because now what Jesus reveals to John through the angel that was sent to him, is seen from heaven's perspective that the churches are no longer involved. But they are and in that context it is worth repeating the text in Ch.22v16, "I, Jesus, have sent My angel to testify to you these things in the churches." What happens next is that John looks and what he sees is an open door in heaven, and he hears the same voice as he heard before like the voice of a trumpet, inviting him to come up into heaven so that he can be shown the things that will take place after this. What a privilege for John to be invited into heaven. The prophets of the Old Testament had seen visions of God, when He had come down to the earth, and Daniel had seen visions of the throne of God, but only John has such an extensive view of heaven and hears things that no one else has heard previously, and is permitted by God to write what he saw. What a privilege too, for the churches then and for us today, to be able to visualise what John saw, because he was instructed to write what he saw in a book. Jesus has been revealed, in His character and nature, in the vision John saw of him in his glory and also in the messages to the seven churches. Now in the next two chapters of Revelation the Father and the Son are clearly revealed as having the future in their hands. There is a certainty about the words of Jesus when He said to John, "Come up here and I will show you things that MUST take place after this." There is no doubt that the things that Jesus is going to reveal about the future WILL take place, because He is the architect and builder of the future. Everything will happen according to His plans and specifications.

John records that on hearing the invitation from Jesus, to view things from heaven's perspective, he was immediately in the Spirit and he saw a throne. This throne was set in heaven and One sat on the throne. It is not without significance that the first thing John saw in heaven was a throne, because the whole of the rest of the book of Revelation, is centred around the throne in heaven, and the edicts that come from God, and the Lamb. Indeed, it is the core revelation of this book that God the Father and Jesus the Lamb, reign from heaven over the events on the earth. So it was very necessary for John to be taken up into heaven, to see behind the scenes and see who is really pulling the strings, who has the real power over heaven and earth. Without this revelation, the churches would only be able to see events taking place on the earth, from a very limited perspective. It would be like viewing present and future events without the aid of a telescope, or indeed a microscope. When the telescope was first invented, people discovered that they could see over the horizon of their normal unaided vision. Similarly, with a microscope, they could see detail that they would be unable to see with naked eye. So with this revelation from heaven, the churches would be able to see far into the future, and also see current events in far greater detail. The churches that were being persecuted for their faith in Jesus, would be able to take courage from the realisation that in fact it was not Rome that ruled or Satan, but Jesus.

The One that John saw on the throne, he describes as being like a jasper and sardis stone. Both these stones are often translucent, and fiery red. They were the first and last stones on the breastplate of judgment that was worn by the high priest in Old Testament times. On this breastplate of judgment, were twelve stones that were engraved with the names of the twelve tribes of the children of Israel. God instituted this, so that the high priest who was to represent the children of Israel before God, would wear these names over his heart as a memorial before the Lord. It could be that God is seen by John on His throne, represented by these two stones, so that His church would be reminded that they are ever in His heart and thoughts. That even though He is a God of consuming fire, His mercy and grace are ever towards His children. This is clearly seen in this book, as even though many of His children are out of line and out of order, yet His message to them is of mercy and grace, in that He calls on them to repent and offers rewards to those who do repent and overcome. Yet to the unrepentant world, those who receive Satan's seal, the message of the rest of this book is one of punishment and judgment, ending in the lake of fire.

Another sign, that God is a God of grace and favour, is seen in the emerald rainbow that is around the throne. Yes the throne of God is surrounded by the symbol of a covenant of grace and mercy which God gave after He had flooded the earth and destroyed all that lived on the land. The first mention of the rainbow in the Bible is in Genesis Ch. 9v13 where God said to Noah, "I set My rainbow in the cloud, and it shall be for the sign of the covenant between Me and the earth." God's covenant was that He would never again destroy the earth with a flood, so He set the rainbow in the clouds as a sign of the agreement. The rainbow around His throne is there, because God is a God of grace and He makes covenants with His people, and keeps His promises. God made a covenant with Abraham, regarding his descendants and the land of Israel, and He will keep to His side of the agreement even though Israel has failed to keep their side many times over. God made a covenant with King David, concerning his throne and royal line, and all those promises will be fulfilled in Jesus, as the book of Revelation makes clear. God has also made an everlasting covenant with His people, through the shedding of the blood of Jesus on the cross that He will, if they put their trust in Him, wash away their sins and bring them safely into His eternal kingdom. God has a rainbow around His throne because central to the character of God, is the fact that He is as good as His word, and He always keeps His promises.

Around God's throne John saw twenty four thrones, and on those thrones he saw twenty four elders sitting. Elders in both the Old and New Testaments are those who, as mature men, represent and lead the people. In Old Testament times they were the men who sat at the gate of a city, because that was the place where official business took place. The elders of the city would be a witness to covenants made between two parties, and would be the judges in disputes, and generally oversee the civic life of the city. They would also be involved in important national occasions, such as the crowning of a king, or in going to war. In the New Testament the apostles ordained elders to oversee the churches that they founded. Paul's letters to Timothy and Titus, are concerned with the appointment of elders, and the qualifications that they needed to have. So we have twenty four elders sitting on thrones around God's throne. As elders were representatives and leaders of the people on earth, it is reasonable to deduce that these elders are those who represent the redeemed people of God, both of the twelve tribes of Israel and the redeemed of the twelve apostles of the Lamb. As representatives of the redeemed they are seen by John as those who are seated in the heavenly places in Christ Jesus, where they reign with Christ deriving their authority from the throne of God. They are clothed in white, as would be expected of those who represent the saints who are always seen dressed in the white robes of righteousness. They have crowns of gold on their heads. Those crowns are given to them as a reward for faithfulness to the Lord. The Greek word for these crowns is stephanos, which means, that which surrounds. They were originally given to athletes at the Olympic Games and were made of laurel leaves, which would quickly fade. These crowns are gold, which indicates that they will endure. The crowns of life, and righteousness that Paul speaks about, are stephanos crowns. Paul said he would receive these crowns because, he had run the race, he had kept the faith and he had finished his course. Like Paul who himself was no doubt an overcomer, these elders, not only represent the redeemed, but the redeemed who are overcomers and have merited their rewards. Their reward being that they sit around the throne of God crowned with golden crowns.

From the throne of God, proceeded lightenings, thunderings and voices. What an awesome sight the throne of God is! With all that John has already seen of the One sitting on the throne, in fiery majesty with an emerald green rainbow surrounding Him, now he records that some of the most majestic natural phenomena known to man, also proceed from the throne. When the Lord came down on Mount Sinai and gave Moses His law, it was as if the throne of God had come down to earth. Which indeed, in a sense it had, for God was announcing to Israel His Royal Law, the Law by which He as their Lord and King He expected them to live by, but which because of the weakness of the sinful nature in man they were not able to do. Moses records, "Then it came to pass on the third day, in the morning, that there were thunderings and lightnings, and a thick cloud on the mountain; and the sound of the trumpet was very loud, so that all the people who were in the camp trembled."(Exodus Ch.19v16) With such terrifying sights and sounds coming from the mountain, God called Moses up to meet Him, where over the next forty days He received Gods laws and instructions to build the tabernacle. Psalm 77v18 says, "The voice of Your thunder was in the whirlwind; the lightnings lit up the world; the earth trembled and shook." When the Lord speaks it is sometimes in the lightning and thunder, and this is what John saw coming from God's throne. When God speaks from His throne all creation trembles before His mighty word, everyone and everything comes into subjection to His word. This is the lesson of this book that as God issues His word of commands from the throne, nothing can stop His will from coming to pass.

Seven lamps of fire were burning before the throne, which are the seven Spirits of God. Like the seven branched golden lampstand, which was to perpetually burn before the ark of God in the tabernacle and also the temple, John saw seven lamps burning before the throne. The seven branched lamp, in its entirety including the oil that produced the flame to give light, represent the Holy Spirit. The Holy Spirit, is not seven spirits, but is the sevenfold Spirit of God.

The lampstand, in the tabernacle was made of one piece of gold, which was fashioned into a lampstand with a central branch and three branches coming out on each side. So the Holy Spirit is one Spirit, but with a sevenfold character as seen in Isaiah Ch11v2, which says, "The Spirit of THE LORD shall rest upon Him, the Spirit of WISDOM and UNDERSTANDING, the Spirit of COUNSEL and MIGHT, the Spirit of KNOWLEDGE and of the FEAR OF THE LORD." The Holy Spirit is the Spirit of the Lord, as the central branch, with six aspects of His character branching out. The Holy Spirit is also represented by the oil which burned from the top of each branch, and of course the Holy Spirit is also represented by the light given from the flames. The whole scene in and around the throne is predominated by fire. We should not think of the Holy Spirit, in terms of just being like a dove or wind or breath although these things do represent His character, but also like fire. He certainly manifested Himself in that way on the Day of Pentecost, when tongues of fire came and sat on all the disciples and they were all filled with the Holy Spirit and spoke with other tongues, as the Spirit enabled them. John the Baptist also said of Jesus, that He would baptise in the Holy Spirit and fire.

There was a sea of glass, like crystal, before the throne. What a dazzling sight this must have been for John, how majestic and awesomely beautiful. With all the splendour of the throne and the One who sat on it, with the seven lamps of fire, plus the lightning all being reflected into the sea of glass. It would have been a mixture of reds, yellows and green from the rainbow, all these colours not only being reflected into the sea, but also refracting and reflecting out from the sea of glass all around heaven, the light reaching as far as John could see. This wonderful mixture of light would have reflected on the living creatures and the elders. This illustrates for us the fact that there is only one source of true spiritual light in the universe, and that is the light that comes from the throne of God, because of the One who occupies the throne. We can only expect to reflect the light of the glory of God, in the face of Jesus Christ. Apart from Him we are in total darkness.

The living creatures that John saw, in the midst and around the throne, were full of eyes in the front and the back. They represent, not only four aspects of the Deity of Jesus, but also the all seeing all knowing aspect of God's attributes. In Proverbs Ch.15v3 Solomon wrote, "The eyes of the Lord are in every place, keeping watch on the evil and the good." Psalm 11v4-7 says, "The Lord is in His holy temple, the Lord's throne is in heaven; His eyes behold, His eyelids test the sons of men. The Lord tests the righteous, but the wicked and the one who loves violence His soul hates. Upon the wicked He will rain coals; fire and brimstone and burning wind shall be the portion of their cup. For the Lord is righteous, He loves righteousness; His countenance beholds the upright." The Lord looks from heaven, He sees all men everywhere. This is not poetic language, this is fact, and the four living creatures around the throne indicate to us that the Lord sees every action, of every person on the earth, from their very first breath to their last. No wonder Jesus, who has all the attributes of God, could say to the seven churches, I know your works!

The first living creature was like a lion, the second like a calf, the third had a face like a man and the fourth was like a flying eagle. The Old Testament prophet Ezekiel saw these very same creatures, and records what he saw in Ch.1 of his prophecy. In Ch.6 of Isaiah's prophecy, he also saw them and called them seraphim. This was the year that King Uzziah died, and he saw the Lord in the temple, high and lifted up. Isaiah saw that the seraphim had six wings, with two they covered their face, with two they covered their feet and with two they flew. They cried to each other, "Holy, holy, holy is the Lord of hosts; the whole earth is full of His glory." Ezekiel also saw them flying, and having wheels within wheels in which was the spirit of the living creatures. Each of the three revelations of these creatures is different in a number of aspects, but the basics are the same. They represent four different aspects of Jesus, three in His humanity, and one in His Deity.

In Ch.5 of Revelation Jesus is described as the Lion of the tribe of Judah. The lion is universally recognised as the king of beasts; especially the male lion with his stately stance and mane, for God has created him with these attributes. His appearance and posture cry out, I am the king of the beasts of the earth. The origin of the phrase, the Lion of the tribe of Judah, is in the book of Genesis Ch.49v8-10. Jacob is speaking of his son Judah and speaks prophetically when he says, "Judah, you are he whom your brothers shall praise; your hand shall be on the neck of your enemies; your father's children shall bow down before you. Judah is a lion's whelp; from the prey, my son, you have gone up. He bows down, he lies down as a lion; and as a lion, who shall rouse him? The sceptre shall not depart from Judah, nor a lawgiver from between his feet, until Shiloh comes; and to Him shall be the obedience of the people." Shiloh is a reference to the Messiah. There are unmistakable references to Judah as a lion and a lion king, in those words of Jacob. The reference to Shiloh, or Messiah, is conclusive, that this prophecy is unmistakably about Jesus, the Lion of the tribe of Judah. To be of the tribe of Judah, Jesus had to be born into the world of the tribe of Judah, and He was. The first living creature displays that kingly aspect of the humanity of Jesus.

The second living creature looked like a calf. The obvious inference here, in Biblical terms, is that of sacrifice for sin. When Ezekiel saw this living creature, he described it as having the face of an ox. These were animals that, in the Old Testament scriptures, were offered as a sacrifice for the sins of the people. But Jesus was the sin offering for the sins of the whole world. The offering of these beasts involved the shedding of their blood, for cleansing. Hebrews Ch.9v22 says, "Without shedding of blood there is no remission," or forgiveness, of sins. So the shedding of the blood of Jesus on the cross makes available to us the means of cleansing for our sins. Then the fat of the animal was burnt on the altar of sacrifice, as an atonement for sin, and a sweet aroma to the Lord. The word atonement breaks down into at onement, and some have taught that that is the meaning of the word atonement. But being at one with God is what reconciliation means. Atonement actually means to cover. When the fat of the animal was burnt on the altar, it covered the sins of the people, in the sight of God on a temporary basis. This covering however, did bring about reconciliation between the people and God, and God's righteous anger and wrath against sin would be appeased. Jesus faced the fire of the wrath of God against sin, when He died on the cross for us, and He made a permanent covering for our sins and brought about reconciliation between us and a Holy God. For God looked upon the offering of the body of Jesus and His wrath against the sin of the world was appeased. The rest of the carcass was taken outside the camp of Israel and was burned. The writer of the book of Hebrews draws an analogy to this part of the sacrifice by saying, "For the bodies of those animals, whose blood is brought into the sanctuary by the high priest for sin, are burned outside the camp. Therefore Jesus also, that He might sanctify the people with His own blood, suffered outside the gate. Therefore let us go forth to Him, outside the camp, bearing His reproach." (Hebrews Ch. 13v11-13) So all who are in Christ Jesus, who is our sin offering, will not face the wrath of God against sin that we read about in Revelation Ch.16. This does not mean that the wrath of God is not already poured out on sin, or that this specific, final and totally devastating outpouring is the only time God manifests His wrath. For Paul writes in Romans Ch.1v18, "For the wrath of God is revealed from heaven against all ungodliness and unrighteousness of men, who suppress the truth in unrighteousness."

The third living creature had the face of a man. How wonderful this is! That man is represented by a creature so close to the throne of God. The other living creatures of the earth are ignorant of the close association God has with the creatures He has created, but we know how closely God has identified with us as distinct from all the animals. For man is clearly very distinct from all other animals in every conceivable way. The Bible teaches in Genesis Ch.1 that man was made in the image of God. It is surely true, that all animals are a wonder of God's creative power, as modern science is constantly discovering. But man was made to be God's Viceroy on earth and have dominion over all the earth, including the other creatures. Man alone has the unique capabilities to have intelligent thought, rather than act by instinct, has the ability to love and hate. Man alone, is able to communicate through intelligent speech and be creative, in all areas of the arts. A whole host of other things separate man from the beasts, not the least of these being, that God desires fellowship with man, because God made man with the capacity to have fellowship with Him. This is exactly what Adam and Eve had with God in the garden of Eden, a relationship of wonderful fellowship, until Eve was deceived and Adam disobeyed God and sin entered the human family. So God associated Himself with man in creation, by creating man in His own image, but because of sin God has also associated Himself with man in redeeming man back to Himself. This intimate association with man is remembered every Christmas time, when Christians remember the birth of Jesus in Bethlehem. The Bible clearly teaches that God, in His Son, became man through the birth of Jesus to the virgin Mary who was engaged to Joseph. This birth took place before Mary and Joseph had sexual intercourse as husband and wife, because Jesus was miraculously conceived in Mary's womb by the Holy Spirit. So Jesus was not the seed of Joseph, as was the case with the other children that were born to Mary, but was the seed of the woman, as predicted by God in the garden of Eden when man first sinned. God said to the serpent, "And I will put enmity between you and the woman, and between your seed and her Seed; He shall bruise your head, and you shall bruise His heel."(Genesis Ch.3v15) Jesus was conceived of the Holy Spirit of the seed of the woman, there can be no ambiguity or confusion over this issue, only faith in the Word of God, or unbelief. Those who deny the divinity of Jesus are unbelievers, for it is pointless in God's sight to believe lesser things, and deny the truth of one of the central planks of the Christian faith. In fact all the living creatures so far represent His humanity, but they would all lose their significance, if Jesus were not God as well. For Jesus as the Lion King of the tribe of Judah, not only ruled as King over all sin during His life on earth, all sickness and disease and even death, as well as the natural elements, but is set to reign over a Kingdom that will last forever. Only God can rule over such a kingdom, on a new earth where sin and all its consequences are no more. As a sin offering He needed to clothe Himself in the likeness of sinful flesh, in order to offer Himself up to God as the only effective sacrifice for sin. The writer to the Hebrews wrote, "For it is not possible that the blood of bulls and goats could take away sins. Therefore when He came into the world, He said; "Sacrifice and offering You did not desire, but a body You have prepared for Me. In burnt offerings and sacrifices for sin You had no pleasure." Then I said, "Behold I have come- in the volume of the book it is written of Me- to do Your will, O God." (Hebrews Ch.10v4-7) It was necessary for God the Son to become a man in order to be our saviour. John Wesley expressed this truth so wonderfully in the carol, Hark the herald angels sing, in the lines,

> Veiled in flesh the Godhead see
> Hail the incarnate Deity
> Pleased as man with man to dwell
> Jesus our Emmanuel
> Hark the herald angels sing
> Glory to the new born King.

The flying eagle speaks of the divinity of Jesus. The eagle is such a majestic bird that is able to soar to great heights and see for great distances. All the other creatures are earth bound, but not the eagle; he is the king of the heavens. The eagle is able to overcome earth forces, but also able to ride out the violent storms in the heavens. With wings outstretched, this mighty bird uses the strong winds to his advantage, and rides the storm as a sailing ship uses the winds to drive it along. He is able to fly higher and higher as his powerful wings harness the winds. The eagle lives for a long time, compared to most other creatures, and is able to renew its feathers and beak many times over. Efficient feathers are of course essential to maintain his mastery of the skies, and a sharp beak necessary for eating its prey. These things remind us of some of the characteristics of God. God rules in the heavens, and the heaven of heavens, in fact there is no place He does not rule. The psalmist says that He rides upon the storm. He is the Ancient of Days, who never tires or grows old, but is the same yesterday and today and forever. John has not seen Jesus in heaven yet, but in these four living creatures he has seen represented all the vital aspects of Jesus our wonderful saviour.

These living creatures have six wings. Isaiah saw them with six wings, two were in order to fly, and the other four were to cover their faces and feet in the presence of a holy God. Ezekiel saw them as burning coals of fire, like the appearance of torches. They ran backwards and forwards in appearance like a flash of lightning. John repeats that the creatures are full of eyes, and are constantly saying, "Holy, holy, holy, Lord God Almighty, who was and is and is to come!"(Revelation Ch.4v8) They proclaim the holiness of the Father, Son and Holy Spirit. Holiness is the fundamental attribute of all three members of the Godhead. In every way they are apart from and above anything that they have created. In knowledge, wisdom, power, authority, riches, honour, and purity, in every conceivable attribute of Godlike character they are incomparable. This is acknowledged by all in heaven, and was only ever challenged once, when Lucifer sinned but he was quickly ejected from heaven along with the rebellious angels. He was once the covering cherub, who walked among the fiery stones on the holy mountain of God, until iniquity was found in him as he aspired to sit on the throne of God. He said in his heart, "I will ascend into heaven, I will exalt my throne above the stars of God; I will also sit on the mount of the congregation on the farthest sides of the north; I will ascend above the heights of the clouds, I will be like the Most High." But God said to him, "Yet you shall be brought down to Sheol, to the lowest depths of the Pit."(Isaiah Ch.14v13-15) God will not allow anyone to challenge His holiness, as the rest of the book of Revelation reveals, and as Satan, the antichrist and the false prophet are yet to find out. God is God, because He is the Holy One, nothing and no one in any way shape or form can be compared to Him.

The triplet of Holy, holy, holy, is followed by another triplet, Lord God Almighty. All the way through scripture God is called the Lord. Several Hebrew words are translated as Lord in the Old Testament, and their meanings are that God is Master, the I Am, or He who Is. In the New Testament the word translated Lord, means Master, Christians calling Jesus Lord and Master in the same way as Jews called God Master and Lord. The living creatures acknowledge the holiness of God, in that He is the only Lord and Master, the I Am. He is the Lord God, God meaning the Mighty One who is to be worshipped. He is the Lord of Hosts; He is the one who created all things. God is sometimes called the Mighty One of Israel, but He is not just mighty, but The Almighty. No one can question Him and say, "What are you doing." No one can challenge His authority.

He has power over all creation, as a potter has power over the clay in his hands. Paul wrote to the church in Rome and said, "But indeed, O man, who are you to reply against God? Will the thing formed say to the one who formed it, "Why have you made me like this?"(Romans Ch.9v20) No one can question God, yet many presumptuous people imagine that they can. Paul also wrote to the same church in Ch.11v34-36, "For who has known the mind of the Lord? Or who has become His counsellor? Or who has first given to Him and it shall be repaid him? For of Him and through Him and to Him are all things, to whom be glory forever. Amen." No one else can make claims like this because there is only one Lord God Almighty, and He is and always will be the One on the throne in heaven.

Who was and is and is to come. This is a constant theme in the book of Revelation, that God is the eternal God, without beginning or ending. Just as a circle has no beginning and no end. This is incomprehensible to the natural mind of man, but so is everything about God, and His creation. Scientists think that they have come a long way in discovering the secrets of the natural world, and one has even claimed that he will have the answer to everything. If anyone seriously thinks that is the case, he is under a strong delusion. Man has not even begun to scratch the surface, of all there is to be known about all that God has created. Indeed new discoveries are being made almost every day, that necessitates the constant revision of science textbooks. Also science cannot even answer the most fundamental questions, such as where did we come from, what is the purpose of life? It is a total cop out to say we arrived here by accident and there is no purpose to life. We are faced with a stark choice. Either the eternal God of the Bible created everything by His own will and for His own purposes, or matter has always existed in some form or other and just keeps on evolving and then disintegrating. Logic would bring us to the conclusion that matter, which has no intelligence, could not possibly produce the massively intricate designs that science itself has discovered, designs that are in the vast expanses of space, and also in the minute world of the atom. The discovery of DNA has shown us, that all living things are designed according to the information contained in the DNA and information has to come from an intelligent source. It makes sense to believe that everything has come into being through the agency of the Almighty Eternal God who is all knowing and all wise. This is the God revealed in the Bible.

As the living creatures never cease to worship God, so also the twenty four elders are also constantly worshiping God. They worship by falling down before Him who sits on the throne who lives forever and ever. Worship is not only expressed in words but also in posture. What is vitally important in worship is the posture of the heart before God. Whatever the physical posture of a person may be, there is no real worship where the heart, the inner being and the mind and will, are not submitted to God. As they fall before the throne, they cast their golden crowns before the throne. These crowns are the rewards that they have received for being good and faithful, some of them having given their lives, and have received martyrs crowns. These they cast before the throne to acknowledge that whatever they have done to merit their rewards, they are debtors to the grace of God that strengthened them and enabled them to be overcomers. Paul expressed in words what these elders expressed by their actions when he wrote, "For I am the least of the apostles, who am not worthy to be called an apostle, because I persecuted the church of God. But by the grace of God I am what I am, and His grace toward me was not in vain; but I laboured more abundantly than they all, yet not I, but the grace of God that was with me."(1Corinthians Ch.15v9-10) Jesus has been urging those in the churches in Asia to be over comers and go for the rewards that He is offering them, so that they too when they stand before the throne of God, will have something to give back to God that by His grace He has given them. The sad thing is that the scriptures indicate that there will be some in heaven who will receive no reward, because their works will be burnt up because they are all made of wood, hay and stubble. (1Corinthians Ch.3v11-15)

The elders by their actions are saying, it is all by the grace of God that they sit around the throne of God. They say as they bow down, "You are worthy, O Lord, to receive glory and honour and power; for You created all things, and by Your will they exist and were created."(Revelation Ch.4v11) The word worthy has to do with weight and worth. In Old Testament times money was gold or silver coins or pieces that were a particular weight. For example when Abraham's wife Sarah died, Abraham bought a field that had a cave in it, to bury Sarah in. Genesis Ch.23v16 records that Abraham weighed out four hundred shekels of silver to buy the field. Even as recently as the 19th century the gold sovereign coin was made of the weight of gold that was worth one pound, so that the Bank of England would give anyone a gold sovereign for a pound note. In saying that God is worthy, the elders were in effect saying that God was worth the weight of all the glory, honour and power that exists in the universe. For God is worthy to receive all the glory, honour and power and they belong to Him. There are those in our predominantly secular and atheistic society and even some in the church, who do not acknowledge God as the creator and therefore do not acknowledge His true worth, consequently they cannot worship Him as the One who is worthy. They have exchanged the truth about God for a lie, in order to try and justify their sinful and ungodly lifestyle. How vital it is for Christians to hold tenaciously to the truth that God created the heavens and the earth, and everything in them in six days as is written in Genesis Ch.1. There is nothing in what is truly science that can refute God's Word, although there is a great deal of speculative science and tentative theory that finds itself in conflict with the unchanging Word of God. Theories abound as to the origin of life and the universe that can loosely be described as evolutionary, big bang theories, all of which are unproven and impossible to prove scientifically. Yet despite this there is in the media a constant barrage of evolutionary propaganda which purports to be science, but what is needed by those who put forward these theories is some good old fashioned integrity. I say this because instead of them asserting that these things are facts, if they were honest they would say we believe these things to be true, but cannot prove it. These things are all unproven by all the norms by which scientific facts are established. Conclusions need to be drawn from reliable data that can be tested experimentally, by those who are independent of any particular agenda. It seems to me that no one is allowed to question the status quo, even though there is a growing body of evidence provided by scientists who are Christians, that the Bible is true, and they are every bit as qualified to speak on these things as those who support evolution. The secularists and atheists have long derided Christians by saying that they have no proof that God is the creator, and with this I agree, Christians cannot prove by scientific means the things they believe, but accept them by faith in God's Word. But I have a question for the evolutionist and atheist, where is the scientific proof for what you believe? Don't evolutionists believe what they believe by faith?

Not only is God the creator, but by His will all things exist. The book of Revelation reveals to us that there is coming a time when God will decide that the time is right to dissolve all that He has created and it will be burnt up in what Peter describes as a fervent heat. He says, "the heavens will pass away with a great noise, and the elements will melt with fervent heat; both the earth and the works that are in it will be burnt up. Therefore, since all these things will be dissolved, what manner of persons ought you to be in holy conduct and godliness."(2Peter Ch.3v10-11) The universe did not come into being with a big bang, but it will certainly end that way. People in the world and the church need to get real and acknowledge that as God is the creator of all things, so He will one day bring it all to an end. Where will you stand in that day in relation to the Holy, Almighty and Creator God. Do you acknowledge His holiness and worth? Wisdom would teach us the fear of the Lord, that it is right to get in line with the four living creatures and the elders and fall down before the One who sits on the throne, and worship Him who lives for and ever.

CHAPTER 10

THE SCROLL AND THE LITTLE LAMB

There is a definite sequence to the things John sees in heaven, for John is in the Spirit and the unfolding pattern of what he sees and when he sees things, is controlled by the Holy Spirit. Briefly recapping, firstly he saw the throne and the One who sat on it. Around the throne were twenty four elders sitting on thrones. Then he saw the Seven lamps of fire burning before the throne, representing the Holy Spirit. After that he saw the four living creatures in the midst of the throne, representing four aspects of Jesus as Savior, but Jesus himself has not been seen yet. Then John hears the worship of the four living creatures, and they worship God for who He is. Then the elders join in the worship and proclaim God to be the creator of all things. This pattern of revelation follows the pattern of the whole of the scripture. The Holy Spirit is teaching us that revelation is progressive, and that to understand the things of God, we have to start at the beginning and build on the foundations of our faith. The foundations of the Christian faith are not in the New Testament, but in the Old Testament, and the foundations begin to be laid in Genesis Chapter one. Having established the revelation of the beginnings the Holy Spirit now brings to John the next thing that he needs to see and write to the churches about.

The Holy Spirit directs John's attention back to the throne of God, and specifically to the right hand of the One who sits on the throne. For in God's right hand is a scroll that is sealed with seven seals, with writing on the inside and outside of the scroll. This scroll is of the utmost importance, as is indicated by it being held in the right hand of God. The significance of this scroll would not be lost on the readers of John's day, for it was typical of a scroll that contained the details of an inheritance. What was contained in this scroll and who would claim this inheritance? This scroll certainly has to do with the earth, for John is shown the scroll as part of the unfolding revelation of things to come on the earth. The importance of the scroll is further reinforced by what happens next. John heard a strong angel making a royal proclamation from heaven, that must have sounded throughout the whole of heaven and earth. The angel cried out, "Who is WORTHY to open the scroll and to loose it's seals." The criteria for opening this scroll, and claiming the inheritance written on it, is not might, wisdom, riches or any other qualification, but the one who opens the scroll has to be WORTHY. God himself has drawn up the inheritance and sealed it with seven seals, and unless someone is found who is worthy in the sight of God to open the scroll, it will remain sealed. What are the implications of the scroll not being opened? I believe that if no one could open the scroll, then the Eden that man lost through sin, would be lost forever. It was always Gods intention to reclaim the earth, after Satan became prince of this world and prince of the power of the air, because of Adam's sin. When Jesus was tempted by Satan, one of the temptations was that if Jesus would fall down and worship him, then Satan would give him the kingdoms of the world and all their glory and power. Jesus did not challenge his right to do just that but replied, "You shall worship the Lord your God, and Him only you shall serve."(Matthew Ch.4v10) Furthermore God Himself had put all of creation under a curse because of sin, and it was always God's intention that the curse would one day be totally eradicated, and the world would once more be free from the curse of sin. So God's intention, in the drawing up of this inheritance of a new earth and Eden regained, is to take away all of Satan's power over the earth, and bring into existence a new earth where righteousness reigns.

But who is worthy to open the scroll and to loose the seals? On the answer to that great question the future of the earth depends. Were any of the cherubim or seraphim, who are around the throne of God worthy, or indeed any of the myriads of angels in heaven? One thing is for certain, as God has made the criteria for opening the scroll that the person must be worthy, Satan is out of the frame. Satan may be the prince of the power of the air, and the pretender to earth's throne as things stand at the moment, but he only has that position because he deceived Eve and caused the downfall of Adam. If someone is found that is worthy, then Satan cannot even hold the position that he has. If Satan is not worthy, is there any man who is worthy to open the seals? How about Abraham, the friend of God, would he be worthy? Or what about David, the king of Israel and composer of so many beautiful psalms, maybe he would be found worthy? What of Daniel, Isaiah, or one of the other prophets. Could it be that one of the apostles would be found worthy, perhaps John himself, who was suffering for Jesus sake? Certainly there were powerful men on the earth, Caesar for instance, or there were Greek intellectuals and philosophers, but would they qualify in the sight of God?

After the proclamation of the angel, there seems to be a pause, and John no doubt holds his breath. Who, if anyone would be found worthy? Would the earth have a brighter future than its sin ridden past? Was there any prospect that Satan would be dethroned? The whole future of the earth hangs in the balance. There is no doubt in my mind, that John expected this situation to be resolved positively, and that someone would be found who was worthy. But he is in for the greatest shock of his life, for no one in heaven or on the earth or under the earth was able to open the scroll, or to look on it. John records that he wept much, because no one was found worthy to open and read the scroll, or look on it. John now knew a sense of utter despair, a feeling of hollow emptiness and hopelessness, because now it seemed that everything was on hold and there was no one worthy to retrieve man's inheritance for him and more than that it would have seemed to John also that the purposes of God would be thwarted. It was probably no surprise to John that no one on the earth or under the earth was found worthy, but as he wept it must have been a numbing blow to John's mind and heart, that no one in heaven was found worthy. John, along with James his brother and Peter, had been particularly close to Jesus and they had all loved and respected Him as their Lord and Teacher and knew that He had come from God and gone back to God. John had been at the cross when Jesus was dying, and heard Him say to him that he should look after Mary, who had carried Jesus in her womb. From that time on, John looked after Mary as his mother and Mary looked after him as a son. After the crucifixion of Jesus and His burial, John had been the first of the disciples to the tomb, and he looked in and saw the tomb empty with just the grave clothes inside. John had also been with the other disciples when Jesus had appeared to them after His resurrection, and also when Jesus had ascended to heaven. Added to all of this, John has not long before seen Jesus in vision, standing gloriously among the seven churches. Knowing Jesus is in heaven, and also alive among His people on earth, it is not hard to understand why John is weeping.

John knows the absolute necessity of some one being worthy to redeem for God and man, the inheritance of rulership and dominion over the earth that Adam gave away to Satan. Would the earth be forever under Satan's heel? Would the powers of darkness win by default, because no one could open the seals, and claim the earth back for God and righteousness as a place where sin and evil would be banished forever? As John continued to weep, with these thoughts going through his mind, he faced a crisis of faith. It was dawning on him that the faith he had placed in Jesus, as the Savior and Redeemer, may have been misplaced. He could not come to terms with a situation where Jesus was not found worthy. After all, was He not the sinless sacrifice, the Lamb of God who takes away the sin of the world? Could it be that after all, some blemish a tiny fault had been found in Jesus, and now He could not finish what He had begun? Where was Jesus anyway? He has seen a dazzling array of things in heaven, but so far he has not seen Jesus. All these thoughts pressed on his mind, as he wept and wept. He now felt alone, almost abandoned, for there he was suffering for Jesus sake and for the testimony that he held, and now when Jesus is needed to step forward it seems that

He is not there. Surely if anyone was going to be worthy to open the scroll it would be Jesus. Jesus is needed to loose the seals in order to finish the outworking of that which He finished on the cross, when He cried out with a loud voice, "It is finished."(John Ch.19v30) The whole plan of redemption, including the redemption of all of God's children from death at the resurrection and the redemption of the creation spoiled through sin needs to take place, and unless the scroll is opened none of these things will happen. John must have wondered if the whole experience was indeed a revelation from God, or just a horrific nightmare! When John had seen Jesus in his glory, He is in the midst of the seven churches, and he had fallen at His feet as dead and Jesus had been offering rewards to those in the churches who would overcome. But where is Jesus now that John is in the Spirit, and in heaven?

Suddenly, as John is still weeping, one of the elders left his throne and came to John with a message. John heard the words, "Do not weep, Behold the Lion of the tribe of Judah, the Root of David, has prevailed to open the scroll and to loose its seven seals."(Revelation Ch.5v5) It must have seemed to John that he had been weeping forever, for he was so traumatized that he had not noticed that the seals were loosed from the scroll and the scroll was now opened. He had not seen what had already happened in heaven, with his head buried in his hands and his eyes filled with tears. John wiped his eyes, and lifted his head up to see that right in the middle of the throne, the four beasts and the twenty four elders, stood a lamb looking as though it had just been slain. This lamb is actually a little lamb, just a young lamb, standing in the middle of all of heaven. The Greek word for lamb, in this instance, means a little lamb. This little lamb, as a man is the Lion of the tribe of Judah. We have already looked at scriptures concerning this title of Jesus in the previous chapter, and it is connected with Him being the rightful ruler of all the earth, in succession to David in his royal line. But He is also the root of David the king, who God promised would have a kingdom that would never end, thus indicating His divinity. Just as the root of a plant causes the growth of a plant and sustains it, so Jesus as God is the one who causes the kingdom of God to come and sustains it eternally. These titles that Jesus has clearly show that He is truly man and truly God.

The question has to be asked, why did God want John to go through this traumatic experience? It was clearly God's intention for John to go through this, for he is in the Spirit and all that is happening to John is Spirit controlled. I believe the answer lies in God wanting to demonstrate to John and all his readers, how absolutely lost and hopeless they are without Jesus. After all, some of the churches which this book was first sent to were playing fast and loose with the Lord. They were being unfaithful to him, by turning to idolatrous practices, valuing money and possessions as being more precious than Him and one church even had Jesus on the outside trying to get into their lives. They needed to feel what John felt when it seemed that Jesus was not there anymore. Needless to say, this is something that many people who claim to be Christians need to experience too. For let me ask you, what hope is there in the future for ultimate salvation, without Jesus? The new earth that the Bible speaks of, will not come about through the preaching of the gospel alone. It will not come about because of the actions of men, in uniting together through religions or political organizations. It will come about because the King of Kings will come, and set up His eternal kingdom, that will never be challenged and will never end. Jesus, as King, is the only hope for the future.

John has no problem in identifying the little lamb, who is in the middle of the throne, it is of course the one he has been longing to see in heaven, it is Jesus. John had already written in his gospel of the time when Jesus came to John the Baptist to be baptized. John the Baptist pointing to Jesus had said, "Behold! The Lamb of God who takes away the sin of the world!"(John Ch.1v29) How reassuring to see Jesus, how comforting. It is always a comfort to the heart of the believer to see Jesus, and it was never so comforting to John to see the Lamb of God in heaven as it was then. I said at the beginning of the chapter, that the revelation that John receives is a revelation that follows a pattern and a step by step unfolding. Jesus had always been in the middle of the throne, but only when God so directed, did John see Him there. This is the pattern for God's dealings with His people.

We do not see everything at once. It is a line upon line and precept upon precept approach that God has in revealing His truth to us.

How wonderful to see a little lamb on the throne in heaven. Jesus is also portrayed as a lion, a kingly animal if ever there was one, but God has chosen to reveal Jesus as a little lamb on the throne in heaven. The Lamb reigns in heaven, because it was not might that raised Jesus to the throne, but humility. He could have used might to deliver himself from the hands of the wicked men who crucified Him. He could, no doubt, have used might to take over the world and proclaim himself king, but He chose to wear a crown of thorns and have the cross for His throne. This was the purpose of God for Jesus and because He fulfilled the purposes of God instead of pleasing Himself, God has highly exalted Him and given Him a name above all other names. This principle, that God always exalts the humble, also applies to His people. Peter wrote, "God resists the proud, but gives grace to the humble." "Therefore humble yourselves under the mighty hand of God, that He may exalt you in due time."(1Peter Ch.5v5-6) How instructive it must have been for the churches to know, that God has exalted the little lamb, to the highest place in heaven. For many of them needed to humble themselves before God, and begin to accept that He is God and Jesus is Lord of all, so that God could exalt them in due time and reward them in heaven.

Furthermore Jesus is the lamb, which looked to John as if it had just been slain. John could see the wounds were still fresh as Jesus ascended to heaven with wounds that were still fresh. He had invited doubting Thomas to put his finger into the nail prints in His hands, and also to put his hand into the spear wound in His side. Jesus wounds will be forever fresh, because his death and the shedding of His precious blood, will forever speak from the throne of God. They speak of His great love wherewith He has loved us. They speak of the atonement He has made for our sins, and the averting of the righteous judgment of God against sin. They speak of His victory over death and hell and of His right to reign. They also speak of His right to loose the seals and open the scroll, because of His life and His death He has been found worthy. This makes Jesus unique, in all of history, He is worthy. No other person is worthy, whoever you may wish to name. No religious leader, no prophet, no sage or philosopher, for all need the redemption from sin that only Jesus provides. If Jesus was not found by God to be worthy, the scripture would have ended with a revelation of despair and it would certainly have all ended in tears. But through His sinless life and death Jesus conquered, and obtained the victory over Satan, He prevailed to take the scroll. Jesus did not have to come and prize the scroll out of God's hand, but the Father willingly gave it to His Son because He is worthy.

John is shown the seven horns and the seven eyes that the little lamb has, and it is revealed to him that both the horns and the eyes, are the seven Spirits of God. The three persons of the Godhead relate to each other in loving submission. The Father is on the throne, and is revealed in awesome fiery majesty. The Son is revealed as a little lamb, because He submits to the Father in everything. The Holy Spirit submits to Jesus the Son, and this is clearly revealed in this picture of the Holy Spirit being the seven horns and seven eyes. It is Jesus who has sent the Holy Spirit into all the earth, as He promised He would. In His heavenly role the Holy Spirit is seen as seven lamps of fire burning before the throne of God. However in His earthly role the Holy Spirit is seen as seven horns and seven eyes. The horns speak of power and authority and the eyes of the Holy Spirit being all seeing and all knowing. John had recorded the words of Jesus, regarding the Holy Spirit, when he wrote, "And I will pray the Father, and He will give you another Helper, that He may abide with you forever- the Spirit of truth, whom the world cannot receive, because it neither sees Him nor knows Him; but you know Him, for He dwells with you and will be in you." (John Ch.14v16-17) This other Helper was a helper who would be exactly the same as Jesus Himself. Jesus knew that He would soon be leaving the disciples, so He comforted them by telling them that they would have the Holy Spirit with them just as He had been with them. In John Ch.16v7 Jesus said, "Nevertheless I tell you the truth. It is to your advantage that I go away; for if I do not go away, the Helper will not come to you; but if I depart, I will send Him to you." In the same chapter in v8, Jesus describes three ways in which the Holy Spirit will exercise power on the earth. Jesus said, "And when He has come, He will convict the world of sin, and of righteousness, and of judgment." Jesus went on to say that the Holy Spirit would convict the world of the sin of unbelief, because they have not believed on Him. In a similar vein Jesus said in John Ch3v19, "And this is the condemnation, that the light has come into the world, and men loved darkness rather than light, because their deeds were evil." The fundamental sin that will condemn men to the lake of fire, is the sin of unbelief. This is not to be confused with doubt or misgiving, because unbelief is the sin which caused the scribes and Pharisees to want Jesus to be crucified. They saw the wonderful things He did and heard the truths that He spoke, but the straw that broke the camels back for them, was when Jesus raised Lazarus from the dead. After the raising of Lazarus, they determined to kill Jesus. One would have thought that they would want to acclaim Him as their Lord and Messiah, but no, because of unbelief they did not want to believe on Him. There is no valid reason, in science, philosophy, religion, or in any human experience, why anyone should not believe on the Lord Jesus Christ and be saved, there is only unbelief. That is why the Holy Spirit has come to convict men of unbelief. The greatest power on earth, is the power the Holy Spirit exercises, when He turns an unbeliever into a believer on the Lord Jesus. He will also convict the world of righteousness, because Jesus was no longer in the world and had gone to the Father. When Jesus was on the earth, because of His perfect sinless life, people who came into contact with Him were aware of God's standard of righteousness. Jesus convicted them of sin, and they were also convinced that perfect righteousness existed in this man. On one occasion Jesus said to His enemies, "Which of you convicts me of sin?"(John Ch.8v46) Jesus could throw out the challenge to those who hated Him, and none of them could accuse Him of any sin. Jesus exhibited before men the righteousness of God, truly Light had come into the world. Because Jesus showed by His life the righteousness of God, He could also fearlessly speak the truths of God that express that righteousness and no one could say that they did not know what was right. But now that Jesus was going back to the Father the Holy Spirit would continue to do this work in the earth. The Holy Spirit would also convict the world of judgment, because the ruler of this world, Satan, is judged. This means that Satan is weighed in the balances and is found wanting. God has determined that Satan who rules in the world is not worthy to hold that position and judgment has been passed, although sentence has not yet been carried out. One of the major events in the book of Revelation is the sentence being carried out and Satan being thrown into the lake of fire. The Holy Spirit has come into the world to convince fallen man that he is on the wrong side. That the prince of darkness, the ruler of this world, is judged and if they do not want to suffer the same fate as him they need to believe on the Lord Jesus Christ. "For God so loved the world that He gave His only begotten Son, that whoever believes in Him should not perish but have everlasting life. For God did not send His Son into the world to condemn the world, but that the world through Him might be saved. He who believes in Him is not condemned; but he who does not believe is condemned already, because he has not believed in the name of the only begotten Son of God." (John Ch.3v16-18.)

Jesus said that the Holy Spirit is the Spirit of Truth that would come. He is the Spirit that searches out the hidden things in the heart of God and man. He is the Spirit that is represented by the seven eyes. He has been sent out into all the earth and He sees everything that is happening in all the earth. He even sees into the hearts of every man everywhere, and nothing can be hidden from Him. Acts Ch.5v1-11, records the death of two people, Ananias and Sapphira. They died because they lied to the Holy Spirit. They had sold a possession and pretended to bring all of the money to the apostles, so that the money could be distributed to the poor in the church, but they had held some back for themselves. This they were quite entitled to do, but their grave error was in trying to deceive the apostles, and make themselves look good at the same time. But Peter said, "Ananias why has Satan filled your heart to lie to the Holy Spirit and keep back part of the price of the land for yourself?"(Acts Ch.5v3) On hearing this Ananias fell dead at the apostle's feet. When Sapphira also lied about the sale of the land, she too died some time later. Let us beware of trying to deceive the Holy Spirit, because if we do sooner or later judgment will follow. The Holy Spirit also reveals the deep things of God. As Paul wrote to the Corinthians, in his first epistle, "Eye has not seen, nor ear heard, nor have entered into the heart of man the things God has prepared for those who love Him. But God has revealed them to us through His Spirit. For the Spirit searches all things, yes the deep things of God. For what man knows the things of a man except the spirit of the man that is in him? Even so no one knows the things of God except the Spirit of God."(1Corinthians Ch.2v9-11)

The Holy Spirit has also been sent into the earth to bear witness to, and confirm with various signs and wonders and miracles, the preaching of the gospel. Hebrews Ch.2v4 says, "God also bearing witness both with signs and wonders, with various miracles, and gifts of the Holy Spirit, according to His own will." Miracles come from God through the Holy Spirit, and are a sign that the gospel is true, and when God sees fit miracles happen as an aid to people believing the gospel. The Holy Spirit is bringing people, of all ages and races to faith in Jesus as their Savior from all over the world, through the preaching of the gospel. For it is the gospel that is the power of God unto salvation to every one who will believe. The Holy Spirit will stay and do this work until the Father decides it is time for reaping. In Matthew Ch.13v24 Jesus begins to tell the story of two harvests in the parable of the wheat and the tares. The wheat represents the sons of the kingdom of God and they will be harvested when Jesus comes with His angels to gather His own. But the tares are also harvested and prepared for burning. John sees a picture of the reaping time of the tares in what is recorded in Revelation Ch. 14v14-16, where an angel reaps the harvest of the earth, a harvest that has rotted and is over ripe. After that there is only the fearful outpouring of the wrath of God, and that is represented by the picture of the clusters of the vine of the earth being reaped, and just as grapes are trodden to make wine, so they will be thrown into the winepress of the wrath of God.(Rev. Ch 14v17-20.)

The elder had said to John that the lamb had prevailed to open the scroll and to loose the seals. But because John had been weeping so much, he had missed the great event. So God graciously allows John to see a replay of the moment when all heaven gasped in wonder as the little lamb came and took the scroll out of God's right hand. This is a pivotal moment in heaven's history for now the rightful inheritor of the earth takes the title deeds of His inheritance, and the rest of earths history culminating in the coming of the King of Kings, can begin to take place. Psalm two is a wonderful prophetic psalm which speaks of the rulers of the earth doing what they, and most men have tried to do, and that is break free from God's rule and authority and from God's anointed King, Jesus Christ. But God laughs at their feeble attempts to thwart His purpose and says, "Yet I have set My King on My holy hill of Zion. I will declare the decree: The Lord has said to Me, You are My Son today I have begotten You. Ask of Me, and I will give You the nations for Your inheritance, and the ends of the earth for Your possession. You shall break them with a rod of iron; You shall dash them to pieces like a potters vessel."(Psalm 2v6-9) When Jesus came and took the scroll, and God released it to Him, this was God giving Jesus the ends of the earth for His inheritance and Satan who has no right to rule will be dethroned.

When did Jesus take the scroll and loose its seals? In answering this question it is necessary to bear in mind that events in heaven do not necessarily take place in an earth time frame, for heaven is in eternity. But John is seeing things in heaven as they are at the time of the seven churches in Asia, and He has been told to write what he sees, and send it to them. We also have another clue, in that the Holy Spirit has been sent out into all the earth. When was the Holy Spirit sent to carry on the work of Jesus in the lives of the disciples? The answer is clearly, the day of Pentecost forty days after He ascended, when the disciples were all filled with the Holy Spirit, and spoke with tongues. When did Jesus assume authority over the earth from the throne in heaven, by taking the scroll and loosing the seals? Peter in His sermon on the day of Pentecost said, "For David did not ascend into the heavens, but he says himself: "The Lord said to my Lord, sit at my right hand, till I make Your enemies Your footstool." Therefore let all the house of Israel know assuredly that God has made this Jesus, whom you crucified, both Lord and Christ."(Acts Ch.2v34-36) I believe Jesus took the scroll when He ascended to the Father's right hand, and what John saw was a replay of what had already happened, in earth time probably about sixty years before, but in terms of eternity was no time at all. God who lives outside of time, is already in eternity when Satan is in the lake of fire, and all His redeemed are safe in His eternal kingdom.

The enthronement of the little lamb in heaven, prompted the four living creatures and the twenty four elders to do something new, they started to sing. In chapter four of Revelation the elders and living creatures had only said words of worship and praise, but after the Lamb is enthroned they start to sing a new song. This is one of the differences in heaven, before and after Calvary. The living creatures had previously praised Father, Son and Holy Spirit, for being the One eternal God. The twenty four elders worshipped God, Father, Son and Holy Spirit, for being the creator of all things. Now the focus of their praise is the Son, who John sees as the Lamb and they start to sing. To accompany their singing they each have a harp. They offer their praise to the Lamb along with the prayers of the saints, for John sees that each one had a harp and golden bowls full of incense, which are the prayers of the saints. Jesus said, "And whatever you ask in My name, that I will do, that the Father may be glorified in the Son." (John 14v13.) Paul wrote to Timothy and said that there was only one mediator between God and men, and that was the man Christ Jesus. Jesus said that prayer was to be offered to God through Him and for whatever reason we approach God, there is only one mediator, and that is Jesus. So we see this principle taught by this picture, of the elders and living creatures, offering the prayers of the saints to God through Jesus as they fell down before the Lamb and worshipped Him.

The song they sang had not been heard in heaven before, for a unique event in heaven required a new song. They sang, "You are worthy to take the scroll, and to open its seals; For You were slain, and have redeemed us to God by your blood out of every tribe and tongue and people and nation, and have made us kings and priests to our God; and we shall reign on the earth."(Revelation Ch.5v9-10) Some versions of the Bible have them singing, "and have made them kings and priests to our God; and they shall reign on the earth." This would seem to make more sense as they are singing this song on behalf of the redeemed, as their representatives around the throne. We can only wonder that the centre of attention is the Lamb. For not only has

He been exalted to the throne, but now is worshipped as the one to inherit the earth. Who before He establishes His kingdom on earth, wealds unprecedented spiritual power on earth, through the Holy Spirit seen as seven horns and seven eyes. Jesus said when preaching the sermon on the mount that the meek shall inherit the earth, and no one was meeker than He was. Satan got it completely wrong when he thought that rebellion and deception would win the day. The way of Satan is pride, of being full of self and exalting himself, but he and those like him will be brought down to the lake of fire. What a lesson for the churches and for all men everywhere for all time.

John looks again and sees and hears the voices of many angels around the throne. They are joined by the four living creatures and the twenty four elders. The angels are so many that they cannot be counted and the host of them stretch as far as the eye can see. John describes their number as one hundred thousand million, all saying with one voice, "Worthy is the Lamb who was slain to receive power and riches and wisdom, and strength and honor and glory and blessing!"(Revelation Ch.5v12) I believe that they are saying Jesus is worthy of every last bit of all these things that the whole of the universe contains. Not only is Jesus more than worth all that the earth is, but He is more than worth all the power right through to all the blessing in the universe. We just cannot calculate the worth of Jesus, for what could possibly be equal to His value. As God the Son, before His birth through the virgin Mary, His worth was incalculable. But since He has been slain for sinners, and redeemed them to God, how much more worthy is He now? He was worthy because of who He was, but now He is doubly worthy because of who He is and what He has done. He reigns in heaven now because of His double worth, the Lamb upon the throne. God has given Him all power and all other powers are under His feet, and derive their power from Him.

He was rich before His birth in Bethlehem. But Paul tells us in 2Corinthians Ch.8v9, "For you know the grace of our Lord Jesus Christ, that though He was rich, yet for your sakes He became poor, that you through His poverty might become rich." Jesus became poor in every way that we might be rich. On His travels around the land of Israel, He had nowhere to lay His head, even though the foxes have holes and the birds of the air have nests. He never laid up treasure on earth, or left and earthly inheritance. He never owned any property, and when He died He was laid in another man's tomb. He shunned the offer of riches and power from Satan, during the temptations in the wilderness. But now, having emptied Himself completely and going through the death of the cross, God has raised Him up from the dead and He is more than worth all the riches in the universe, and more than worthy to receive them.

Jesus is worthy of all wisdom. Wisdom is skill and Jesus will receive all the skill and ability He needs to reign on the throne in heaven, over the affairs of earth for He is worthy. No one will ever outwit Him or outmaneuver Him in all of history, the arch enemy Satan will be no match for Him. He will skillfully weave all of the purposes of God, through all the rebellion of man and Satan, to achieve His ends.

Jesus is also worthy to receive all strength. Strength is the force to subdue all other powers and principalities that are opposed to Him and bring them into submission to His purposes. Jesus did not get to the throne by force, but now that He is on the throne He will use divine force, the power of His word, to crush His enemies as the final chapters of Revelation record. All the powers of nature, which He created are at His disposal and at His command, and He uses them with ever increasing force to destroy the wicked of the earth. Spiritual powers and rulers, whether good or evil, are at His command and they do His bidding. He uses them to inflict His righteous judgments on the nations, the kingdoms, the peoples and religions of the earth that reject Him as Lord and King. This culminates in the Judgment of the Great Whore and Babylon the Great. In the end the Lord God omnipotent reigns, because He is worthy to receive all strength.

Jesus is worthy to receive all honor. Honor is esteem, ones true value. Jesus is worthy to be valued at His true worth, even though He rarely is. The name of Jesus is most frequently heard in this world being used irreverently and flippantly, and this is a reflection of a complete lack of esteem for the King of Kings and Lord of Lords. Men honor other men for discovering one or two of the secrets of the material world

He has created. I say, one or two, because even with the escalation of knowledge that has occurred over the last one hundred years, men have not even begun to scratch the surface of all that could be known. Men honor each other for acts of bravery, for feats of endurance, and even for acts of unselfish self-sacrifice. But what can compare with the sacrifice of God the Son, in emptying Himself and paying the price in suffering, for the sins of the world. Men honor each other for great works of art and music, but few honor the one who, when He made them in His image, invested in them the ability to create such wonderful things. He alone is worthy of all honor and esteem.

Jesus is worthy also of all the glory. Glory is brilliance, weightiness, a radiance that is truly substantial. Glory is an attribute of God and of no other, and Jesus is worthy to receive all the glory. Stars have a glory, and some are more glorious than others, but they all receive their glory from their creator. Psalm 8 says that God has set His glory above the heavens. He is speaking of the glory of the starry host, which is above the earthly sky. The psalmist also goes on to say that God has crowned man with glory and honor, in that He gave him dominion over the works of His hands. It is plain to see that in numerous ways the glory that God invested in man, far exceeds the glory of any other living being that He created to live on the earth. When Jesus emptied Himself and came to earth to be our savior, He divested Himself of the glory He had with God the Father. In John's gospel Ch.17v5 Jesus prayed, "And now, O Father, glorify Me together with Yourself, with the glory which I had with You before the world was." God answered that prayer, for Jesus is worthy to receive all the glory, and outshine every other man, every star and anything that He created, for He is worthy.

Jesus is also worthy to receive all blessing. That means He is worthy to be spoken well of. The Greek word which has been translated as blessing is the word eulogia, which is similar to the word eulogize. Eulogize means to speak or write in praise of someone, so all the hosts of heaven are now blessing the Lamb that was slain for He alone is worthy. We cannot praise Jesus enough, because of what He has done and as we look at the sevenfold approbation that Jesus receives in heaven, it is an example to us that we should fully recognize His worth as they do.

But the praise does not climax there, for John now sees well into the future when all of creation will praise the One who sits on the throne and the Lamb. For John heard every creature in heaven and earth and under the earth attributing blessing and honor and glory and power to Him who sits on the throne and to the Lamb forever and ever. This is John seeing what will happen when the kingdom of this world has become the kingdom of our God and His Christ, when every tongue will confess that Jesus Christ is Lord to the glory of God the Father. This is the climax of all time and of the purposes of God in heaven and earth. This is the climax of all revelation, to John, to the seven churches and to all the church throughout time. God has spoken very clearly to the seven churches, mostly in bringing them to order and repentance, because they in some way have not grasped the worth of His Son. In the revelations that have come to John so far in heaven, God has continued this same process. Jesus once said to the disciples, "You believe in God, believe also in me."(John Ch.14v1) God is saying much the same thing to the seven churches, I am worthy and so is My Son. As you worship me, worship Him also, for He is worthy. The four living creatures say, "Amen" to the praise and worship offered to God and the Lamb. The seven churches, and the church throughout time, should do no less. The twenty four elders fall down and worship Him who lives forever and ever, and we should do the same.

CHAPTER 11

THE OPENING OF THE SIX SEALS

What is past or present or future can begin to be somewhat puzzling when, as John was, you are in the Spirit in heaven. To illustrate my point, while John was weeping one of the elders came to him, and told him that the Lion of the tribe of Judah had prevailed to open the scroll and loose the seals. This was something that had already happened. After this John sees the Lamb take the scroll, from the right hand of the One who sits on the throne, and the scroll has not yet been opened. These things John records in Chapter five. Now we come to chapter six and John sees the lamb open one of the seals. Confused? Well there is no need to be confused when you recognize that in heaven things do not need to be revealed in order of time. For what God is interested in doing through this book is revealing Jesus, and the truths the church needs to know. As we progress further into Revelation, I will be able to clearly demonstrate that what we see in chapters five and six, is common to the rest of the book. Revelation is not a catalogue of chronological events, but the unveiling of events that must take place, which are the prelude to the second coming of Jesus and the establishing of His eternal kingdom in the new heaven and new earth.

These events occur because Jesus is worthy to open the seals. If the rest of the book of Revelation had been revealed to John as a play in a theatre, it would be a play of three acts. After each act, there are interludes, when things that have occurred during the previous act are explained in some detail. Act one is the opening of the seven seals, act two is the blowing of the seven trumpets and act three is the pouring out of the wrath of God from the seven golden bowls. Essential to the whole play is the opening of the seals, so let the curtain rise and let the drama of the history of the last two thousand years as seen from heaven begin.

I believe it is necessary to look at the opening of the first four seals together, because there is a pattern of events that occur, and there are so many things that they have in common. Firstly as the lamb opens each of the first four seals, one of the four living creatures issues a command, with the words, "Come and see." Some versions of the Bible have the command as just the one word, "Come." In the context it would seem to me that either is appropriate. The words, "Come and see", would be addressed to John, for him to see what is about to happen as a result of each of the seals being opened. The word, "Come", would be addressed to the horses and their riders to come. The first living creature to speak, it would seem to me is the one with the face of the lion, the one that speaks of kingship. His voice sounded to John like thunder much like the roar of a lion. It is possible that the second living creature to speak was the one with the face of a calf, the one that speaks of sacrifice and atonement and peace with God. The third had the face of a man and could be the one who speaks next, which leaves the fourth creature the flying eagle to speak last, the former representing the humanity of Christ and the latter the divinity of Christ.

What happens next is the same for all of the four seals as they are opened. When the living creatures say, "Come and see", a horse appears each with a rider. I believe it is necessary first of all to consider each horse, because I believe that these horses have been seen by someone else before John saw them. The prophet Zechariah saw these horses in Ch6 of his prophecy. He saw four chariots coming between two mountains of bronze. They had the same colours as the four horses that John saw, white, red, black and pale. Zechariah asked the angel that was talking with him, "What are these, my lord?" The angel told Zechariah that they were four spirits of heaven who go out from the Lord of all the earth. The Lord of all the earth in the context of Revelation, is the Lamb, and they come forth as the Lamb opens the seals. In Zechariah they are seen pulling chariots, but in Revelation they are seen with riders on them. Only one of the riders is actually identified to John, and that is the rider of the black horse, and his name is Death and Hades follows in his train. I believe there should be consistency when interpreting who these riders are. The horses are spiritual beings, and as is indicated by Death being identified as one of the riders, so I believe the other three riders are also spiritual beings. To identify any of the riders as people who have lived or will live on the earth, from the scripture itself or from the context, is impossible. For instance, there is nothing to enable anyone to positively identify the rider of the white horse, from the one verse that he is mentioned, and that goes for the riders of the red and black horses too. To attempt to identify any of the three of them is, I believe, only conjecture and supposition, and I said in the introduction to this book that I would not be indulging in either of these things.

The important thing to note is that the riders come form heaven, when the lamb opens a seal and the livings creatures call for the riders to come. It is undeniable that each of them comes as a direct result of actions in heaven, which may come as a shock to the system of some people, who have a sentimental view of Jesus meek and mild and lying in a manger. The fact is that He is no longer in the manger, or on the cross or in the tomb, but on the throne in heaven working all things according to the counsel of His own will. What is extraordinary also is that the One exercising such power is a little lamb! The riders are those that bring death and destruction on the earth, through conquest, slaughter, poverty, famine, pestilence and wild beasts. These are certainly destructive spirits that have been given their power and authority from the throne of God, and they have been in operation in the earth since Jesus opened the seals. The first rider has a bow and is given a crown, and he goes out as a conqueror bent on conquest. The second rider is given power to take peace from the earth, and he is given a great sword. The third rider is holding a pair of scales to measure out the earth's food and luxury goods. The poor will always be with us and the rich who profit from olive oil and wine are to go unscathed. The forth rider is Death, with his captives in Hades the place of the dead. Death is given power over a quarter of the earth, to kill with sword, famine, pestilence and wild beasts. This sounds much like the story of the history of the earth, since the time that Adam sinned, as these four riders work together in the earth. I see no reason, from these scriptures to relegate all these things to some future time, as hundreds of millions of souls have perished throughout the history of the earth due to these things. The difference now, since Jesus the Lamb has opened the seals, is that these spiritual powers are now under His control as He opens the seals and history is being brought to the glorious conclusion of the Lamb on the throne. There are many people who question the existence of God in the face of human misery and tragedy, and the reason for this is that they do not have a biblical understanding of the God of the Bible. They have not read Revelation and do not understand that the Lamb is in control on the earth. Why doesn't God stop all the trouble in the world, people say, if He is a God of love? The answer is that according to this revelation of Jesus Christ, God will stop all the trouble, but in His own time and in His own way. It has been nearly twenty centuries since Jesus took His place in heaven, as far as earth time is concerned, but the Lord is not going to break His promise and will come again to reign in righteousness. If your longing is for a world without sin and strife then you need to receive Jesus as your saviour now, so that you can enjoy the new earth with God and the Lamb forever.

There is an important point that needs to be made regarding all of the above. It is this, that although the lamb is in control, even so, what is happening on the earth is still the work of men and God will hold men responsible for their actions. This, I believe is the theme of the opening of the first five seals, what is described is the work of man towards his fellow man. It has been described as man's inhumanity to man. The view of it that we have, in this sixth chapter of Revelation, is the view from heaven. The spirit of conquest has gone out from heaven and men down through history have been controlled by it. This is confirmed by what Jesus said would characterize the age from the destruction of Jerusalem to His second coming. There are a number of things Jesus mentions in Matthew Ch24, one of which is that nation will rise against nation and kingdom against kingdom. There are some who would relegate this to just our modern day or sometime in the future, but surely this is to deny the whole pattern of human history. Of course what makes the conquest of one nation by another more terrifying in our time, is the awesome array of sophisticated weapons that are now available for mass destruction. What we have today also, is the ability to have war on television, destruction seen almost as it happens. Along with conquest, comes the slaughter of countless millions of souls, and this has been happening without any cessation throughout history. There has never been a time of peace on the earth, and Jesus said to His disciples, "And you will hear of wars and rumors of wars. See that you are not troubled; for all these things must come to pass, but the end is not yet."(Matthew Ch.24v6) If the number of those who had perished in war, throughout the last twenty centuries, could be calculated it would be a mind numbing figure. We are told that today, two thirds of the world's population is malnourished or starving, but I would venture to suggest that this has always been the case. Jesus said there would be famines and pestilences, famine as we know is by no means a modern phenomena. It has often been caused by the constant wars that have raged between nations and tribes and peoples. The other third of the world has enough and more than enough. The rich nations have such a surfeit of food that various food mountains have accumulated over the years. Some restaurants advertise, eat as much as you like, and people gorge themselves and grow fat, while others starve. The rider with the balance is in the earth, and the olive oil and wine abound as they always have.

There are many who have died at the hands of wicked men, for the sake of their testimony, because they would not deny Jesus Christ who bought them with His own precious blood. At the time of writing this book of Revelation, John himself was suffering persecution and eventual death for Jesus sake. The Church at Smyrna was suffering in a similar way, and under Rome Christians suffered terrible deaths. In every age the saints of God have given their lives for the sake of the truth and their love of the Lord. They have also not been immune to the ravages of war and indiscriminate killing. Of course many people of many faiths and persuasions have been persecuted for their beliefs, but when the Lamb opens the fifth seal John sees something that is unique to those who have died for Jesus sake. What he sees under the altar, that is before the throne of God, is the souls of those who were killed for the testimony that they held and for the word of God. They cry out to God with loud cries, "How long, O Lord, holy and true, until You judge and avenge our blood on those who dwell on the earth?"(Revelation Ch.6v10) It should be noted that they are calling on God to avenge their blood. This is in line with the scripture that Paul wrote in Romans Ch.12v17-20, "Repay no one evil for evil. Have regard for good things in the sight of all men. If it is possible, as much as depends on you, live peaceably with all men. Beloved do not avenge yourselves, but rather give place to wrath; for it is written, "Vengeance is Mine, I will repay," says the Lord. Therefore, "If your enemy is hungry, feed him; if he is thirsty, give him a drink; for in so doing you will heap coals of fire on his head." It is quite scriptural for God to take vengeance on the enemies of His children, and for His children to ask Him how long before He does so and leave the matter in God's hands. It should be noted that what John is seeing is the result of mans hatred toward his fellow man, just as it was with the previous four seals that were opened.

White robes are given to them and they are told to wait, until the full number of those who would killed as they had been, has been completed. There under the altar are the souls of those who were slain in the time of the apostles and the early church, right up to our own day. There are those who faced crucifixion under the Romans, and also faced the lions in the arenas of Rome. There are those who faced the fires and the torture of the inquisition. There are some who have been slain by the sword of armies that have marched under the banner of Islam, and in our own day have been shot to pieces or blown to pieces by those of the same beliefs. Another belief system, that has sought world domination in modern times, is communism and God's children have suffered and still do suffer persecution and death where this system holds sway. The number of the souls under the altar will continue to swell, until Jesus comes for His Church, but meanwhile they are at rest with pain and sorrow a thing of the past. The writer to the Hebrews wrote a fitting tribute to them in Ch11 from v35-38 "Others were tortured, not accepting deliverance, that they might obtain a better resurrection. Still others had trial of mockings and scourgings, yes, and of chains and imprisonment. They were stoned, they were sawn in two, were tempted, were slain with the sword. They wandered about in sheepskins and goatskins, being destitute, afflicted, tormented- of whom the world was not worthy." In our modern day we could no doubt add to the catalogue of ways that God's people have suffered, They have been gassed, starved, shot, electrocuted, drowned, poisoned and the list could go on.

In all these things we have to bear in mind that John is writing to the seven churches in Asia, and to the church universal throughout the ages, to teach them that despite all of man's inhumanity to man Jesus reigns. Conquerors will conquer, and then pass away. All the Caesars have come and gone. Alexander the Great, Genghis Khan, all the Popes who have held sway in Europe, all the great emperors of the east, all the great rulers of the ancient civilizations of the Americas, have all passed away. Stalin, Hitler, the Japanese Emperor who was regarded as a god, are no longer with us. But there are others waiting in the wings of the stage of time, for their opportunity to step out from the masses and claim the conquerors crown. Great conflicts have come and passed into history, but despite man's best efforts conflict is still with us. The poor are still with us and so are the rich, despite all that has happened over the last one hundred years, nothing has basically changed. We wish those well who seek to eradicate poverty and make it history, but I fear they fight against powers that are too strong for them. Death continues to reap through the activities of man in his greed for power and riches, and his hatred for his fellow man. But Death cannot touch those who die for Jesus sake, they on the other hand are not in Hades, but under the altar in heaven resting where Jesus reigns. All these things characterize the activities of man toward man in this current age, from the time Jesus ascended till the time that He will return. When John sees the sixth seal opened by the Lamb, in earth time we have come to that great event, the second coming of Jesus Christ.

There are three occasions when the second coming of Jesus is documented by John in the book of Revelation, and this is the first of those occasions. The second occasion is in Ch11, when the seventh angel sounds. The third occasion is in Ch19, when John saw heaven open and Jesus coming riding on a white horse. Here in Ch.6 John sees a great earthquake and the sun became black as sackcloth of hair and the moon became like blood. He also sees the stars of heaven falling to the earth, as a fig tree drops its figs when it is shaken by a strong wind. These events are unmistakable, they are events that take place at the second coming of Jesus. What John saw coincides exactly with what Jesus predicted in Matthew Ch.24v29-30 where Jesus said to His disciples, "Immediately after the tribulation of those days the sun will be darkened, and the moon will not give its light; the stars will fall from heaven, and the powers of the heavens will be shaken. Then the sign of the Son of Man will appear in heaven, and then all the tribes of the earth will mourn, and they will see the Son of Man coming on the clouds of heaven with power and great glory."

Then John saw the sky recede as a scroll being rolled up, and every mountain and island being moved from its former place. What an awesome sight, and this is predicted for us in other scriptures also, at the time of the second coming of Jesus. Isaiah Ch.34v4 says in the context of God's final judgment on the earth that, "All the host of heaven shall be dissolved, and the heavens shall be rolled up like a scroll; all their host shall fall down as the leaf falls from the vine, and as fruit falling from a fig tree." In a similar vein Isaiah again predicts in Ch.51v6, "Lift up your eyes to the heavens, and look on the earth beneath. For the heavens will vanish away like smoke, the earth will grow old like a garment, and those who dwell in it will die in like manner; but My salvation will be forever, and My righteousness will not be abolished." Peter writes in his second epistle words that echo the words of Isaiah. 2Peter Ch.3v10, "But the day of the Lord will come as a thief in the night, in which the heavens will pass away with a great noise, and the elements will melt with fervent heat; both the earth and the works that are in it will be burned up."

In the face of all this cosmic upheaval the kings of the earth, the mighty men and all those with rank and riches right down to the lowest slave, all of them hid themselves in the caves and among the rocks. John heard as they cried out to the rocks and mountains to fall on them, so that they might be hidden from the face of Him who sits on the throne, and from the wrath of the Lamb. Isaiah Ch.2v10-21 speaks of the same events and a few sample verses will give a flavor of the whole passage. Verse12 says, "For the day of the Lord of hosts shall come upon everything proud and lofty, upon everything lifted up- and it shall be brought low." Verse19 says, "They shall go into the holes of the rocks, and into the caves of the earth, from the terror of the Lord and the glory of His majesty, when He arises to shake the earth mightily."

"For the great day of His wrath has come, and who is able to stand?"(Revelation Ch.6v17) The answer is that no one left on the earth in that day will be able to stand, for the day of the grace of God will be passed, and there will only be wrath and eternal punishment for those on the earth to face. If you are among those who are saved by the grace of God, then Paul's words to the Thessalonian church will apply to you when he wrote, "For God did not appoint us to wrath, but to obtain salvation through our Lord Jesus Christ." (1Thessalonians Ch.5v9.) We have now come to the end of act one in the great drama that is unfolding before John's eyes. It has brought us to the second coming of Christ, and has involved what God has decided to include of man's actions toward his fellow man. There now follows an interlude, where God wants the churches to understand something about the age of His grace, before the seventh seal is opened and acts two and three can proceed.

CHAPTER 12

THE SEALED SERVANTS AND THE SECURE SAINTS

The previous chapter ended with the return of Jesus Christ, with all the terrible consequences for those who are left remaining on the earth. The theme of the chapter was the activities of man in respect of conquest, war, famine and the relative indifference of those who have more than enough. How things changed when the once powerful and influential and self sufficient men and women who have rejected Jesus Christ, are then faced with His wrath at His coming and cry out for the rocks to cover them. What John sees next is something that must occur before Jesus returns and then something that occurs after His return. As I have mentioned in the previous chapter, it is no problem for God to show things to John that are far in the future, and then to switch back in time to something that occurred previously and then to show John something in the future again. Once this facet of the writings of John in Revelation is grasped, it makes the book a whole lot easier to understand.

The first American astronauts to travel to the moon saw the earth, as only a very few people have ever seen it. One of them, quite overcome with the view, read from Genesis Ch.1v1, "In the beginning God created the heavens and the earth." He could have not read anything that was more appropriate, despite the whining of those who hate the Word of God. However I believe that he was not the first man to see the earth in such a way. John was in the Spirit in heaven, and what God showed him next is the earth before its destruction at the return of Jesus. He sees four angels at what he describes as, the four corners of the earth. This is not to infer that John saw the earth as a square, but to help us to visualize the scene. He observes that what they are doing is holding back the four winds of the earth. We have already seen a considerable amount of activity on the part of angels in the book of Revelation, and there is a whole lot more to come. God could of course do without angels, as He could do without anything or anyone else, but He has chosen to create them as His servants. Psalm 103v20-21, well describes the purpose of the angels God has created. It reads, "Bless the Lord, you His angels, who excel in strength, who do His word, heeding the voice of His word. Bless the Lord, all you His hosts, you ministers of His, who do His pleasure." The writer of the book of Hebrews Ch.1v14 says, "Are they not all ministering spirits sent forth to minister for those who will inherit salvation?" In what John sees next the angels are directly ministering to those who are to inherit salvation.

They are holding back the four winds. There are basically four wind systems that operate in the earth. The very strong winds that blow away from the two Polar Regions, and the two winds that circulate from the equator northwards and then back towards the south. The phrase, the four winds of the earth, is one that occurs a number of times in the scripture. For the most part they are used metaphorically of winds that scatter God's people because of their sin, or His enemies as judgment comes on them. In Daniel Ch.7v2 the four winds of the earth stir up the Great Sea, and four beasts arise out of the sea, which represent the four great kingdoms of Babylon, the Medes and Persians, Greece and finally Rome. Matthew and Mark both record the words of Jesus that, with a great sound of a trumpet the Lord's chosen ones will be gathered from the four winds, from one end of heaven to the other. In this instance however, there is no reason to believe that the meaning of the four winds is metaphorical or symbolic, as there is plenty of collaboration from other scriptures that the earth is in for some pretty heavy punishment before the end comes. This of course is due entirely to man's rebellion against God. That the wind can be extremely damaging must be, especially in these days, obvious to everyone. In recent times the world has become aware of the heavy loss of life and property that has occurred in New Orleans, and the surrounding areas, because of hurricane winds. Even in our modern times we are no match for the wind. However the four winds could also be referring to the winds of judgment that come as a result of the sounding of the trumpets by the seven angels, that John sees in chapter eight of Revelation. For the four angels are told not to hurt the earth, the sea or the trees till the servants of God have been sealed. In the judgments of the first four trumpets sounding it is the earth and the sea and trees that are affected. The fifth angel sounds, and the people who are not sealed with the seal of the living God are judged. This places the trumpet judgments in the same time frame as the sealing of God's servants.

As the four angels are restraining the four winds of the earth, John saw another angel ascending out of the east, having the seal of the living God. He cried out in a loud voice to the others not to harm the earth or the sea with the winds until the servants of God are sealed. God had given the four angels permission to harm the earth with the four winds, as part of the build up of judgments that are coming on the earth culminating in the return of Jesus. Who are these servants? What does it mean to seal the servants of God on their foreheads? Why does God want His servants sealed before the coming judgment? The answers to these questions are not given in the text in Revelation, but I believe we can find some answers elsewhere in the scriptures as we progress through the chapter.

Who are these servants? The word for servant in this passage, is the usual word in the Greek, it is the word doulos. It literally means a slave, so those who are to be sealed with the seal of God are His slaves. Romans Ch.1v1 has Paul calling himself the servant or slave of Jesus Christ. This is the word that is used for the servants of God in the very first verse of the book of Revelation. "The Revelation of

Jesus Christ which God gave Him to show His servants, things that must shortly take place." How wonderful that God wills to reveal the amazing things of heaven and of His purposes to His slaves. How different to the way earthly slaves were treated, their masters would not be revealing their plans to them. How wonderful too that God wants to make such revelations known to churches that are far from being in His will and need to repent and still call them His servants. The particular servants referred to in this chapter are from the twelve tribes of the children of Israel. John hears the number of them, one hundred and forty four thousand. Although I have some sympathy with those who view these as God's spiritual Israel, after all, this book is written to the church and is about the church, yet I believe there are good reasons to believe that these sealed servants are Israelites of the nation of Israel. In the next section of Revelation chapter seven a great multitude which no man can number are in view, from every conceivable part of the earth, which includes Jews from the twelve tribes. There is an emphasis on the vast multitude coming from every nation, as a contrast to the limited number coming from just one nation, Israel, that are seen first. Also just as the church at the beginning was made up exclusively of Jews, and for most of the intervening two thousand years has been made up predominantly of Gentiles, so I believe the scriptures teach that shortly before Jesus returns the Jews will again come into their own in the church and play a prominent part.

What does it mean to seal the servants of God on their foreheads? The word seal means to impress, and usually was associated with an impression made in soft wax by a particular person's seal, that denoted his ownership of the thing that had the seal on it. God wants to seal His servants in order to have his seal of ownership on them. This is a common theme in the New Testament. Paul writing to the Corinthians in his second letter Ch.1v21-22 says, "Now He who establishes us with you in Christ and has anointed us is God, who also has sealed us and given us the Spirit in our hearts as a guarantee." The word guarantee in the Greek has an inferred meaning to an engagement ring, so God has given His servants the Holy Spirit as an engagement ring, because they are part of the bride of the Lamb.

Ephesians Ch.1v13-14 says, "In Him you also trusted, after you heard the word of truth, the gospel of your salvation; in whom also, having believed, you were sealed with the Holy Spirit of promise, who is the guarantee of our inheritance until the redemption of the purchased possession, to the praise of His glory." This sealing of course does not involve any literal seal on the forehead, but is the sealing of the Holy Spirit, God's seal of ownership.

Why does God want His servants sealed before judgment comes? The angel comes from the east and cries loudly to the four angels that have been granted permission to hurt the earth, to hold back the winds until the servants of God have been born again of God's Spirit and incorporated into the church. This time is a time of the outpouring of grace towards Israel, before a time of judgment comes on the earth. It is consistent with the character of God, that there is an outpouring of grace before judgment. It is also consistent with God's character that He will want to clearly define who His people are in order to preserve them, when judgments are designed to punish the wicked. God has done this in the past, for example, when God preserved the children of Israel in Egypt, when He poured out His wrath on the Egyptians. The plagues that came upon the Egyptians did not come near the Israelites who were in the land of Goshen. God also recognized the difference between righteous Lot, who lived in Sodom and the rest of the men who lived there, and made a way of escape for Him so that he was not destroyed with the wicked. 2Peter Ch.2v9 speaking of Lots deliverance from Sodom says, "Then the Lord knows how to deliver the godly out of temptations and to reserve the unjust under punishment for the day of judgment."

This time of grace toward Israel is of immense importance in God's purposes. Paul, when he wrote to the Roman church devoted three whole chapters to the place of Israel in God's purposes, and to their future place in the church. At the beginning of Ch.9, Paul expresses an extremely strong desire for his countrymen the Israelites, that they might be saved. This desire is expressed when he writes that he has great sorrow and continual grief in his heart, and goes as far as to say that, he could even wish himself to be accursed from Christ if it meant that his countrymen would come to Christ. At the start of

Ch.10 he writes, "Brethren, my heart's desire and prayer to God for Israel is that they may be saved." Chapter11 begins with the words, "I say then, has God cast away His people? Certainly not! For I also am an Israelite, of the seed of Abraham, of the tribe of Benjamin. God has not cast away His people whom He foreknew."

This sealing of the servants of God that John saw taking place, is an act of sheer grace on God's part. This is true of all God's dealings with men throughout all of time since Adam sinned. Noah found grace in the eyes of the Lord. Abraham was chosen by God, not because of anything in himself that was better than anyone else. Paul writes in Romans Ch.9v15-16, "For He says to Moses, "I will have mercy on whomever I will have mercy, and I will have compassion on whomever I will have compassion." So then it is not of him who wills, nor of him who runs, but of God who shows mercy." Despite God's mercy towards Israel in the past, when Jesus came the first time to His own, His own did not receive Him. This eventually lead, through the ministry of Paul the apostle, to the Gentiles being included in the church. Paul writes in Romans Ch.9v25-26, 'As He says in Hosea: "I will call them My people, who were not My people, and her beloved, who was not beloved. And it shall come to pass in the place where it was said to them, you are not My people, there they shall be called the sons of the living God." This is Hosea prophesying that the Gentiles would be called sons of the living God, but of Israel He says, "All day long I have stretched out my hands to a disobedient and contrary people."(Romans Ch.10v21) Is there any hope for God's chosen people Israel, or is there always only a remnant that is destined to be saved?

Moving on to Ch.11 Paul asks the question. Has God cast away His people as far as the church and salvation is concerned? The answer comes immediately without any hesitation, certainly not! Even though there is as Paul explains in Ch.11v5, "at this present time there is a remnant according to the election of grace." In v11 Paul again asks, "I say then, have they stumbled that they should fall? Certainly not! But through their fall, to provoke them to jealousy, salvation has come to the Gentiles." Paul goes on to explain that their fall has meant that the Gentiles have come into the riches of the kingdom of God. He says their casting away has meant the reconciling of the whole world to God, the embracing of the Gentiles. He then goes on to liken Israel to a cultured olive tree, the natural branches, and the Gentiles to a wild olive. Israel are the natural branches, because if any people should have responded to God's Son, it was Israel. Ch.9v4 says, "Who are Israelites, to whom pertain the adoption, the glory, the covenants, the giving of the law, the service of God, and the promises." They were God's special people, that He had separated for himself a holy people, they were the natural branches. Paul explains that some of the natural branches were broken of, and branches of a wild olive were grafted into the olive tree, in order to receive the goodness and life of the root of the olive tree. But if the natural branches who are Israelites do not continue in unbelief, God is able to graft them in again. Paul explains a mystery to the Roman Gentile Christians, that he does not want them to be ignorant of and it is this, blindness in part has happened to Israel until most of the Gentiles have been saved. Israel is again going to feature predominantly in the church. In Romans Ch.11v26 Paul writes, "And so all Israel shall be saved, as it is written: The Deliverer will come out of Zion, He will turn away ungodliness from Jacob; for this is My covenant with them, when I take away their sins." This is going to be a wonderful time of the overflowing of grace, "For if their casting away is the reconciling of the world, what will their acceptance be but life from the dead?"(Romans Ch.11v15) There is coming a time when all the elect of Israel will be saved, and if God so chooses, this could be every Israelite alive on the earth at the time.

With these things in mind let us now return to Revelation Ch.7v4. John says, "And I heard the number of those who were sealed. One hundred and forty-four thousand of all the tribes of the children of Israel were sealed:" There are some significant things to take note of here. Firstly, it appears to me that the number one hundred and forty-four thousand, although it could be taken literally without detracting from what I have written previously, it seems to me that there is more significance to it if it is regarded as a symbolic figure. Ten is the number of completeness or perfection, and one thousand is ten cubed. One hundred and forty four is the square of twelve, twelve being the number of the tribes of Israel. One hundred and forty-four thousand can therefore be viewed as the number of completeness in every way, as far as Israel is concerned, The twelve thousand from all the tribes representing all the elect of Israel that shall be sealed by the Holy Spirit, as Paul wrote, "So all Israel shall be saved."(Romans Ch11v26) These will be terrible times for the earth, as it faces the judgment of God, but also glorious times for the church as the grace of God is poured out on Israel. It is also worthy of note, that for the first time since Israel became a divided kingdom after the death of Solomon, the twelve tribes are together again. This is an indication that what John is seeing is the reconciling of the tribes once again in Christ, in His body, one in the Spirit. Ezekiel Ch.37 tells a very familiar story, the story of the dry bones. Much like John is in the Spirit, so Ezekiel is brought out in the Spirit to a valley, full of dry bones. The Lord asks Ezekiel, "Can these bones live?"(v3) Ezekiel's answer is, "O Lord God, You know" The Lord tells Ezekiel to prophesy to the dead bones, which he proceeds to do. As he did so there came a rattling noise as the bones came together, then sinews and flesh covered the bones, and finally skin covered them over but there was no breath in them. Ezekiel is then told to prophesy to the breath and say, "Come from the four winds, O breath, and breathe on these slain that they may live."(v9) As Ezekiel did this breath came into them and they lived, and stood on their feet a vast army. Incidentally, the four winds can also bring life, as well as destruction, as they are held back from destruction in order to bring life to Israel. Then the Lord said to Ezekiel, "Son of man, these bones are the whole house of Israel."(v11) God is going to resurrect the WHOLE HOUSE OF ISRAEL, "So all Israel shall be saved," Israel is united again. Again the word of the Lord comes to Ezekiel, and what the Lord says is not so well known but every bit as significant. God tells Ezekiel to take two sticks of wood and to write on one Judah and Israel, and on the other for Joseph the name of his son Ephraim. He is told to join them together, and God said they will become one in your hand. When the people of Israel ask you what this means, God said tell them that I am going to make them all one in My hand. God promises to gather them from wherever they have been scattered in the earth, to their own land, and that the Lord will revive them spiritually and cleanse them. God says, "Then they shall be My people, and I will be their God." (Ezekiel Ch.37v23). The nation of Israel is today back in their land, but as yet the angel has not arisen from the east with the seal of the living God, so they still as a nation have no life in them. But one of the most exciting things that will ever happen in the history of the church will happen when Israel is revived and they stand on their feet a mighty army. I believe that once again Israel will be the leading light in the church, as they were at the beginning.

The next thing that John sees is in a sense not unrelated to what he has just seen. There is no essential difference between sealed servants and secure saints, for those who are sealed are just as secure as those who are safely with the Lord in heaven. It is just their location that is different, but what a difference! John sees a great multitude which no one could number from every conceivable people and nation and tribe standing before the throne. I believe John is seeing a picture of the saints when all is done and dusted, when Satan is in the lake of fire and all the enemies of Jesus Christ have been put down and defeated forever. Not only is there a big difference between the physical location of the two groups, but a difference in time location too. The saints that John saw before, when the Lamb opened the fifth seal, were under the altar and crying out, "How long, O Lord, holy and true, until You judge and avenge our blood on those who dwell on the earth?"(Revelation Ch.6v10) Here there is no further call for vengeance on the enemies of the saints, but they are crying out in praise to God and saying, "Salvation belongs to our God who sits on the throne, and to the Lamb."(Revelation Ch.7v10)

As usual the saints are dressed in white robes, and interestingly they have palm branches in their hands. It would seem to me that John is seeing the saints celebrating the victory of the King of Kings and Lord of Lords. You may recall that when Jesus had His triumphant entry into Jerusalem that the crowds waved palm branches and cried Hosanna, which means the Lord saves, Hosanna in the highest they cried. They thought that Jesus was coming as their king to save them from the oppression of Rome, but Jesus had come to save them from a far greater oppression that of Satan and sin. How appropriate that this great multitude should have palm branches in their hands as they cry out, "Salvation belongs to our God," or our God saves. What a salvation they have experienced we shall see in a while. But as ever in heaven one note of praise leads to another and so the angels that are around the throne and the elders and the living creatures join in the praise and worship too.

First of all they say, "Amen!" Well, who would not say amen to what the saints have just been crying out so loudly in heaven? Amen and amen is what I say, for salvation has come at last and complete salvation at that. This is what the scriptures are all about, the story of salvation for mankind who was lost and ruined by the fall into sin. God has accomplished what He set out to do, salvation is complete and what John sees here is just a foretaste of the picture of full salvation that he sees a little later on. For what God has accomplished in salvation they all then go on to attribute to Him, "Blessing and glory and wisdom, thanksgiving and honor and power and might." They end by saying that it should, "Be to our God forever and ever. Amen"(Revelation Ch.7v12) God and the Lamb are now the only ones who are worshipped. In the Greek there is the definite article before blessing and all the other things that belong to God, indicating that all the blessing and all the glory and all of all the other things belong to God. God is now all in all.

John is asked by one of the elders who the vast multitudes that cannot be numbered are. John is unsure, and replies, "Sir you know." The elder then informed John that, "these are the ones who come out of the great tribulation, and washed their robes and made them white in the blood of the Lamb."(Revelation Ch.7v14) For such a vast multitude that no man could number, it is likely that they are the redeemed of the church from all the ages. Tribulation is the lot of life on earth, although some pass through considerably more trouble than others. Job said that man was born to trouble as the sparks fly upward. Paul wrote that those who will live a godly life will suffer persecution. Jesus said to His disciples that in the world they would have trouble, but that they were not to fear because He had overcome the world. There is a time of trouble that Jesus spoke of, that is coming very near the end of the age, just before He returns. In Matthew Ch.24v21 Jesus said, "For then there will be great tribulation, such as has not been since the beginning of the world until this time, no, nor ever shall be." In Ch.24v29-30 Jesus further explains, "Immediately after the tribulation of those days the sun will be darkened, and the moon will not give its light; the stars will fall from heaven, and the powers of the heaven will be shaken. Then the sign of the Son of Man will appear in heaven, and then all the tribes of the earth will mourn, and they will see the Son of Man coming on the clouds of heaven with power and great glory." The saints who are alive on the earth at that time will experience some of that tribulation; many will give their lives for the sake of their testimony.

The elder continues to say to John that they have all washed their robes and made them white in the blood of the Lamb. All of these men and women, boys and girls have been saved in the same way, through the blood of the Lamb. There is no other way to be able, in the end, to stand before the throne of God, only through the blood of the Lamb. "Therefore they are before the throne of God, and serve Him day and night in His temple."(Revelation Ch.7v15) Serving God day and night does not mean there is day and night in heaven, but the idea is that they are serving God constantly. Also there is no literal temple in heaven, as one would imagine a temple to be on earth, but the thought that is being conveyed by these words, is that the redeemed are serving God by praising and worshiping Him. God will live among His people, which is one of the themes that is taken up later on in Revelation. Ch.21v3 says, "And I heard a loud voice from heaven saying, Behold the tabernacle of God is with men, and He will dwell with them, and they shall be His people. God Himself will be with them and be their God."

The elder goes on to say that, "They shall neither hunger anymore nor thirst anymore; the sun shall not strike them nor any heat; for the Lamb who is in the midst of the throne will shepherd them and lead them to the living fountains of waters. And God will wipe away every tear from their eyes."(Revelation Ch.7v16-17) That sounds like heaven to me, and in the last chapters of Revelation John sees much more detail, of the wonderful life that the blood washed saints will enjoy.

What John wrote to the churches in Asia first of all, was intended to be an encouragement to them to overcome. One of the constant themes in his messages to them was, he who overcomes will be rewarded. Now that John is seeing into heaven and is being told how wonderful things are there, Gods intention is that His people will make every effort to arrive in heaven not by the skin of their teeth, but with abundant rewards. Peter in his second epistle Ch.1v10-11 wrote, "Therefore brethren be even more diligent to make your call and election sure, for if you do these things you will never stumble; for so an entrance will be supplied to you abundantly into the everlasting kingdom of our Lord and Savior Jesus Christ." Let us also be spurred on by visions of heaven and of being in the immediate presence of God our savior and the Lamb.

CHAPTER 13

THE SEVENTH SEAL

You will recall that when the Lamb opened the sixth seal, the scene was set for His return to the earth in power and glory, and of the end of the age. Chapter seven of Revelation is a brief interlude in which John saw and heard the sealing of the one hundred and forty four thousand, the saving of the whole house of Israel, and the multitude that no man could number of the redeemed of all the ages from every nation under heaven. Chapter eight begins in a most unexpected way. After all the wonder of the praise and worship of the heavenly hosts, and the various sounds that come from the throne of God that sound like thunder and voices, there is complete silence in heaven. It seems almost unimaginable that there should be silence in heaven. But what a dramatic silence it must have been, every bit as dramatic as the great earthquake and the sun becoming black and the moon turning red like blood, the stars falling to the earth and the sky receding like a scroll. I suggested previously that this silence could be heaven taking in the awesome things that have happened. The whole of the heaven catching its breath, coming to terms with the new situation, that finally God reigns supreme with the Lamb in the midst of the throne. Silence can also be deafening, when words are not necessary to convey a message. The message of this silence is, our God reigns! Silence can be very profound and this silence surely is. It is like the silence on the battlefield when the war is over and the victory is won. The guns fall silent, the cries of soldiers has ceased, mortar rounds are no longer exploding and bombs are no longer falling, the enemy is defeated. The silence may also be just a natural break between scene one of the great drama of history and scene two. For after what John says was only half an hour of silence there is even more drama to follow. Again it is typical of Revelation, that having come to the end of the age with the sixth seal, John is brought back a few years in time to a period of intensified judgment on the earth with the blowing of the seven trumpets.

For contained in the opening of the seventh seal are the things that come upon the earth when the seven angels that stand before God blow the trumpets that they are given. But before they blow their trumpets something else has to happen which is of great interest. An angel with a golden censor came and stood at the altar, and while he waits there he is given a great deal of incense, that he should offer the incense with the prayers of all the saints. Some have suggested that this angel could be Jesus, as this is a priestly function to offer incense on the altar before the throne of God. But all through Revelation, if Jesus is being referred to He is clearly identified by either His name or a well recognized title, so I believe this is an angel performing this duty.

John saw the smoke of the incense ascending to the throne of God, with the prayers of the saints. The prayers of saints that are hard pressed upon the earth are heard by God in heaven. They ascend as a sweet smell in the presence of God. It would appear that there is a close connection between the prayers of the saints and what follows. God can act independently if He so chooses, without the prayers of the saints, but our aim as children of God should be to be so in tune with God that we ask for the things that He wants to do. In this way we become partners in the fulfillment of God's purposes in the earth. The angel then took the golden censer and filled it with fire from off the golden altar, and then he threw the censer to the earth. That which had been the conveyer of the prayers of the saints, now becomes the conveyer of judgment to the earth. God is a God of judgment, and when we pray, "Your kingdom come, Your will be done on earth as it is in heaven," part of the answer to that prayer is God pouring out judgment on the earth in righteousness. When the angel threw the censer John heard noises and thunderings and lightnings, things he had heard before coming from the throne of God. Also there was an earthquake, the mountains and hills quaking at the presence of the Lord, as the rule and reign of Christ is approaching.

The sounding of trumpets has often been associated in the scripture with a proclamation of war, or the crowning of a king, or the ushering in of the year of jubilee. There were other times when trumpets would be sounded, such as to sound an alarm, or at the feast of trumpets, and also the priests would blow trumpets as part of the worship to God. If there is a significance to the trumpets that the angels blow, it would most likely be as a declaration of war, for the earth is about to suffer significantly as are those who do not have the seal of the living God.

The question arises, when is it that the angels begin to blow their trumpets? We are given a clue in Revelation Ch.9v4, when John hears that with the sounding of the fifth trumpet locusts arise from the bottomless pit, that have the same abilities as scorpions to hurt people. But they are commanded only to hurt those who do not have the seal of the living God. This equates to the time of the revival of Israel's spiritual fortunes, when all Israel will be saved and sealed by the Holy Spirit. This has been discussed in the previous chapter, and takes place just a short number of years before Jesus returns. So we can say that the trumpet judgments begin to come on the earth not long before the Lord returns. We will see that the trumpet judgments differ in character from what happened on the earth when the seals began to be opened. The opening of the first five seals resulted in the unfolding of earth's history of the conquest of one nation by another, of wars, of famines and pestilences, the angel of Death claiming a quarter of earth's population and many martyrs giving their lives because they were faithful to Jesus. The Lamb upon the throne is in control, but man is responsible for his actions on earth that precipitate these things. It is the unfolding of the history of man, after he had for the most part, rejected the Savior Jesus Christ. There is nothing in the opening of the seals that affects the earth, apart from the opening of the sixth seal, which ushers in the new age and the new heaven and earth. With the sounding of the trumpets, the earth environment is significantly damaged, and so are those who do not belong to the Lord. This is all leading to the final wrapping up of the old earth and heavens. God is turning up the heat on rebellious man. Will he continue to defy God, or will he repent of his evil ways? The trumpet judgments are also directly administered from heaven, and man has no part to play in what follows. Another difference, as compared with the opening of the five seals, is that demonic powers are brought directly into play in the outworking of God's purposes. These powers of darkness are under the control of the Lamb, they may seek to do their own will, but inevitably do the will of the Lamb on the throne. Although we have seen the effect of the four horsemen on the earth for a long time, none of the seven angels has yet sounded their trumpets, but when they do there will be no doubt that the end of the age is near.

So the seven angels prepare to blow their trumpets. The first angel sounded and hail and fire followed the sounding of the trumpet, this was mingled with blood. This mixture was thrown to the earth and a third of the trees were burned up and all the green grass. As we are coming towards the end of the age of the old earth, and God is pouring out a measured degree of judgment, there is no reason to believe that what John saw from heaven is not intended to be taken literally for the old earth will literally be replaced by a new earth in which there will be righteousness. Trees play a vital role worldwide in the absorption of carbon dioxide, and the release of oxygen into the atmosphere, keeping the air we breathe viable to support life. The impact of a third of the earth's trees suddenly being destroyed will be considerable on the worldwide production of oxygen and absorption of carbon dioxide. A double whammy will be the fact that for these fires to burn they need oxygen, and vast amounts will be used up by these enormous fires. On top of that the pollution of the atmosphere from the smoke of vast forests burning out of control will also cause considerable disruption to the balance of the atmosphere. If as a result of this judgment there is an unbreathable atmosphere in some parts of the world, it is likely that people will suffocate much as they did in the awful firestorms in places like Dresden in World War Two. With the destruction of a third of the world's forests wildlife, the delicate balance of the whole eco system of many regions of the world will also be affected. It is also possible that there will be a danger of serious soil erosion taking place in those regions, that will mean that whatever may grow there in the future would be much less than in the past. Forests cannot be replaced very quickly so millions of square miles of land around the world will be changed forever. We are also told that all the green grass was burned up. The last line of the hymn 'Jerusalem' so beloved of England cricket fans, speaks of England's green and pleasant land. Ireland is called the emerald isle, because of the abundance of green pasture there is there due to the plentiful rainfall. All around the world, where there is enough rainfall, there is the wonderful contrast of the blue of the sky and the green of the grass. Imagine all that lovely green grass gone, and in its place a blackened charred earth smoldering from the fire cast down to the earth. Think of the effect on all the cattle and other animals that depend on the grasslands of the world for their food. Then think also of the knock on effect of animals dying because of the fires and starvation, of the way that millions of people will suffer because of their dependence on these animals for meat, milk and other byproducts. This is only the first of the trumpet judgments and already there is a major crisis around the world.

We are not told the time scale over which these events occur so we do not know how quickly each one of the angels sounds their trumpets in heaven. The second angel sounded and John saw something like a great mountain, burning with fire, was thrown towards the earth, and hitting the earth in one of the oceans. From the description it would appear to be a massive meteor. There is a great deal of research being carried out today on the possibility of huge meteors hitting the earth. It is known that there are very many large chunks of rock in space, and that one will inevitably one day hit the earth, although the projections are that this kind of event will not occur any time soon. However from John's vantage point in heaven and in the Spirit, we can see that this is going to happen, and not too far in the future. The effect of the meteor is to turn the sea into blood, destroying all marine life over a vast area as well as all shipping. John sees that one third of sea creatures are killed and one third of ships are destroyed. What a calamity this will be, coming hard on the heels of what has previously happened on land! Many millions of people around the world depend, to a greater or lesser degree, on the harvest of the sea for their food so the repercussions of this dreaded occurrence will be widespread. Added to that the loss of life when thousands of ships will be lost at sea will be a devastating blow to the morale of the world. Many will see these things as chance happenings and will curse their bad luck. Still others will seek to find a scientific answer to the horrific turn of events that are occurring. Governments all around the world will come under enormous pressure to alleviate suffering and bring relief to millions of people. Only two of the trumpets have sounded, and already the armies, air forces and navies of the world will be more than at full stretch, as well as all available medical resources in an effort to begin to cope with what is happening around the world. But the destruction is only partial and many will be still untouched and hope that these are just passing events that will not touch them.

So far men and women, to a large extent, have only been indirectly affected by what has already happened. But what happens next will directly affect millions of people. John hears the third angel sound and what he sees is a great star falling from heaven, burning like a torch and it fell on a third of the rivers and springs of water. The star has a name and its name is Wormwood. Whatever this star is, it is able to pollute a third of the world's fresh water supply. The result of this pollution is that many men died, many could quite easily be hundreds of millions of people, all depending on a third of the earth's fresh water resources. Water is, after all the most basic of all our needs. We can go without food for weeks, but without fresh water we cannot last many days. Now some people may begin to think that these things are perhaps not mere chance happenings, but how many would come to the conclusion that Jesus the Lamb on the throne in heaven, is pouring out the judgments that those who have rejected Him on the earth deserve. One can perhaps imagine the international tension that this event will bring about. The greatest threat to nations these days is considered to be that of international terrorism, and one of the ways that terrorists could strike would be through the widespread pollution of the water supply. People will not take seriously the fact that these things are being sent from heaven, because for the most part people will not believe that the God of the Bible even exists, or they will have some false idea of God as a sugar daddy who is far too kind to punish the world for its sin and rebellion. Only those who take the Bible seriously and believe in the God of the Bible will know what is really going on.

Then John hears the fourth angel sound in heaven. From his vantage point in heaven John sees that the sun, moon and stars do not give their light on the earth as they did previously. For a third of the normal hours of daylight are turned to darkness, and for a third of the hours of night there is no moonlight or starlight. This is going to be somewhat baffling to astronomers and scientists in general. All the technologies of that day will no doubt be brought to bear on this phenomena, but it is doubtful that anyone will come up with any right answers. For this is an act of God and the Lamb, which will strike fear into the hearts of many as the street lights and the car head lights have to be turned on about four hours earlier each day. People will possibly search in vain for the moon during the night, when it should be giving its pale reflected light. No one will be able to give any explanation for the absence of any light from the billions of stars, that should be shining throughout the hours of darkness but like the moon will not be shining for four hours each night. The earth will be a colder place because not only does the sun give light to the earth but very necessary warmth. This will no doubt have an effect on the food production of the world, as millions of farmers struggle to get their crops ripened in season, one third of light and heat suddenly being withdrawn is not insignificant. This would in turn lead to even more food shortages than the world has to cope with today. How will the various UN agencies be coping with one disaster upon another is a matter of conjecture, as the most likely effect will be that each member country will be desperately trying to deal with its own problems, and have no resources left to contribute to any united effort to bring relief.

The next thing John sees is an angel flying through the midst of heaven, heaven no doubt referring to the skies. John hears that he cries out loudly, "Woe, woe, woe," to those living on the earth, because of the three trumpet blasts that are still to sound in heaven. As if things were not bad enough there is still worse to follow.

Chapter nine of Revelation begins with the sounding of the trumpet of the fifth angel, which is deemed to be the first woe. John saw a star fallen from heaven to the earth. This star is actually a spiritual being who is given the key to the bottomless pit. He then proceeds to open the pit and release a great deal of smoke into the atmosphere out of which come locusts. There is a further degradation of the light of the sun on the earth, due to the amount of smoke coming out of the pit. This is the first harnessing of demonic powers on the earth, against the men who do not have the seal of the living God. They are commanded not to hurt the grass of the earth, or any green thing or any tree. This of course would be the normal thing for locusts to do. It is worth noting that there must have been sufficient time between the blowing of the first trumpet and this fifth one, for the grass of the earth to recover, this will give us some idea of the time scale involved in these events. The locusts were not permitted to kill anyone, but they are given authority to torment men for five months. The question arises, where do these locusts get their authority to torment men from? In answering this question it is necessary to start by stating who it is that has the key to the bottomless pit. The answer clearly is the Lamb on the throne, who has the keys of death and Hades and every other key. Keys of course denote authority, so to say that the Lamb has all the keys, is to say He has all authority in heaven and earth. The Lamb gives the key to the bottomless pit to the fallen angel and gives his demonically controlled hordes authority to hurt men for five months. In giving them authority to do these things, He is also stating the limitations on the power that they are given. They are not allowed to kill, and they can only operate for five months.

It may come as rather a culture shock to some people, to realize that the powers of darkness are under the control of the Lamb in heaven. This is one of the great themes of the Bible that Satan and all the powers of darkness come under the authority of heaven and always have. From the start of Satan's rebellion, when he was cast out of heaven, he has never been free to do what he wants to. He has always only been able to operate within the limits that God permitted, and whether they like it or not, they have always only been able to do that which will bring about the purposes of God. There is an erroneous idea that some people have, that God and Satan are equal and opposite, like the two sides of a coin. You do not have to read very much of the Bible to realize that this idea holds no water, for in Genesis Ch.3v14 God says to the serpent, "Because you have done this, you are CURSED more than all cattle, and more than every beast of the field; on your belly you shall go, and you shall eat dust all the days of your life. And I will put enmity between you and the woman, and between your seed and her Seed; He shall bruise your HEAD, and you shall bruise His heel."(emphasis in capitals mine) God put Satan under a curse and predicted that the Seed of the woman, who is Jesus the Lamb, would bruise his head and defeat him. So here in Revelation, at the sounding of the fifth trumpet, the powers of darkness are doing the bidding of the Lamb on the throne.

Something else that some will find hard to swallow is that men are being tormented by the Lamb. People have been conditioned to believe that Jesus is all kindness and mercy and cannot come to terms with a lamb acting like a lion. But Jesus is the Lamb of God for the purposes of being the sacrifice for the sins of the world. But for the purposes of bringing about the new heavens and earth and establishing His eternal kingdom, He is the Lion of the tribe of Judah, who will fight and prevail against all His enemies. In these circumstances it is the right and sensible thing to seek the Lord while He may be found and call upon Him while He is near, for the wicked man to turn from his wickedness and sin, and to repent and turn to the Lord for to those who repent of sin there is forgiveness and pardon. The Bible makes it clear that unless we have repented of sin and received Jesus the Lamb as our savior, we are the enemies of God and under condemnation. Romans Ch.5v10 says, "For if when we were enemies we were reconciled to God through the death of His Son, much more, having been reconciled, we shall be saved by

His life." Again in Colossians Ch.1v21 Paul writes, "And you, who once were alienated and enemies in your mind by wicked works, yet now He has reconciled." Before we are reconciled to God we are His enemies, and it is not sensible to be an enemy of God.

So severe is the pain inflicted by these locusts, with a sting in their tails that men will want to die but death will elude them. There will be no medical remedy for what these locusts inflict despite the best efforts of the worldwide scientific community, and the effect will be to drive men crazy and desperate for relief from pain. This affliction will come on all who are not the sealed servants of God and will include presidents and paupers, religious people and atheists, the law abiding and criminals, the only discriminating factor will be the seal of the living God. They will operate on a worldwide basis among all nations. These locusts will proceed to do their work in military formation and their wings will sound like the sound of many chariots. They have a leader whose name is Abaddon, who is the angel of the bottomless pit. Reading the full description of these locusts, as John saw them, they are very strange creatures with golden crowns and faces like men, with women's hair and lions teeth. They also had breastplates like iron and tails like scorpions. But the important thing to bear in mind is that they are led by a demon who is under the control of the Lamb on the throne.

Then John heard the sixth angel sound his trumpet and he then heard a voice coming from the horns of the golden altar that is before the throne of God. The angel of God who sounded the trumpet is told to release the four angels who have been bound at the river Euphrates. The fact that these angels have been bound denotes that they are demonic powers that God has not permitted to do anything until His appointed time. Revelation Ch.9v15 makes it clear that they have been held back by God right down to the appointed hour, and when the trumpet sounds God releases them to go and kill a third of mankind, that will be over a billion people. These four angels have at their disposal an army of two hundred million. There is no point in conjecturing as to what country this army may come from as the Bible does not tell us, or to speculate as to what their weapons are. What John sees is that a third of mankind is killed by weapons that produce fire, smoke and brimstone, brimstone having a connection with sulphur. We hear much today about weapons of mass destruction, and we have seen even in today's conventional weapons how destructive they can be, but at the time of the sounding of the sixth trumpet there will be mass slaughter on a scale never envisaged before or even thought possible. In view of all this that has befallen the world one would have thought that men would be even a little bit inclined to want to seek God and turn from their wicked ways. Especially as they will not have failed to notice that all the saints of God, who are sealed by the Holy Spirit and are serving God, were untouched by the plague of stinging locusts that caused them such distress.

But what does John observe about the rest of mankind who have survived all these plagues so far. He writes that they did not repent of their evil ways, which he aptly describes as the work of their hands. It is men who are responsible for the evil deeds done in the world, because they love darkness rather than light. They continued to worship demons and idols made of gold, silver, brass, stone, and wood. They refused, in other words, to acknowledge the God of heaven and worshipped the works of their own hands. The idols of today may not necessarily be made into the shapes of animals or men, but they are the material possessions and the things that men value and set their hearts on and strive to posses. This is the root cause of all the other evils in the world, the refusal of man to accept that God is God and He is the only one who is to be worshipped. Therefore neither did they repent of their murders, murder not meaning necessarily killing someone, but as Jesus pointed out, to hate someone in your heart you are as culpable as if you had killed them. Murder where someone is actually killed has become common place in the world today and around the world law enforcement agencies are so stretched solving crimes of murder that most other crime pays because the police cannot even begin to investigate the majority of other crimes. These things are set to get worse and not better. Men still continued to engage in all kinds of things connected with the occult and witchcraft, things which God has forbidden and called an abomination in His sight. But sinful man ever seems to love to do the things that God hates. There is a massive interest today in all things to do with demonic powers, even though people may not recognize them to be demonic. From astrology to black magic, the new age and crystals and all kinds of superstitions, there is a vast market. It is rather a paradox that in this age when people have never been so well educated, they still want a spiritual dimension to their lives, even if that spiritual dimension has its source in the demonic. Sexual immorality, in all its forms, is another thing that men refuse to turn away from. Adultery, fornication, homosexual acts perpetrated by both men with men and women with women, rapes, indecent assaults on children and pornography of all kinds, all these things are abounding in our day and will get worse as the end of the age approaches. Despite the best efforts of those who try to halt the moral decay in societies around the world and in spite of all that men have suffered, they still will not repent. Finally John says that they will not repent of stealing from each other. Theft is probably the most common crime that is committed around the world and John sees that still nothing has changed.

There is an argument that punishment does not change people and with this the scriptures agree. It is discipline that changes people, and this is what God gives all His children. Discipline is loving correction and patient teaching, where there is a willingness on the part of the person being disciplined to change, because he or she knows that the one who is doing the disciplining loves them and wants the best for them. This is the kind of relationship that exists between God and His children. This is why God is disciplining those in the seven churches who are involved in some of these things and calling on them to repent. God is showing His people how he will deal with them as opposed to unbelievers who are unrepentant. God is not disciplining the world of men who have rejected Him or trying to change them, but is giving them their just deserts, therefore we should not be surprised that they will not change their ways. God also wants to warn people today of the things that MUST come to pass, so that they will seek Him and be found of Him before the trumpets begin to sound in heaven. They will sound without any warning and the results will be devastating for billions of people. God so loved the world, but His patience will not be extended forever and the day of grace will have an end and that day is fast approaching. Have you repented and turned to God through Jesus the Lamb who was slain for your sins? If not, it is still not too late, but Revelation Ch.14v14-16 speaks of the time of the harvest of the earth, and it is an over ripe harvest, speaking of a world that is only ripe for judgment. This judgment will be expressed in terms of the vintage that is thrust into the winepress of the wrath of God. What is written in Jeremiah Ch.8v20 is very pertinent, "The harvest is past, the summer is ended, and we are not saved."

CHAPTER 14

NO MORE DELAY

Angelic activity is evident throughout the book of Revelation and it continues apace. The sixth angel has sounded his trumpet and the second woe has passed. Before the sounding of the seventh trumpet John sees another mighty angel coming down from heaven, clothed with a cloud. His face was shining like the sun and the combined effect of the radiance of his face and the cloud created a beautiful rainbow around his head. This magnificent angel also had feet like pillars of fire. How awesome are these magnificent spiritual beings that God has created to do His bidding, although John is rebuked on two occasions for falling down to worship before an angel, yet faced with creatures of such glory it is maybe understandable. Some have suggested that this angel is Jesus himself, but the scriptures always make it clear when Jesus is in view, and here John was seeing an angel.

John saw that he had a little book in his hand that was open. All the things that God has revealed to us are an open book, but as we shall see there are things that God has decided to keep secret and that is God's prerogative. He set his right foot on the sea and his left foot on the land. Everything about this angel speaks of power and authority.

I imagine him to be like a colossus, a being of tremendous stature. He cries out with a loud voice that sounded like the roaring of a lion and when he cried out John heard seven thunders utter their voices. John has been hearing thunder coming from the throne of God, and this is where I believe, the thunders came from. John is used to writing down all that he is seeing and hearing and so he automatically begins to write down what the thunders said. But he heard a voice from heaven forbidding him to write what the seven thunders have said, but instead he is told to seal up what he had heard. There are two very important things that need to be noted at this time.

Firstly as indicated beforehand there are things that God has revealed and things that he has decided not to reveal. If we are not prepared to accept this important principle we can end up in a lot of error and confusion. Deuteronomy Ch.29v29 says, "The secret things belong to the Lord our God, but those things which are revealed belong to us and to our children forever, that we may do all the words of this law." This scripture clearly defines the boundary between the things that God has made plain to us as His children, and the things that belong to Him, and are out of bounds for us. This scripture also makes it clear that God has revealed enough for us to live in obedience to Him and this is what is important. Many children of God have gone astray in the things they believe, and consequently in the way they live, because they would not content themselves with receiving the things that God has freely given us but wanted to push the boundaries of spiritual knowledge and understanding beyond what God has revealed.

Secondly it is important to note that John heard what the seven thunders said, and was obedient to the Lord in not revealing what he heard. What a privilege it was for John to be trusted by the Lord with one of His secrets. John kept this secret all the rest of his life and it went with him to his grave. I believe there are things that God may reveal to us that are to be kept to ourselves. We are so fond of wanting to share everything that God says to us, but maybe there are things that God wants to say to us that are just for us, so we need to be obedient at all times.

This mighty angel then raised his right hand to heaven and swore by Him who lives forever and ever who created heaven and earth and everything in them, that there would be no more delay, but at the time of the sounding of the seventh angel the mystery of God would be finished as He had said to His servants the prophets. God has everything planned out in the minutest detail so that everything will go according to what He has preordained. No more delay, nothing can stop the mystery of God coming to the fruition that He has foretold. This mystery of God foretold by the prophets is the time of the consummation of all things, this is the time Paul refers to in his letter to the Ephesians when he wrote, "Having made known to us the mystery of His will, according to His good pleasure which He purposed in Himself, that in the dispensation, (or the administration), of the fullness of the times He might gather together in one all things in Christ, both which are in heaven and which are on earth-in Him." (Ephesians Ch.1v9-10) There is a new administration of the eternal kingdom of God coming, this is the thing that was hidden in the past, but is now revealed. It is the good will and purpose of God that all things will be gathered together in Christ Jesus, and no book in the Bible reveals this more plainly and graphically than the book of the Revelation of Jesus Christ. Paul teaches this mystery again in 1Corinthians Ch.15v24-28 and says, "Then comes the end, when He delivers the kingdom to God the Father, when He puts an end to all rule and authority and power. For He must reign till He has put all enemies under His feet. The last enemy that will be destroyed is death. For He has put all things under His feet. But when He says all things are put under Him, it is evident that He who put all things under Him is excepted. Now when all things are made subject to Him, then the Son Himself will also be subject to Him who put all things under Him, that God may be all in all." In Revelation Ch.11 we will see the fulfillment of these words that Paul wrote when the kingdoms of this world have become the kingdoms of our Lord and of His Christ.

This is the same message that we read in the book of Daniel on a number of occasions, firstly in Daniel Ch.2. At the beginning of king Nebuchadnezzar's reign, in only his second year as king, God gave him a dream which troubled him and so he needed to have the meaning of the dream explained to him. There was an added complication however; the king could not remember what he had dreamt, so he needed someone to tell him what he had dreamt as well as what it meant. When all his usual Chaldean mystics could not tell him the dream or explain it, a man with the Spirit of God in him was found to whom the Lord revealed what the king had dreamt and gave the meaning of the dream, this man was Daniel. Daniel went before the king and said that there was a God in heaven who reveals secrets and that what the king had dreamt concerned the latter days. Daniel said that what the king had seen was a great image that was truly awesome. The head was of gold, its chest and arms were of silver, its belly and thighs were of bronze, its legs were of iron and its feet were iron and clay. Then an amazing thing happened in the dream, a stone was cut out without any human involvement which struck the image on its feet and the feet were broken in pieces. This resulted in the whole image being crushed by the stone so that it became like wheat chaff and was blown away by the wind, so that when the wind died down there was not a single trace of any of the image. Then the stone that struck the image became a great mountain that filled the whole earth.

At first sight this seems like a typical dream, because dreams always seem to have a touch of reality and a great deal of fantasy. But then Daniel began to explain the dream. Nebuchadnezzar was the head of gold for God had made him a king of kings with such power, strength and glory that would never again be rivaled. Then four other kingdoms would come after the Babylonian kingdom that would be inferior, but they would rule over the earth as the Babylonian kingdom had. The fourth kingdom would be as strong as iron and would break and crush all other kingdoms. The feet would be a fifth kingdom, partly strong like iron and partly fragile like ceramic clay, and also be divided as iron and ceramic clay will not bond together. The kingdoms that ruled the world after the Babylonians were the Medes and Persians, the Greeks came next and then the Romans. The feet of iron and clay, representing as it does a divided kingdom of strength and fragility, is yet to emerge, although some have thought that the European Union is that kingdom. If it is it is still in embryo as there is no clearly defined ten kingdom federation, although it does have the characteristic of being constantly divided and the prediction in Daniel is that this union of ten kings will not adhere to each other. But on the other hand the European Union does not represent a revival of the old Roman Empire. But the scripture tells us that in the days of this kingdom of ten kings, the God of heaven will set up a kingdom that shall never be destroyed or replaced by any other kingdom and that it shall break in pieces every other kingdom and shall stand forever. These are the days of no more delay when the kingdoms of earth will have run their course, all of them having been weighed in God's balances and been found wanting, just as the Babylonian empire was.

The king who replaced Nebuchadnezzar as king of Babylon was Belshazzar and in the first year of his reign Daniel himself had a vision of these kingdoms, and he records what he saw in Daniel Ch.7. What he saw was the four winds of heaven whipping up the Great Sea, which we know as the Mediterranean Sea. Out of the sea came four great beasts. The first was like a lion and it had the wings of an eagle, the second was like a bear with three ribs in its teeth. The third was like a leopard with four wings on its back and it also had four heads, the fourth beast Daniel describes as being terrible and exceedingly strong with huge iron teeth. It was devouring and trampling all that was left of the other kingdoms and was different from the former beasts. It also had ten horns, which are ten kingdoms. The lion is Babylon, the bear is the Medes and Persians and the leopard is Greece and the fourth beast that was very terrible is Rome. But Daniel now sees something very interesting that was not shown to Nebuchadnezzar in his dream for as he looked at the ten horns a little horn arose which rooted up three of the ten and it had the eyes of a man and began speaking great things. It is explained to Daniel that the ten horns are ten kings which correspond to the ten kings represented by the ten toes of the image, but Daniel sees that one king shall rise up and exalt himself, and in the last days make war with the saints of God. This kingdom of ten kings shall subdue the whole earth and then be dominated by one who not only makes war against the saints but also speaks pompously against God. This little horn is identified in the New Testament on various occasions as the Antichrist and in the book of Revelation particularly as the Beast, which is associated with the number 666, the number of a man. But despite all his pompous words Daniel Ch. 7v26 says, "But the court shall be seated, and they shall take away his dominion, to consume and destroy it forever. Then the kingdom and dominion, and the greatness of the kingdoms under the whole heaven, shall be given to the people, the saints of the Most High. His kingdom is an everlasting kingdom, and all dominions shall serve and obey Him." In the same chapter Daniel records seeing much the same scene of the throne of God as John had seen with the myriads of angels attending Him and Daniel sees the court of heaven seated and the books opened for God is about to pronounce judgment on the pompous little horn. He is taken and destroyed and cast into the lake of fire. Then Daniel says, "I was watching in the night visions, and behold, One like the Son of Man, coming with the clouds of heaven! He came to the Ancient of Days, and they brought Him near before Him. Then to Him was given dominion and glory and a kingdom, that all peoples, nations, and languages should serve Him. His dominion is an everlasting dominion, which shall not pass away, and His kingdom the one that shall not be destroyed."(Daniel Ch.7v13-14)

This is a message to the churches that God is in absolute control of the events on earth and that nothing, no power, no earthly kingdom or authority can delay the coming of God's kingdom. That these things will come about because events in heaven will determine events on earth. The sounding of the seventh trumpet will be the death knell to all who have exalted themselves against God.

But although there are predictions of the end, the prophecy of John recorded in Revelation is not about to finish, because John hears a voice from heaven which told him to go to the angel and take the little book from his right hand. So John obeyed and went to the angel and asked for the little book. The angel told John to eat it and that it would be as sweet as honey in his mouth, but it would be bitter in his stomach. Having eaten the little book John experienced exactly what the angel had predicted, and was told that he was to prophecy again to many peoples, nations, tongues and kings.

CHAPTER 15

THE TEMPLE AND THE TWO WITNESSES

There are many parallels between what John records in Revelation Ch.11 and some things written in the book of Zechariah. The beginning of the chapter concerns the temple of God. John is given a measuring rod and told to measure the temple, the altar and those worshipping in the temple. Measuring the temple of God in the Old Testament is something that occurred with every temple that was built. The forerunner of the temple, the tabernacle in the wilderness, was to be measured precisely according to the pattern that God gave to Moses. Solomon's temple was made to precise measurements according to the detailed plans that David received from the Lord, and passed on to his son Solomon. There are no details given regarding the measurements of the temple that was built after the Jews returned from exile, but the exhortation of the prophet Haggai was for the people to rise up and build. The people had been hesitant and were more concerned with building their own houses, but God promised great blessing if they will attend to His house. The word of the Lord by the prophet Zechariah that came at the same time was, "Not by might nor by power, but by My Spirit, says the Lord of Hosts." Zech. Ch.4v6. The temple that was built at that time was certainly built under the direction of the Holy Spirit, and Ch.4v7 says, "Who are you, O great mountain? Before Zerubbabel you shall become a plain! And he shall bring forth the capstone with shouts of "Grace, grace to it." In the same chapter Zechariah wrote in v10, "For who has despised the day of small things? For these seven (the seven eyes of the Lord) rejoice to see the plumb line in the hand of Zerubbabel. They are the eyes of the Lord, which scan to and fro throughout the whole earth." All these temples were destroyed because of the sin and rebellion of the people of Israel and some believe that the temple referred to here in Revelation is a temple that is yet to be rebuilt. Certainly there are Jews in Israel at this time who would build another temple if the site where the temple once stood was available, but most people believe that the Muslim mosque, The Dome of the Rock, occupies that ground.

There can be no doubt from the New Testament that God has no use for another earthly temple of stone and wood, however beautiful and magnificent it would be. There is nothing in the scripture to indicate that God ever wants to go back to any kind of sacrificial system of worship, or an earthly priesthood, or reinstate an old covenant that He has done away with, in the place of what He has called a new, better and everlasting covenant in the blood of Jesus. Hebrews Ch.8v8-13 says, "Because finding fault with them, He says, Behold the days are coming, says the Lord, when I will make a new covenant with the house of Israel and with the house of Judah- not according to the covenant that I made with their fathers in the day when I took them by the hand to lead them out of the land of Egypt; because they did not continue in my covenant, and I disregarded them, says the Lord. For this is the covenant that I will make with the house of Israel after those days, says the Lord: I will put my laws in their mind and write them on their hearts; and I will be their God, and they shall be my people. None of them shall teach his neighbor, and none his brother, saying, Know the Lord, for all shall know Me, from the least of them to the greatest of them. For I will be merciful to their unrighteousness, and their sins and their lawless deeds I will remember no more. In that He says, A new Covenant, He has made the first obsolete. Now what is becoming obsolete and growing old is ready to vanish away."

There is so much scripture in the book of Hebrews to indicate that God is never going back to something that He has done away with. Hebrews Ch.9v11 says, "But Christ came as High Priest of the good things to come, with the greater and more perfect tabernacle not made with hands, that is, not of this creation." The following verses make it clear that the blood of animal sacrifices could not bring about eternal redemption as His blood did. Neither could the blood of animals cleanse the conscience of the sinner. Verse 15 says, "And for this reason He is the mediator of the new covenant." Animal sacrifice was only ever intended to be a temporary thing until Christ came, because He is the once and for all sacrifice for sin. He is also the great High Priest, after the order of Melchizedek, and His priesthood will never be superseded. Neither will God go back on His word that all believers are priests and have direct access to God the Father, and do not need any kind of earthly priesthood. We have already read in Revelation Ch.1v6 that Jesus has made His blood washed people a kingdom of priests to God the Father. Peter also teaches the same truth in his first epistle Ch.2v5 where he describes believers as a holy priesthood, offering to God spiritual sacrifices, acceptable to God through Jesus Christ.

It was important for the tabernacle and the temples that were built, to be built according to the measurements and pattern that God required. God had especially said to Moses, make sure that you make the tabernacle according to the pattern that I showed you when you were on Mount Sinai. Measuring the various aspects of the temples would ensure that they were made to God's standard. John is told to rise and measure the temple to determine whether it was up to God's standard. He was given the reed that was like a measuring rod, because it would be worse than useless to measure something that was holy and belonging to God, with an earthly standard. There is such an important lesson here for everyone. How futile it is for men to pass any opinion on the things of God, or the Word of God with what in effect is their earthly measuring rods. How can the value or measure of the things of God be calculated using earthly standards? God has His own standards and He measures things that are Holy by His standard. The temple of God is Holy, as it is His habitation.

God lived among His people in the tabernacle in the wilderness and the glory of the Lord was seen in the pillar of cloud by day and of fire by night. Solomon's temple was dedicated and the glory of the Lord filled the house. The prophet Ezekiel saw the glory of the Lord depart from Solomon's temple, because of the gross wickedness of the people of Israel, but the glory of God returned, when the new temple was built after the return of Judah to Jerusalem in the days of Haggai and Zechariah. Haggai Ch.2v7-9 says, "and I will shake all nations, and they shall come to the Desire of All Nations, and I will fill this temple with glory, says the Lord of hosts. "The silver is Mine, and the gold is Mine," says the Lord of hosts. The glory of this latter temple shall be greater than the former, says the Lord of hosts. And in this place will I give peace, says the Lord of hosts." But because of the sin and unfaithfulness of the people the glory of the Lord departed again. For when Jesus died the veil of the temple was torn in two from the top to the bottom, and one of the things that is absent from the record of that event, is any reference to the glory of the Lord being manifested.

The temple that John is told to measure is the temple of God, the temple where God lives. This can only be a reference to the church, as this book is a revelation of Jesus Christ and is written to the seven churches of Asia. Unlike all the other temples of the Old Testament, where there are very detailed measurements of every part, only the temple and the altar are measured and uniquely he is told to measure, or number, the worshippers. No detail is given of what the measurements are, unlike all the other records of temple dimensions, where they have been stone and timber constructions. There are many references to the church being the temple of the Living God. In 1Peter Ch.2 Peter says that Jesus is a living stone, rejected by men, but chosen by God. That Jesus is the chief cornerstone and anyone who believes in Him will not be put to shame. In v5 Peter says that those who do believe are also living stones being built up into a spiritual house. further adding in v10 that believers were once not a people but are now the people of God. Paul agrees wholeheartedly with what Peter writes when he wrote to the Ephesian church. In Ch.2v19-22 he says, "Now therefore, you are no longer strangers and foreigners, but fellow citizens with the saints and members of the household of God, having been built on the foundation of the apostles and prophets, Jesus Christ Himself being the chief cornerstone, in whom the whole building, being fitted together, grows into a holy temple in the Lord, in whom you also are being built together for a dwelling place of God in the Spirit." What significant words these are, a dwelling place of God in the Spirit. Again Paul speaks of the church as the temple of God when he asks the question of the Corinthian church, "Do you not know that you are the temple of God and that the Spirit of God dwells in you? If anyone defiles the temple of God, God will destroy him. For the temple of God is holy which temple you are." (1Cor. Ch.3v16-17) In his second letter to the Corinthians Paul wrote, "And what agreement has the temple of God with idols? For you are the temple of the living God. As God has said: "I will dwell in them and walk among them. I will be their God, and they shall be my people." Therefore "Come out from among them and be separate," says the Lord. Do not touch what is unclean, and I will receive you. I will be a Father to you, and you shall be My sons and daughters, says the Lord Almighty."(2Corinthians Ch.6v16-18) The churches in Asia would have understood this reference to the temple of God as referring to the church, and would have had it very much in mind that Jesus himself had taken the measuring rod of His word and His glory and found many of them to have come short of His standard.

Significantly John is told not to measure the court of the Gentiles, the outer court, which has been given to them. John is told that the Gentiles will trample the holy city for three and a half years. This seems to me to indicate that the Gentiles will tread under foot, and despise the holy things of God. This crusade against God, I believe, will be led by the beast otherwise known as the antichrist. So with the measuring line he is told only to measure that which is holy, the temple of God. What follows in the rest of Ch.11 may at first sight seem unrelated to John measuring the temple of God, but there is a close connection between the temple of God and the two witnesses, which I will discuss later in the chapter. The temple in this context is the church near the end of the age, before Jesus returns for His bride.

Jesus says that He will give power to His two witnesses and they will prophecy also for three and a half years. I believe that as the two same periods are mentioned in the same context that we are meant to understand them as running concurrently. Even in the darkest times God has never left himself without witnesses. We may think that things are dark enough now, in the way the holy things of God are despised and trampled under the feet of evil men, but the scriptures say that evil men will get worse and worse. Jesus also always gives power to His witnesses to fulfill their mission. In Acts Ch.1v8 Jesus says to the disciples, "But you shall receive power when the Holy Spirit has come upon you; and you shall be witnesses to Me in Jerusalem, and in all Judea and Samaria, and to the end of the earth." Acts Ch.2 records the disciples receiving the power of the Holy Spirit, as they were all filled with the Holy Spirit and they spoke with other tongues. The story of the Acts is the story of the church being filled with the Holy Spirit, and being witnesses to Jesus, to the end of the earth. The story of the Acts did not finish with what Luke wrote, although I am not saying that the scripture should be added to. But simply that in every generation God has had His true witnesses who have been empowered by His Spirit. Jesus is highlighting two particular witnesses here in Revelation, for a particular reason. Firstly they are said to be, "the two olive trees and the two lampstands standing before the God of the earth."(Revelation Ch.11v4) This is a very obvious reference to Zechariah Ch.4, where the angel comes to Zechariah and wakes him to see a lampstand and two olive trees either side of the lampstand. When he asks the angel the meaning of what he is seeing the angel replies with the word of the Lord, "Not by might nor by power, but by my Spirit says the Lord of Hosts."(Zechariah Ch.4v6) Later when Zechariah asks the meaning of the two olive trees and the branches that drip oil into the receptacles joined to the pipes, that feed the oil to the seven lamps, he is told they are the two anointed ones that stand before the God of the whole earth. The literal translation of the Hebrew is that they are sons of fresh oil.

These two witnesses, like the branches of the olive tree that Zechariah saw, are sons of fresh oil who are lights in a dark world. The oil I believe is symbolic of the power of the Holy Spirit that flows through those who are branches of the cultured olive tree which represents the chosen people of God. The lampstands also represent the two witnesses who through the power of the Holy Spirit bring light to the world, and I believe particularly to the people of Israel. By the power of the Holy Spirit they are to prophesy, I believe to the people of Israel, and play an important part in God's plan in the sealing of the one hundred and forty four thousand, the saving of the whole house of Israel. They will, I believe, have their ministry focused in Israel and Jerusalem, and bring a spiritual revival to all the elect of Israel, whether that is every single Israelite or not. They will preach the good news of Jesus the Messiah and Savior of Israel and of all men of every nation, and their ministry will be backed up by significant signs and wonders.

It is futile to speculate as to who they may be, as many have done. It really does not matter who they are, what matters is that they are anointed ones with a mission from Jesus. They have significant powers that they will exercise at will, against those who oppose them. Against them there are significant evil powers, so God ensures that they are more than well equipped to deal with any opposition from the devil, the antichrist and the false prophet. It is worthy of note that the devil has his two witnesses, in the shape of the antichrist and false prophet, but these two are more than a match for them. In their armoury they have the fire of God with which they are able to kill any who want to destroy them. They are invincible until they have finished their work, as are all the people of God who are His witnesses. They have the power to stop the rain from falling anywhere in the earth, as well as being able to turn that most precious of all commodities, water, into blood. All the plagues known to man are also at their disposal, to inflict them upon those who oppose them. Needless to say they will be intensely hated by the devil and his henchmen, who will be powerless to stop their witness to Jesus and many thousands coming to faith in Jesus as their Messiah, Savior and Lord.

When they have finished their testimony the beast will make war against them and kill them. Jerusalem will be under the control of the antichrist; John describes Jerusalem as spiritually Sodom and Egypt, where also the Lord was crucified. They will not be deemed worthy of burial and so their bodies will begin to rot in the heat of the day, and lie in the streets of Jerusalem for three and a half days. There will be no doubt intense media interest in their deaths, far more than in what they achieved for God in their lives. You could say, what has changed? For the most part the secular media has no interest in reporting the good things that God is doing around the world. But if a Christian falls into sin in a public way, they suddenly become very interested, or if it seems that the godly have suffered any kind of reverse, they are right there like vultures. So I believe it will be when these two witnesses are killed by the antichrist. There will be headlines around the world like, "The tormenting two killed at last," or "They thought they were invincible," and "The dynamic duos demise." Interestingly John indicates that their dead bodies will be seen around the world, which of course they will by satellite transmission as the world's television news media will converge on Jerusalem. There will be ecstatic joy and rejoicing around the world among those who hate the things of God and Christians. So powerful was their ability while they were alive to torment the wicked of the world, that it will seem like Christmas, New Year and all the other holidays and everyone's birthday has all come at once and the world will go wild in celebration. Gift shops of all kinds will run out of stock as people rush out to give gifts to each other to mark this momentous time. Their hero, the antichrist, has defeated their tormenters. People all around the world will now cement their belief in the antichrist, and believe that he is more powerful than God.

It is not hard to imagine that the TV cameras will still be very much focused on the dead bodies of these two when after three and a half days, the breath of life from God enters them and they stand on their feet. All around the world people will be tuned into what is happening in Jerusalem so we can envisage millions of people simultaneously seeing them stand up alive, and all of them feeling the same stomach churning fear at the same time. John says, "and great fear fell on those who saw them." (Revelation Ch.11v11) John then heard a voice from heaven saying to the two witnesses, "Come up here," and they ascend to heaven in a cloud.

It is not so very long, within the hour of these two ascending to heaven, that there is a great earthquake and a tenth of the city of Jerusalem is destroyed and seven thousand people are killed. Not many people will need convincing that there is an inevitable connection between the resurrection of the two and God's judgment on Jerusalem. John says that the rest of the people were afraid and gave glory to God. God has achieved His purpose in Israel and the two witnesses have done their work well and now they go to their reward.

If you are still wondering about the connection between the measuring of the temple and the two witnesses the connection is this. In the book of Zechariah we have the record of God's dealings with the Jews in Jerusalem, after their return from exile in Babylon, and the building of a new temple. Joshua was the high priest and Zerubbabel was the civic leader of the people. In chapter three there is a picture of Satan opposing Joshua and condemning him because of his sin. But the Lord rebukes Satan and gives Joshua clean clothes to wear and admonishes him to walk in the ways of the Lord. How important it is for spiritual leaders to be clean and pure before God. The hands of Zerubbabel have laid the foundations of the temple and God says that his hands shall also finish it. God rejoiced to see the plumb line in the hands of Zerubbabel as he built the temple. Joshua and Zerubbabel were the two anointed ones of their day and God had charged them with the completion of the temple and the spiritual leadership of the people.

The two witnesses we read of in revelation are the two anointed ones of their day and they are also charged with the building of a temple, but not a temple of stone and wood, but of living stones, who are joined to Jesus Christ and become part of the temple of the living God by the Holy Spirit. For although they are hated by their enemies, they are hugely successful in bringing the sons of Israel to faith in Jesus Christ and into that living temple that will soon be completed. It is also reasonable to believe that their impact is worldwide and many people will hear the gospel and be saved. Jesus said in Matthew Ch.24v14, "And this gospel of the kingdom will be preached in all the world as a witness to all the nations, and then the end will come." Some have predicted the extinction of the church but world wide it has never been stronger than it is today, and it is set to grow even more with the saving of the whole house of Israel.

CHAPTER 16

THE SEVENTH TRUMPET

With the sounding of the seventh trumpet, which is also the third woe, we have again arrived at the time of the second coming of Jesus to the earth. This same event has been arrived at before and discussed in chapter 11, The opening of the six seals. Why does the book of Revelation refer to this event again, as it will once more after this occasion? The reason is that God is revealing, in three stages, different aspects of His purpose. In the history of the heavens and the earth there have been three major players. There is of course God the Father, Son and Holy Spirit also the angelic hosts comprising the two thirds majority who serve the Lord and the third that fell along with Satan and there is also mankind As I mentioned in a previous chapter, when the Lamb starts to open the seals, and the rest of the revelation unfolds, it is like a play with three acts. Act one is God working out His plans and the actors are mankind from the time of Jesus accession to the throne in heaven and His second coming to set up His eternal kingdom on a new earth. In act two the players are angelic, both those who serve the Lord and those who are under Satan's command. But as we have seen those under Satan can only work at the behest of the holy angels of God. We have come to the end of act two in the great pageant of redemption and the powers of darkness are defeated.

The cries of victory are coming from heaven, and this is now the place of the focus of John's attention. Revelation Ch.11v15 says, "Then the seventh angel sounded: And there were loud voices in heaven, saying, "The kingdoms of this world have become the kingdoms of our Lord and of His Christ, and He shall reign forever and ever!" This is the time of the stone that hit the image on its feet, and destroyed the image, and then grew and filled the whole earth. This is the time of the vision that Daniel saw in Ch.7 of his prophecy. He says in v13-14 of that chapter, "I was watching in the night visions, and behold, One like the Son of Man, coming with the clouds of heaven! He came to the Ancient of Days, and they brought Him near before Him. Then to Him was given dominion and glory and a kingdom, that all peoples, nations, and languages should serve Him. His dominion is an everlasting dominion, which shall not pass away, and His kingdom the one that shall not be destroyed."

At the sound of the loud cries of final victory over all the kingdoms of earth, the elders who were seated on their thrones fell on their faces and worshipped God saying, "We give You thanks, O Lord God Almighty, the One who is and who was and who is to come, because You have taken Your great power and reigned. The nations were angry, and Your wrath has come, and the time of the dead, that they should be judged, and that You should reward Your servants the prophets and the saints, and those who fear Your name, small and great, and should destroy those who destroy the earth."(Revelation Ch.11v17&18)

The elders are worshipping God and thanking Him for taking His rightful place as supreme ruler in the universe. The powers of darkness have been, in the end, singularly unsuccessful in trying to rule in heaven and on earth. It is quite in order for them now to thank God for the final victory over Satan and all his followers. If you are not on the Lord's side, you are most definitely on the loosing side and will suffer the consequences. The nations were angry for they did not want to acknowledge God as the supreme ruler. They had chosen the antichrist and followed him to destruction, being deceived by the devil. They had chosen to invest only in the things of this world, and now those things are no more, for all the world and its works are consumed by fire. The nations were angry but there was nothing that they could do to hinder the kingdom of God and His Christ. Their anger is futile, just as man's opposition to God always has been futile. But the wrath of God has come, and the elders are thankful to God that those who deserve to taste His wrath will now do so. God's anger is not futile, but purposeful and directed against those who are His enemies.

Paul writes to the church at Thessalonica twice, and in his second epistle Ch.1 he goes into some detail regarding the outpouring of the wrath of God at this time. In v6 he says, "Since it is a righteous thing with God to repay with tribulation those who trouble you." Paul is speaking to the Christians of His day and saying that as far as God is concerned those who oppose and cause His children trouble and persecute them, God is quite within His rights to repay them in kind. This is not vindictiveness, this is justice and the God of the Bible is a God of justice. The second coming of Jesus to the earth will be a time of the execution of justice and retribution In v7 Paul then tells the Christians that they will have rest when the Lord is revealed from heaven as he comes with His mighty angels. Although Paul speaks as if Jesus will come in their day, the fact that Jesus still has not returned means that the truth Paul is expressing will certainly be applicable to the hard pressed saints that are alive when Jesus returns. In v8 we see the Lord taking vengeance on those who do not know, or acknowledge God, and do not obey the gospel of our Lord Jesus Christ. Paul says that Jesus will take vengeance in flaming fire on the ungodly, and that they will be measured and assessed according to the gospel. There is only one gospel and that is the gospel of our Lord and Savior Jesus Christ, that He is the Way the Truth and the Life. That He is the only mediator between God and men, and the only Savior. Obeying the gospel is believing on the Lord Jesus and living in such a way as to acknowledge Him as Lord. This entails living in obedience to God's Word and obeying the leading of the Holy Spirit. Paul wrote to the Romans and said that those who are led by the Spirit of God are the sons of God. The only really important question for any one to answer in their lives is, am I living in obedience to the gospel of Jesus Christ, for God is a God of vengeance, and when Jesus returns those who are living in disobedience to the gospel will experience the full wrath of God. Paul goes on to say in v9 that those who do not obey will be punished with everlasting destruction. Everlasting destruction is not extinction, but everlasting loss and ruin, in the lake of fire which burns forever and ever. This everlasting destruction is from the presence of the Lord and from the glory of His power, this is the second death, an eternal separation from God. Nothing could describe eternal ruin better then eternal separation from God the creator, the Savior and loving shepherd of His people.

Paul says that Jesus is coming to be glorified in His saints and to be admired among all those who believe. When Jesus returns to the earth He will come in a cloud of glory, surrounded by His glorified saints which will make His coming all the more glorious, and also with myriads of angels. There will be no holding back on the majesty and splendor of His second coming, unlike His first coming as a baby. Charles Wesley wrote that in His first coming He was, "veiled in flesh," but now He comes to reign and He comes in power and great glory. And how His saints will admire Him, for they know the long road that He has trod to arrive as King of Kings. He took no short cuts, no bowing down to Satan in order to have the kingdoms of this world, but He comes to reign with His garments stained with His own life blood. They will admire the humble road that He has walked, in order that He might be highly exalted and given a name above all names that at the name of Jesus every knee shall bow and every tongue confess that Jesus Christ is Lord to the glory of God the Father. They will admire His submission to the Father and His long patience for the harvest of the earth, for He will come at the time set by the Father. Jesus said exactly that when speaking to His disciples and Matthew records it in his gospel Ch.24v36, "But of that day and hour no one knows, not even the angels of heaven, but My Father only." They will admire the exercise of His power when He executes justice in the earth. In 2 Thessalonians Ch.2v8 Paul describes the fate of the antichrist, who he calls the lawless one, and says the Lord will consume him with the breath of His mouth and destroy him with the brightness of His coming. On that day only Jesus will be the centre of admiration among His saints, for these and no doubt countless other reasons that we cannot even begin to imagine.

The elders then thank God that the time has come for the dead to be judged. All who have died throughout the long ages of time will be judged. This is a cardinal teaching in the scriptures and the Bible has much to say on the subject. There is only one judgment for the unbelievers and Satan and all his fallen angels and we shall refer to it in more detail later when dealing with Ch.20 of Revelation. But it is sufficient to say that the time of the great judgment when God sits on His great white throne has come, and for unbelievers there is only one verdict, everlasting destruction in the lake of fire. There is such inevitability about this judgment, the time has come. It has not come yet, but many people in the world are just like prisoners on death row, the time will come, and for those who have died not believing in the Lord Jesus the scripture is clear, after death the judgment. Hebrews Ch.9v27, "And as it is appointed for men to die once, but after this the judgment." In other words the only thing the unsaved have to look forward to after death, is judgment.

This is also the time for the saints and prophets to be rewarded. This is the time that Paul wrote about when he said, "For no other foundation can anyone lay than that which is laid, which is Jesus Christ. Now if anyone builds on this foundation with gold, silver, precious stones, wood, hay, straw, each one's work will become clear; for the Day will declare it, because it will be revealed by fire; and the fire will test each one's work, of what sort it is. If anyone's work that he has built on it endures, he will receive a reward. If anyone's work is burned, he will suffer loss; but he himself will be saved, yet so as through fire."(1Corinthians Ch.3v11-15) Again Paul wrote to the Corinthians and said, "Therefore we make it our aim, whether present (with the Lord) or absent (from the Lord) to be well pleasing to Him. For we must all appear before the judgment seat of Christ, that each one may receive the things done in the body, according to what he has done, whether good or bad." (2Corinthians Ch.5v9-10) Lastly in Romans

Ch.14v9-12 Paul wrote, "For to this end Christ died and rose and lived again, that He might be Lord of both the dead and the living. But why do you judge your brother? Or why do you show contempt for your brother? For we shall all stand before the judgment seat of Christ. For it is written, "As I live, says the Lord, every knee shall bow to Me, and every tongue shall confess to God." So then each one of us shall give account of himself to God." All these scriptures make it clear that the time of rewards for the saints is a time of judgment when their works will be tested in the fire. John mentions that those who will be rewarded are those who fear the name of the Lord both small and great. How important the fear of the Lord is in the lives of His people. Some of the saints in the seven churches had lost this vital ingredient to the Christian life, and would be saved so as by fire, but would enter the eternal kingdom without any reward. How will you enter the eternal kingdom, let Peter have the last word, "Therefore brethren be even more diligent to make your call and election sure, for if you do these things you will never stumble; for so an entrance will be supplied to you abundantly into the everlasting kingdom of our Lord and Savior Jesus Christ."(2Peter Ch.1v10-11) The things that Peter talks about in this chapter make it clear that it is not the volume of work that we do for the Lord that will be rewarded, or whether or not we have been admired by the church. What will qualify us for an abundant entrance into the kingdom is the maturity of Christian character that we have achieved through giving all diligence to allowing the Holy Spirit's power to work in us.

John then sees the temple of God in heaven opened and the Ark of the Covenant was seen in heaven. This is not of course a literal temple building in heaven or a literal ark, but it symbolizes Gods dwelling place and the mercy seat and atonement of Christ and His righteous character in judgment. This is a day of mercy towards His children and judgment toward sinners. And there were lightnings, noises, thunderings, an earthquake and great hail. All these things are associated in other scriptures with the end of the age and the Lord's coming.

In the next chapter there is another of the interludes that is characteristic of the book of Revelation, in order to explain in more detail things of importance.

CHAPTER 17

THE WOMAN AND THE DRAGON

The twelfth chapter of Revelation begins in stark contrast to the end of the previous chapter, because having come to the end of the age and the coming of Jesus in the previous chapter; we come to an interlude that explains in more detail and from a different angle things that have already happened during the sounding of the trumpets. John describes what he calls a great sign that appeared in heaven, which should be understood as the sky, rather than heaven where the throne of God is. He saw a woman clothed with the sun, with the moon under her feet, and on her head a garland of twelve stars. There are a number of ways of interpreting this sign, which is an indicator or token of something. But which ever way one interprets what John saw, there can be no doubt that this woman represents the nation of Israel, especially as the chapter proceeds this becomes abundantly clear. There could be a reference here to the dream that Joseph had, where he dreamt that the sun and the moon and eleven stars bowed down to him. The sun and the moon referring to his father and mother and eleven brothers. The sun and the moon here in Revelation referring to Israel and Rachael and the twelve sons of Israel. If it is then we are going back to the beginnings of the nation of Israel that came from the twelve brothers. God had a most significant plan in forming the nation of Israel, which is why the call of Abram, and the covenant with him and his sons after him is so vital to the outworking of His plans.

John saw that the woman cried out in labour and in pain in giving birth to a child. In v5 we read that this child is a male Child who was to rule all nations with a rod of iron. This clearly identifies the Child as being Jesus Christ the King of Kings and Lord of Lords. The calling of the nation of Israel to be the people of God was primarily in order to bring the Messiah, the Savior of the world and ruler of the kings of the earth into the world. A major theme of the Old Testament is the tracing of the chosen line of the Messiah, the Savior Jesus Christ. God did not choose Israel because they were a powerful nation, or a great nation. Neither did He choose them because they would be a model of godliness and obedience to Him, because they were none of these things. God chose them in order to reveal His character and to make Himself known to Israel and to the rest of the world. Paul in Romans Ch.11v22 speaks of the goodness and severity of God. Severity on Israel because of their disobedience and rejection of Jesus Christ, and goodness toward the Gentiles who had been outside of the old covenant made with Israel. In v33 Paul speaks about the depth of the riches of the wisdom and knowledge of God, that His judgments are unsearchable and His ways past finding out. In all of God's dealing with Israel He is revealing His character and attributes. God has revealed His grace and favour to the entire world and His judgments and anger against sin. All of the attributes and characteristics of the God of the Bible are revealed through His dealing with Israel. It can be said with absolute certainty that the God who reveals himself in the Old Testament is exactly the same God who reveals Himself in the New Testament.

The emphasis in this chapter is on who will rule the world. John could have been told to write a number of things regarding the Child that was born of the chosen nation. But what he did write was that the Child that was born of the woman would rule the nations with a rod of iron.

John saw another sign appear in heaven, which was of a fiery red dragon with seven heads on which were crowns and ten horns. With a swish of his tail he drew a third of stars of heaven and cast them down to the earth. Very often in the book of Revelation the stars symbolize angelic beings and it is so in this case. When Satan sinned in heaven he took with him a third of the angels that God had created, and it is entirely reasonable to believe that they are demonic spirits, and the principalities and powers of darkness that Paul speaks of in Ephesians Ch.6v12. Satan knew there was considerable significance in the birth of Jesus Christ, even if it was not recognized by the vast majority of people at the time. He would have been aware of the angelic activity that surrounded the conception of Jesus, as well as his birth. Angels were very active at the time in announcing to Mary that she would become pregnant by the agency of the Holy Spirit, and also in making sure that Joseph who was her husband would not break off their engagement. When Jesus was born Satan did his best to make sure that He would not survive His infancy. Through the evil character of Herod, Satan sought to take the life of the infant savior, who was not just destined to rule over Israel but the world. So John saw that the dragon stood before the woman to devour the Child as soon as it was born. If Satan could destroy Jesus before Jesus could destroy his power then he was not going to miss this opportunity. Satan must have thought that he had a great chance to thwart God's plans, as the plan of God involved the Son of God coming into the world as a helpless baby. A helpless baby in the hands of a Jewish couple who were not rich and powerful, and lived in an occupied country. Naturally speaking we would think the whole operation was rather dicey, especially as Mary had to undertake a considerable journey to Joseph's home town of Bethlehem, when she was late on in her pregnancy. We are told however that the Child was caught up to God and His throne. This is not I believe just a picture of Jesus ascension to heaven, but is a statement of the fact that all through His earthy life Jesus was invincible until the time that He laid down His life, in order to take it up again.

God was well able to protect His Son, and see all of His plans through to completion. Apart from the time that Herod tried to kill Jesus there were a number of occasions when Jesus life was threatened. On one occasion a mob from his own home town of Nazareth tried to throw Him over a cliff. Not long before His death, the Jews in Jerusalem took up stones to stone Him, because of His claim to be the Son of God, which in their eyes made Him equal with God. Jesus of course did not disagree with their conclusion, because He is equal with God the Father. Possibly the most life threatening time was when Jesus sweat great drops of blood, while He was in agony of soul in the garden of Gethsemane, and it was necessary for angels to come and strengthen Him, so that His life would not end before He shed His blood on the cross. Of course in a literal sense Jesus was caught up to the throne of God, after He had finished His work of redemption on earth, from where He reigns until all His enemies become His footstool.

Revelation Ch.12v6 is rather vague in some ways. It would be reasonable to assume that Satan is angry with the woman, the nation of Israel, through whom God has successfully carried out His plan to bring the Savior into the world. This Savior is not just the Savior from sin for all who will believe, but is also destined to rule the nations. Satan has always wanted to rule on earth, as was seen by his actions in the Garden of Eden, but now his ambitions are thwarted. He cannot get to Jesus, who is now on the throne in heaven, but he can persecute the woman, who is the nation of Israel. This explains why John saw that she fled into the wilderness. No specific wilderness is in view, but it is a place prepared by God. Again who it is that feeds the woman is not specified, but as on other occasions when no detail is given, no detail is necessary to convey the truth that God intends us to know. God did not say who the two witnesses are just as there were no details regarding the temple that John measured. We do not know what the thunders uttered, when the angel who had the little book cried out. Plainly we are not meant to know and we should be satisfied with that.

Although there is no detail and it would be wrong to be dogmatic, I believe the truth that God wants to convey is that Israel will have to flee from their land and be in the wilderness of the wide world, where God will look after them and provide for them. This is of course what happened, after AD70 when the Romans destroyed Jerusalem and the temple and the Jews were scattered around the world for nearly nineteen hundred years. There are admittedly difficulties with this interpretation, because of the time of three and a half years, but those who place this time of fleeing into the wilderness in the future, have the difficulty that the woman flees straight after the Child is caught up into heaven. However it would be true to say that in all the centuries that the Jews have been scattered around the world, they have experienced persecution and difficulties, both from the so called church and secular rulers who have been anti Semitic. This culminated in the holocaust of the Second World War, when six million Jews were killed by the Nazis. But through it all God has fed His chosen people and they still exist as a distinctive nation because of their culture and faith.

Things that happen on earth have their counterpart in heaven, and when John saw that war had broken out in heaven between Michael and his angels and the dragon and his angels we can conclude that something is happening on earth that has precipitated this war. From the book of Daniel we discover that the arch angel Michael is the angel who stands up for Israel. Daniel Ch.10v13 speaks of Michael coming to the aid of an angel of God who had been in conflict with a demonic power who ruled over Persia. The conflict centered around the angel coming to Daniel to reveal to him what would happen to Israel in the last days. Satan, through this prince of Persia, was trying to hinder the angel coming to bring God's message to Daniel, but Michael's intervention broke the deadlock. In v20-21 of the same chapter the angel tells Daniel that he has to engage further with the prince of Persia and later with the prince of Greece, but he says that no one upholds me against these except for Michael your prince. In saying that he meant that Michael was the prince of the people of Israel. Daniel Ch.12v1 confirms this when in the last times, Satan's wrath will be vented against Israel like it has never been before, "At that time Michael shall stand up, the great prince who stands watch over the sons of your people;" This is again another indication that it is correct to interpret the woman as the nation of Israel

The result of the conflict was that Satan lost the war, and that was not all he lost. He also lost his place in heaven. It might be a surprise to some that he ever had any place in heaven after he rebelled against God. But there are a number of scriptures that indicate that when he sinned he was cast out of the highest heaven, where the throne of God is, to a lower sphere of the heavenly realm. Job Ch.1v6 speaks of a day when the sons of God came to present themselves before the Lord, and Satan came to present himself among them. The sons of God in this scripture are the angels of God, and Satan still at that time had access to the presence of God at a certain level as the angels did. The same occurrence is recorded in Job Ch.2v1, where Satan comes before the Lord. So up until this time Satan had access to the presence of the Lord, but John sees that after this conflict he looses his place in heaven. (Revelation Ch.12v8)

When will this conflict take place? This is a question that will find its answer in things that have already been discussed in chapter twelve of this book, the sealed servants and the secure saints. The conflict is between, Satan and Michael who stands up for the people of Israel, so I believe that this conflict arises because of something very significant happening in Israel. In verse 10, we read that with the casting down of Satan out of heaven John hears loud voices in heaven saying things that are very similar to what he has already heard in heaven. In Ch.11v15 when the seventh angel had sounded his trumpet there were loud voices in heaven saying that the kingdoms of this world had become the kingdoms of our Lord and His Christ, and that He would reign forever and ever. Now in Ch.12v10 John hears in heaven, "Now salvation, and strength, and the kingdom of our God, and the power of His Christ has come, for the accuser of our brethren, who accused them before our God day and night, has been cast down." As on other occasions in this book of Revelation, John hears or sees the same events a number of times, because God wants us to see them from different angles. The fact that the war is between the angel who stands up for Israel and that it is clearly near the time before Jesus returns, I believe this conflict is over Satan's opposition to the saving of the whole house of Israel, and this will be further confirmed by events that John sees in the rest of this chapter. But Satan loses the war, and loses his place in heaven, and he loses his ability to accuse the brethren before God.

Satan's fortunes take another serious knock, because not only has he lost the war in heaven, but he also looses the war on earth with the saints. For we read in v11, "And they overcame him by the blood of the Lamb and by the word of their testimony, and they did not love their lives to the death." With the outpouring of grace and the Spirit of the Lord on Israel, Satan through the agency of the beast and the false prophet, ruthlessly attack and seek to destroy those who receive Jesus as their Messiah and Savior, in those days. All through this book we are constantly reading of those who have given their lives for the sake of their testimony, and from what we read countless numbers will give their lives during this final period before Jesus returns. But not only will there be countless numbers of Israel saved but also among all nations. The prophet Joel speaks of these days in Ch.2v30-32 when he says, "And I will show wonders in the heavens and in the earth: Blood and fire and pillars of smoke. The sun shall be turned into darkness, and the moon into blood, before the coming of the great and awesome day of the Lord. And it shall come to pass that whoever calls on the name of the Lord shall be saved. For in Mount Zion and in Jerusalem there shall be deliverance, as the Lord has said, among the remnant whom the Lord calls." Although many will give their lives it is not a defeat, but wonderful victory. For through the blood of Jesus the Lamb, they have been cleansed from all their sin and been sealed by the Holy Spirit and their place in the presence of the Lord is assured forever. It was also their testimony that they boldly proclaimed, even in the face of death, that enabled them to overcome Satan. They like the thousands of martyrs before them did not give in to the temptation to renounce Jesus and save their lives, and they shall walk with the Lord in white. They loved the Lord more than their lives, what wonderful grace will be upon our brothers and sisters of those days. John writes that it is cause for great rejoicing in heaven that Satan has been defeated in heaven and defeated on earth by the saints. One can only imagine the ecstasy of the elders, the four living creatures, the angels and the host of the redeemed who have come out of all their trouble and pain on earth, to know that Satan is cast down, and it is the beginning of the end for him.

But there is no cause for rejoicing for those on the earth, but only a cause for woe. John writes, "Woe to the inhabitants of the earth and the sea! For the devil has come down to you, having great wrath, because he knows that he has a short time."(Revelation Ch.12v12) Like a wounded wild animal Satan is cast down to the earth, and is allowed to vent his wrath for a little while, and this we have already seen in the sounding of the trumpets, the last three being called the three woes. But he knows that there will only be a very short time now before he is cast into the lake of fire forever, and he will be determined to vent all his spleen on whoever he is allowed to.

So John sees that when he is cast down he persecutes the woman who gave birth to the male Child. Satan persecutes Israel, not just because ancestrally they are the chosen people of God, but specifically because they have turned to the God of their Fathers, through His Son Jesus Christ. Israel is again the centre of spiritual revival in the earth. But as God knew how to look after His Son, so He knows how to look after His people. Not all will suffer martyrdom but some will be miraculously saved and preserved, For we read that God gave the woman two wings of a great eagle that she might fly into the wilderness to her place where she is nourished, for what John describes as a time and times and half a time, from the presence of the serpent. Just as God preserved His people through nineteen centuries and fed them, so through this short period of time, near the end, God knows how to preserve His own.

John saw that the serpent did not give up in his attempts to destroy these saints of God. He spewed water out of his mouth like a flood. to carry them away, but the earth helped the woman and opened its mouth and swallowed the flood of water. Whatever the reality of the persecution of Satan against these Jewish saints is, one thing is for sure, God is using all those things that belong to Him in order to bring Satan's plans to nothing. Because of his failure to destroy the Jewish saints we read that the dragon was enraged with the woman but could do no more to touch her. Instead he turned his attention to what John describes as the rest of her offspring, who have the commandments of God and the testimony of Jesus. The rest of her offspring are the Gentile Christians, who are saved from every kindred, tongue, tribe and nation. He made war with them, no doubt using all the instruments of earthly rule and authority at his disposal. But all the church on earth at this time are those who overcome him by the blood of the Lamb and the word of their testimony, for they keep the commandments of God and have the testimony of Jesus.

Why should John be writing these things to the seven churches? There are a number of reasons I believe why he should. Firstly it is God's word to them and God wants them and us to know the things that are going to take place before He comes. In the first and second interludes there has been s strong emphasis on the nation of Israel and for good reason. Firstly God wants the Gentile Christians in the seven churches to know their roots, that their faith is rooted in the faith of Abraham, Isaac and Jacob and the truth in the Old Testament. That they have sprung out of what was firstly a Jewish church, and they owe the gospel that they have heard to the church that sprung up in Jerusalem and spread out from there. It is especially important for some of the churches, considering the fact that they face opposition from what John describes as a synagogue of Satan. Secondly he wants them to understand that in the end times Israel will again come into its own spiritually and again play a leading role in the church, although at the time of John writing the Revelation, there were many Gentile believers, and in the churches in Asia they were probably the majority. The church as a whole today needs to wake up the reality of the wonderful future that God has in store for the Jews again in the church, and pray for the nation of Israel. I believe that the reason why God has brought the Jews back to the land of Israel in our day, is in preparation for the amazing outpouring of grace and mercy on them, and it is in order that we should pray for this to happen.

CHAPTER 18

THE BEASTLY DUO

In the next part of what is an extended interlude between the sounding of the trumpets and the pouring out of the vials of the wrath of God, John is very much back down to earth and is standing on a sandy seashore. The Holy Spirit has placed John here in order to observe a beast rising out of the sea. It must have been an awe inspiring sight, to see what would have seemed to John an enormous creature, which had seven heads and ten horns and on the horns were crowns. Now if that sounds familiar, seven heads and ten horns, it should do for the fiery red dragon Satan, had seven heads and ten horns with crowns on them. So there should be no doubt as to who has sent this beast on to the earth. Also on his heads was a blasphemous name. John must have wondered if he was dreaming when he saw this beast, for its appearance was very strange. It was like a leopard, but it had the feet of a bear, and its mouth like the mouth of a lion. Then we read that the dragon gave him his power, throne and authority. This is all part of Satan's final fling that he is allowed to have before being sent to the lake of fire.

We have also come across the leopard, bear and lion before when we were looking at the book of Daniel and the kingdoms that would arise. The lion was Babylon, the bear was the Medes and Persians and the leopard was the Greek empire. This beast has some of the characteristics of all of them and represents the leader of an empire that will dominate the world in the future. This may surprise many people considering the fact that the majority of the major powers in the world today are democratic powers, whereas these kingdoms from the past were anything but democratic. But even the democratic powers have a tendency to centralize the power that they have, especially in Europe. Many of the laws and regulations that govern the lives of people who live within the European Union are determined, not in the individual countries, but centrally by EU bodies such as the commission or the European Parliament in Strasbourg. It is also true that the European court of justice has powers that override any powers that the courts in the individual member countries have. There is every reason to believe that the EU is moving in the direction of ever closer union, until it will effectively become a European super state. Although the EU is the most advanced union of countries in the world, there are moves all around the world in various regions, for countries to co-operate in trade agreements and to form blocks that have the potential to develop into EU type unions. So despite all the effort on the part of the democratic powers to democratize the world, the prediction of the Bible is that there is a worldwide kingdom that is going to arise that will be headed by the beast seen here by John. This is the kingdom that Nebuchadnezzar saw in his dream that was the feet of the image, the image that was struck on the feet and then disintegrated completely and was then blown away by the wind. This beast we are told has ten horns, horns being powers or individual kingdoms that have joined together under the authority of the beast, just as the image had the usual ten toes of human feet. At the moment the emergence of this final kingdom which Daniel predicted, in his interpretation of Nebuchadnezzar's dream, is not in view but it will come and when it does I believe it will come quickly. It will precede the coming of Jesus Christ as King of Kings, as Daniel wrote, "And in the days of these kings the God of heaven will set up a kingdom which shall never be destroyed."(Daniel Ch.2v44) The dragon is allowed to give this beast his power and authority, so when this kingdom emerges it will be energized by Satan and will act in accordance with Satan's will. Paul the apostle writes of this beast in 2Thessalonians Ch.2v9-10 saying, "The coming of the lawless one is according to the working of Satan, with all power, signs, and lying wonders, and with all unrighteous deception among those who perish, because they did not receive the love of the truth, that they might be saved." Needless to say this will mean that he will be the expression of all that is evil and deceptive. There are many unsavory regimes in the world today, but when this man begins to rule, he will supercede anyone that has been before him in evil works.

From the makeup of this beast we can see that he will emerge with the speed of the leopard, just as the kingdom of Greece conquered the ancient world at lightning speed. There has been a great deal written about the emergence of the beast, some of which is entirely fictitious. It has been the vogue in recent years for Christian writers and film makers to theorize about the coming of the beast, otherwise known in other scriptures as the antichrist, or the lawless one. While they may, to some extent entertain Christian audiences and to some extent challenge them, it has to be remembered that they are fiction and the Bible does not give detail about how this kingdom comes about. I have my own ideas, but the purpose of this book is not to put forward my ideas, but to seek to explain what the Scriptures teach, because there is a great danger that people will be hindered in their faith by ideas and conjectures that do not come to pass. We should not believe what the Bible predicts because in some way we can see current events shaping up to fulfill prophecy, but we should believe because it is the word of God. It is sufficient to believe what John the apostle wrote, "Little children, it is the last hour; and as you have heard that the Antichrist is coming, even now many antichrists have come, by which we know it is the last hour."(1John Ch.2v18)

John saw that one of the heads of the beast was mortally wounded, and v14 of Revelation Ch.14 says that he received the wound by the sword. Then lo and behold the deadly wound was healed, and all the world wondered and marveled and followed the beast. Of course what John sees is figurative of an event in the life of the beast, that looks for all the world, as if his career as world dictator could be at an end. Of all the references to the antichrist in the scriptures, this is the only reference to this event in his life. Whether it is something political or personal to him we do not know, but one thing is for sure, it is something from which he recovers that makes all the world marvel as if it were some great miracle. The world's adulation of the beast, John says is in fact the worship of the dragon. They worship the devil and Satan, who gives authority to the beast. Well this is all that Satan has ever longed for, to be worshipped as God and he is in his element. It is quite remarkable that in what will be an even more technically advanced age, knowledgeable and sophisticated, all around the world men will worship Satan. However this will only be because of his strong deception and the fact that God has actually decided that men will be deceived. We have already looked at the Scripture that Paul wrote to the Thessalonians when he said that because men would not receive the love of the truth they would be deceived. Added to the deception from Satan, God Himself will send them strong delusion, that they should believe the lie. We can already see similar things today where men have refused the truth of God's Word. For several hundred years now it has become more and more popular to refuse to believe the truth of God as the Creator. Consequently men have believed a lie and a delusion that permeates almost every branch of science, the lie of evolution. I call it a lie, because not only has it been propagated sometimes by downright deceptions, but is always only backed up by suppositions and theories, and there is not a shred of actual scientific evidence to sustain it. The lie that men will believe, is that Satan is God and the antichrist is the Messiah and savior of the world. John heard that in those days men will say, "Who is like the beast?" In the eyes of the world this man will be the bee's knees, the best thing since sliced bread. He will stand head and shoulders above all other leaders in charisma and intelligence; he will be a past master in handling all the delicate negotiations necessary to bring everyone on side. How can the world be united, people often wonder today, certainly the UN is not able to do the job. But this man will do it, by stealth and cunning, by deception and lies. All religions, all shades of political opinion will unite under his banner, all except the saints of the most High God, who keep the commandments of God and have the testimony of Jesus Christ. They will be the only thorn in his side.

Who is able to make war with him? The talk in the pubs and clubs, in the parliaments and centers of power, on the TV and media in general will be, is there any one more powerful than him. The inference in the question is, no, there is no one who can resist this man. Of course the vast majority of people will see this as an advantage because they now worship this man and give him all their allegiance. He has the feet of a bear and is bear like in the power that he wealds. The bear is one of the most powerful animals on the earth, with such brute strength that almost all other animals would find hard to resist.

He was given a mouth speaking great things, this man is not afraid to shoot his mouth off. It is a popular pastime for some to insult God and Jesus Christ and to say and write blasphemous things. A notorious example, Jerry Springer the opera, was broadcast in 2005 by the BBC, for which they quite rightly received a mountain of protests. But when this man comes onto the scene, the expression, you ain't seen anything yet, will be quite appropriate. Paul writing to the Thessalonians in his second epistle Ch.2v3-4 says, "Let no one deceive you by any means; for that Day will not come unless the falling away comes first, and the man of sin is revealed, the son of perdition, who opposes and exalts himself above all that is called God or all that is worshiped, so that he sits as God in the temple of God, showing himself that he is God." This man will speak against all that men of all religions have held sacred in order to promote himself. In Daniel Ch. 7v23-25 he records what he saw in a night vision, "Thus he said, 'The fourth beast shall be a fourth kingdom on earth, which shall be different from all other kingdoms, and shall devour the whole earth, trample it and break it in pieces. The ten horns are ten kings who shall arise from this kingdom. And another shall arise after them; he shall be different from the first ones, and shall subdue three kings. He shall speak pompous words against the Most High, shall persecute the saints of the Most High, and shall intend to change times and law. Then the saints shall be given into his hand for a time and times and half a time." Like Daniel prophesied, John also saw that he was given authority to continue in this way for forty two months. John is very specific in saying that he opened his mouth in blasphemy against God, blaspheming His name and His tabernacle and those who are in heaven.

Although he gets his authority from the dragon to do these things, it is of course Jesus who is still in overall charge on the earth and permits the beast to do these things. Daniel had already written that this man would persecute the saints of the Most High. His treatment of the two witnesses will be typical of his attitude towards all of God's children in the church at that time. But what he does he does because he is permitted to, just as all those who have persecuted God's children, have only been able to because they have permission from God to do so. Just as with the two witnesses, if God chooses to give His children immunity from persecution, He can do that, and when God so chooses He can allow them to be defeated by their enemies. But what God does is not random and without purpose, but as Paul wrote, "And we know that all things work together for good to those who love God, to those who are the called according to His purpose." (Romans Ch.8v28) We might wonder what purpose there is in suffering, why should God allow His people to suffer sometimes? Paul has some answers to that question in Romans Ch.8. In verse 18 we says, "For I consider that the sufferings of this present time are not worthy to be compared with the glory which shall be revealed in us." The book of Revelation is full of the fact that Christians will suffer persecution and sometimes give their lives for the faith, but equally it is full of descriptions of the glory that awaits those who are faithful and keep their testimony. In Paul's estimation there is no comparison between temporary suffering on earth and eternal glory. I believe there is a correlation between the glory and reward that Christians will receive in heaven, and their willingness to suffer on earth for the sake of Christ Jesus. God's grace and glory is also manifested in the lives of those who suffer for His sake, and Paul writes that nothing can separate us from His love. He asks the question, "Shall tribulation, or distress, or persecution, or famine, or nakedness, or peril, or sword?" "As it is written: For your sake we are killed all day long; we are accounted as sheep for the slaughter." "Yet in all these things we are more than conquerors through Him that loved us. For I am persuaded that neither death nor life, nor angels nor principalities nor powers, nor things present nor things to come, nor height nor depth, nor any other created thing, shall be able to separate us from the love of God which is in Christ Jesus our Lord." Why does God allow His children to suffer? Part of the answer is that those who are given the grace to go through such things receive great reward. Those who suffer also strengthen the hands of the weak, and as the old saying goes, the blood of the martyrs is the seed of the church. At the time of John writing this book to the seven churches, two of them are suffering persecution, I believe that these things would be a comfort to them, Knowing the truth that their persecutors are in God's hands, and to do what they are doing they need God's permission and that God has set boundaries on their authority.

John goes on to say that not only was he allowed to speak so pompously and blaspheme, and allowed to make war on the saints, but he was granted authority over every tribe tongue and nation. All the inhabitants of the earth worship him, although John adds that it is all those whose names are not written in the Book of Life, from the foundation of the world. Those whose names are in the Book of Life will not be deceived because they have been sealed by the Holy Spirit and have the Spirit of Truth in them. What John writes next is a phrase that has occurred in every one of the special messages to the seven churches, and reminds us that he is still writing to the churches and to all of God's children. "If any one has an ear, let him hear." What does the Holy Spirit want us to hear? The message of this chapter so far has been of the beast, empowered by the dragon, who makes war on God and the saints in the church of Jesus Christ. But what the Holy Spirit wants us to hear is that those who make war on God and the saints of God, will have to face the consequences, as Revelation Ch.13v10 makes clear, "He who leads into captivity shall go into captivity, he who kills with the sword must be killed with the sword." But when the beast and his entourage face the sword of the Lord, the consequences for them will be infinitely greater and more deadly than anything they have been able to dish out to the saints. Their captivity will be forever in the lake of fire, where they will be tormented day and night forever. The rest of v10 says, "Here is the patience and faith of the saints." The saints of God who have suffered in the past have done so with patience and faith. They have endured the persecution and imprisonment, the torture and ridicule of sinners because they believe that it is right to commit their souls to God, and leave the vengeance to Him. The writer to the Hebrews expresses this truth so well in Ch.10 v30-39 where he writes, "For we know Him who said, "Vengeance is Mine, I will repay," says the Lord. And again, "The Lord will judge His people." "It is a fearful thing to fall into the hands of the living God." The writer to the Hebrews then encourages the saints to endure suffering and continues in v32, "But recall the former days in which, after you were illuminated, you endured a great struggle with sufferings: partly while you were made a spectacle both by reproaches and tribulations, and partly while you became companions of those who were so treated: for you had compassion on me in my chains, and joyfully accepted the plundering of your goods, knowing that you have a better and an enduring possession for yourselves in heaven. Therefore do not cast away your confidence, which has great reward. For you have need of endurance, so that after you have done the will of God, you may receive the promise." "For yet a little while, and He who is coming will come and will not tarry. Now the just shall live by faith; but if anyone draws back My soul shall have no pleasure in him." "But we are not of those who draw back to perdition, but of those who believe to the saving of the soul." It will be a fearful thing for the beast and his followers to fall into the hands of God, but by the grace of God and the power of the Holy Spirit and Word of God, the saints of those days will patiently endure and overcome him. Overcoming is a theme in the book of Revelation, and while Jesus exhorts His children to overcome and receive the rewards of doing so, He also gives them the means of grace to obey and endure.

Then John saw another beast coming out of the earth, he looked like a lamb with two horns but he spoke like a dragon. In other words this man is not all that he seems to be. Like the first beast he has a big mouth and in other scriptures in Revelation he is called the false prophet. He is able to exercise the same authority as the first beast, but is under his authority. His role is to mimic the role of the Holy Spirit, who has all the attributes of God and is God, but subordinates himself to Jesus and fulfills the role of revealing and exalting Jesus. So Satan now has his fake trinity, himself, the antichrist and the false prophet. John says that this false prophet causes all the earth to worship the first beast, whose deadly wound was healed. Ironically when so many people will reject the truth of the resurrection of Jesus, they will be fooled by the antichrist and his 'so called' resurrection. But this second beast will do such an effective job, in convincing the world that the beast is some kind of god, that they will worship him. Worship means to bow down to, to give adulation, love and affection, to commit yourself to someone or something. Men have always been susceptible to worshipping something that they can see, rather than the true God who is immortal, invisible and the only wise God. So Satan gives sinful man that which accommodates his idolatrous desires, and God allows him to do it.

This false prophet is able to perform great signs, in order to deceive the world. Show us your God, prove what you say is true, is the taunt that Christians have often been faced with from a hostile world. Well, God has nothing to prove, and He does not perform miracles on demand from sinful men, He is God after all said and done. He will do what He wants to do and when He wants to do it. But to a world of sinful men and women the false prophet will be doing just what they want to see. Seeing is believing people say, and this false prophet will give the world all the proof they need to believe in the antichrist as God. Having said all that, God of course will not have left himself without a witness at this time and the two witnesses, discussed in chapter fifteen, will manifest the power of God in many miraculous signs, which will result in judgment on the antichrist. But although the world generally will hate the two witnesses for the plagues that are inflicted by them, they will be so taken up with the antichrist, that they will not believe God's witnesses. The same situation has always existed in the world. People did not necessarily believe on Jesus when they saw His miracles, they did not believe because they wanted to continue in sin, and their spiritual eyes had been closed, that seeing they might not see and hearing they might not hear. For Jesus also said, that he that has ears to hear let him hear, but the majority do not hear, for broad is the way that leads to destruction and there are many that walk that broad way, but narrow is the way that leads to life and there are few that find it. This is also the time of the trumpet judgments, when men either have the seal of God, or the mark of the beast. So God himself is also showing his power and authority as He unleashes demonic powers against His enemies, although they do not recognize what is happening.

This false prophet tells the world that they should make an image of the beast, and that all those who will not worship the image would lose their lives. This kind of thing is not without precedent. The book of Daniel tells of the image that King Nebuchadnezzar set up in the plain of Dura. It was probably and image of himself, and when the people heard the sound of all different kinds of music, they were to fall down and worship the image. Three God fearing Jews refused to worship the image, and were cast into a furnace, but God delivered them and changed the King's mind about who was God. Even in our day people still worship images of men and animals, something which of course is strictly forbidden by God. He is granted power by Satan, to cause the image to have breath and to speak. We have heard in recent times of the image of a Hindu elephant god supposedly drinking milk, and the number of the images of Mary that have supposed to have shed tears, or some such thing, are legion. It was even reported some time ago that there was some excitement in the Muslim community in Britain, over a tomato that when it was cut in half, had the name of Allah in it. All these things cause a stir from time to time among various religious groups, but will pale into insignificance compared with the show that Satan will put on for the world with this talking image of the beast. In Nebuchadnezzar's day Shadrach, Meshach and Abednego, the God fearing three who refused to obey the king's command were delivered from the fire, but in the days of the antichrist many will be killed because they refuse to bow down. This does not mean that God does not care about His children, but that His plan at that time will be that the antichrist will to all appearances, be going from victory to victory over the saints of God.

It is the false prophet that introduces what has become known as the mark of the beast. God has already sealed His own, and the seal of the saints is what it always has been, it is the seal of the Holy Spirit. This is not a visible mark in their flesh, but is the seal by which God recognizes His own. For to every one who He receives He gives His Holy Spirit. Every one who is led by the Spirit is a son of God, and they will refuse the mark of the beast. The consequence of refusing the mark of the beast will be that the saints will not be able to buy or sell. This will be a severe economic sanction against the children of God, but for those who are not killed, God will be able to provide for His children. Jesus once said to His disciples, don't worry about what you shall eat or drink or what you are going to wear, God feeds the sparrows so He is well able to look after you. In the days of famine in Israel, during the time of Elijah, God used the ravens to feed Elijah for God has all of His creation at His disposal to look after His children. People will either have the mark of the name of the beast or the number of his name. This mark will either be on their right hand or their forehead. There has been much conjecture about this mark of the beast, and it is a favorite topic among writers and prophetic groups. It may or may not have to do with any of today's technology, it could conceivably be a technology that is yet to come, that enables the beast to control the world economic system. For he causes all, small and great, rich and poor, high and low to receive this mark. The implications of this much power are enormous. It will not be just the housewife buying the groceries and the motorist buying petrol, but the factory owner buying his raw materials and merchant buying the things he sells. It will also be the international conglomerates that deal in billions of pounds every quarter, oil companies, computer giants, those who trade in world commodities; all will come under the control of the antichrist. His number is 666 and it is the number of a man. "Here is wisdom, John writes; let him who has understanding calculate the number of the beast."(Revelation Ch.13v18) There is no point, as some have done, in speculating who the beast may be. There are no doubt many names that can be calculated in various ways, to total 666. The most important thing to note is that it is the number of a man and as such he is no match for God. When he emerges from the sea of the billions of people in the world, at a time when the catastrophes of the trumpet judgments are hitting the earth, he will be recognized along with the false prophet.

A valid question is, what are the circumstances that will facilitate his coming, and what will be the context of his emergence onto the world scene? It will be Satan that will be the prime mover behind this man, as he gives him his power and authority. But the timing will also be right, and the world will be ready to accept this man who will be a ruthless dictator. Some have conjectured in books and films, that the coming of Jesus for the church and the sudden, mysterious, silent disappearance of millions of people will be the catalyst for the appearance of the antichrist. However this could not be the case for a number of reasons. Firstly, the Bible knows nothing of a sudden, mysterious and silent disappearance of millions of people. The coming of Jesus for the church will be a glorious, earth shattering event which will be accompanied by shouts and the sound of a trumpet and millions of people rising in glorified bodies to meet the Lord in the air. The whole of the rest of the world would have to be in a state of total and complete unconsciousness to miss such an event. Secondly there has been nothing in the book of Revelation, so far, that speaks of the coming of Jesus for the church, so it is reasonable to believe that it still has not happened.

The context in which, I believe, the antichrist comes to power is the trumpet judgments. In chapter thirteen of this book, these judgments are dealt with in detail, but suffice it to say that what happens to the earth and the catastrophes that occur, will stretch all governments and their agencies to the limit. But along comes this diplomatic genius, this loud mouth politician with his thoroughly convincing prophet at his side, and the world thinks that it has its savior. In view of all the emergences that arise, he unites the world so that Muslim, Roman Catholic and Hindu and all the rest of the world's religions, plus the left and the right and centre of politics all come together, prepared to follow this man who speaks great things and does great things.

Only the true church of God, who are in Christ Jesus, will not follow this man and his prophet, because they already have a savior and they are looking for His appearing. True believers will heed the words of Jesus to His disciples in Matthew Ch. 24v21-27 when he said, "For then there will be great tribulation, such as has not been since the beginning of the world until this time, no, nor ever shall be. And unless those days were shortened, no flesh would be saved; but for the elect's sake those days will be shortened. Then if anyone says to you, "Look here is the Christ!" or "There!" do not believe it. For false christs and false prophets will rise and show great signs and wonders to deceive, if possible even the elect. SEE, I HAVE TOLD YOU BEFOREHAND. Therefore if they say to you, "Look He is in the desert!" DO NOT GO OUT; or "Look, He is in the inner rooms!" DO NOT BELIEVE IT. For as the lightning comes from the east and flashes to the west, so also will the coming of the Son of Man be" These words of Jesus are so succinct and pertinent to the situation of the church at all times, but it will be especially so for the saints alive on the earth during the reign of the antichrist.

CHAPTER 19

THE SEALED SING WHILE ANGELS PREACH AND REAP

John is again looking at a scene in heaven and what he sees is the Lamb standing on what he describes as Mount Zion. The context of this Mount Zion is not the one on earth because the ones who are singing with the Lamb are before the throne of God. With the lamb are one hundred and forty four thousand, who have the Lamb's Fathers name on their foreheads. This is obviously the name of God the Father and they have His name because they belong to Him. This brings to mind the words of Jesus when He prayed before going to the cross as the Lamb of God, They are recorded in John Ch. 17v10, "And all Mine are Yours, and all Yours are Mine, and I am glorified in them." Although this group of saints are not clearly identified with the twelve thousand from each of the twelve tribes of Israel, the whole house of Israel that are saved during the reign of the antichrist, it is reasonable to believe that they are.

They are now seen in heaven because the antichrist beast has done all he can do against them. He has waged his war and only succeeded in transporting those saints into the presence of Jesus the Lamb. Jesus once said to His disciples, "And do not fear those who kill the body but cannot kill the soul. But rather fear Him who is able to destroy both soul and body in hell."(Matthew Ch.10v28) It is the antichrist and those who are his followers that now have everything to fear, as their only prospect is the lake of fire forever.

John hears a voice from heaven like the sound of many waters and like the sound of loud thunder. He hears a similar sound again in Revelation Ch.19v6, and it comes from a great multitude in heaven who are saying, "Alleluia! For the Lord God Omnipotent reigns!" At this time also the multitude of the saints must be celebrating something wonderful. John also hears the sound of harpists playing their harps. What an amazing combination of sound, the roar of the sound of many waters and the sound of thunder and somehow in all this cacophony of sound John still hears the sound of harps being played. All this sound was accompanied by singing, the singing of the one hundred and forty four thousand. All this must have been tremendously exhilarating for John, who is on the island of Patmos for the sake of his testimony. He has not been able to fellowship with other Christians for some while, not been able to join in praising God with others, and he will never have witnessed such scenes on earth. These saints, who have endured the persecution of the antichrist years, and have arrived safely in heaven, are privileged to be singing a new song before the throne of God. The four living creatures and the elders are also enjoying this musical feast. This new song is exclusive to this privileged group, for no one else was able to learn it. They have been redeemed from the earth and have gone through great suffering and their song is probably a song that gives expression to their unique experience. It will no doubt be a song of praise to God and the Lamb for their great deliverance from the power of Satan and the mark of the beast and the eternal burnings of the lake of fire. There can be no doubt that the sufferings of the saints in the days of the antichrist will be in excess of anything ever suffered by those who have given their lives in previous times. This is why in a number of scriptures in Revelation the saints of this period are given special prominence, although it is clear that all who have suffered and overcome will be rewarded.

This group before the throne are those who have not been defiled with women, for they are virgins. This may sound at first rather curious, for there is nothing in scripture to indicate that sexual relations with a woman, within the holy covenant of marriage, is anything but pure and holy and undefiled. Not everything in this book is to be interpreted literally and here is a case in point. What this means is that these people have kept themselves holy to the Lord. In the Old Testament infidelity and fornication is a type of being unfaithful to God, especially in regard to the worship of other gods. These saints are undefiled because they have remained faithful to the Lord. They are virgins because they have kept themselves pure since the time they received Jesus as their Lord and savior. Under the power and influence of the antichrist and false prophet, there will be those who will claim to be the church, but will be wolves in sheep's clothing, and worshipers of the antichrist. Having an outward pretence of piety, but in reality full of sin and vile practices. These men, who are faithful to the Lord and follow Him, will in comparison be pure and holy virgins, not having defiled themselves with the prevalent evil of their day. Paul had this desire for the Corinthian Christians when he wrote to them in his second epistle Ch.11v2. He said, "For I have betrothed you to one husband, that I may present you as a chaste virgin to Christ." These redeemed from the earth are the very best example to all the saints for their faithfulness to the Lord. The words, "Well done, good and faithful servant," (Matthew Ch.25v21) are the words that every child of God should want to hear from the Lord when they reach their heavenly destination.

These are the ones who follow the Lamb wherever He goes. This is another expression of the faithfulness of this group. They are true disciples of the Lamb. Jesus called the apostles to be with Him and to follow Him wherever he went during His earthly ministry. Again they are a perfect example for all Christians for we are all called to follow Jesus wherever he may lead us. In the case of this one hundred and forty four thousand they have followed the Lord in martyrdom and laid down their lives as Jesus did. They are described as first fruits to God and to the Lamb. They are first fruits, not because they are the first of the harvest of saints to reach the heavenly shores, but because of their fidelity and first class quality of relationship with the Lamb. They have loved the Lord with all their hearts, soul and mind; they are the very best of the harvest of the earth. The first fruits of the harvests of the children of Israel were to be presented to the Lord, and were to be of the very best quality, for nothing second class was to be given to the Lord. The Lord has redeemed for Himself a group, out of the fires of persecution, saints of the very best quality. They are exemplary and we should all aspire to be as they will be, because James says that "Of His own will He brought us forth by the word of truth, that we might be a kind of first fruits of His creatures." (James Ch.1v18) It has often been the case that saints of rare quality have come out of times of great tribulation, and it is certainly true in this case. In their mouth was found no deceit, for they are without fault before the throne of God. Can this be possible, that such a standard of holiness can be achieved, I believe so? This is not meant to contradict other scriptures that make it clear that men can never reach a state of sinless perfection, as God is sinless and perfect. But by walking in the Spirit and not fulfilling the lusts of the flesh and the mind, there is no limit to the sanctifying power of the Holy Spirit in our lives. Paul wrote that all that he was he was by the grace of God, and he said the grace of God worked in him mightily. He also said that he had not attained to perfection, but one thing he did, and that was to forget the things of the past, and press on to that which lay ahead, which was the prize of the high calling in Jesus Christ. The writer to the Hebrews said words to the effect, that by looking to Jesus and laying aside the sins that easily beset us we should run the race that is set before us. If we do these things we can, by the grace of God, follow the example of these holy saints of God. There is of course a sense in which all of the saints shall stand before the throne of God without fault, because the saints are clothed in the righteousness of Christ. Jude v20-25 says, "But you beloved, building yourselves up on your most holy faith, praying in the Holy Spirit, keep yourselves in the love of God, looking for the mercy of our Lord Jesus Christ unto eternal life. And on some having compassion, making a distinction; but others save with fear, pulling them out of the fire, hating even the garment defiled by the flesh. Now to Him who is able to keep you from stumbling, and to present you faultless before the presence of

His glory with exceeding joy, to God our Savior, who alone is wise, be glory and majesty, dominion and power, both now and forever. Amen." The saints are beset with sin and imperfection, but God is still able to keep us and present us to himself a spotless bride. But that is no reason for any Christian not to strive to attain to the very highest standard of holiness that is achieved by the one hundred and forty four thousand the redeemed of Israel from the last of the last days.

Verse 6 of chapter fourteen indicates that the interlude, which explains in detail some of the important events that are occurring during the time of the trumpet judgments, is coming to a close. I say this because John starts the verse by saying, then I saw another angel. It is a while since he has observed the activity of angels, and when the angels are active events are on the move. God has made every effort to reach out to men and women in these last of the last days. Although He is pouring out His judgments, and He is righteous in doing so, He has not forgotten mercy. Even harsh judgments can be a mercy, if men will turn from their sin, because they realize they are only getting what they deserve. God has sent His two witnesses to prophesy to Israel and they have turned to God, and whosoever calls on the name of the Lord will be saved. What an impact for good the saved of Israel will have on the world, only that time will tell. Paul writing to the Romans said, "For if their being cast away is the reconciling of the world, what will their acceptance be but life from the dead?"(Romans Ch.11v15) Spiritual revival in Israel will breathe new life into the church and the world, despite the terrible conditions of the time. But further to all this manifestation of the mercy and grace of God, comes angelic preachers. An angel flying in the midst of heaven, having the everlasting gospel to preach to all the nations of the earth, every tongue, tribe and people. What a manifestation of the grace of God this will be. Never before has God gone to such great lengths to make his gospel known. We live in a day of tremendous advances in technology, when the gospel can be broadcast around the world by radio and television, through satellites in space. More and more people are being reached by these means, but not every one will be reached. Many around the world are too poor to have radios and televisions and just about manage to stay alive from day to day. How will they be reached? Jesus said in Matthew Ch.24v14, "And this gospel of the kingdom will be preached to all the world as a witness to all the nations, and then the end will come." This task will be completed by this angel and before the end comes the entire world will have heard the everlasting gospel.

This angel will not need a pulpit but will preach from the sky, and I believe every one will hear his voice. He will speak to the world, in every language and dialect and his booming voice will speak out God's message. The false prophet, who incites men and women to practice idolatry and worship the beast, will not have things all his own way. There will be a battle for the hearts and minds of every one around the world. On the one hand the beast will intimidate and deceive and on the other hand God will be displaying His power through the two witnesses and the angelic preachers. The beast will use all the worldly power available to him to dictate to everyone what they should do, and God will use the supernatural power available to Him, to clearly show the world who is God. Those without the mark of the beast will not be able to buy or sell, but those with the mark of the beast are heading for the lake of fire. Who will the world believe, and whose message will get through to the nations, will fear of the antichrist or faith in God prevail?

The message of the angel is, "Fear God and give glory to Him, for the hour of His judgment has come; and worship Him who made heaven and earth, the sea and the springs of water."(Revelation Ch.14v7) "Fear God," the angel cries, this is a direct challenge to the satanic pretender to earth's throne and has always been the fundamental message of the gospel. Who will you serve has always been the most basic of all the questions every man and woman is faced with in their lives? Jesus said, "No one can serve two masters; for either he will hate the one and love the other, or else he will be loyal to the one and despise the other. You cannot serve God and mammon."(Matthew Ch.6v24) This is one issue in life that every man and woman cannot be neutral in, everyone must choose, and at this most critical time in earth's history the choice could not be starker. It will not be a choice as to which religion you follow, or which political party you vote for, but who will you serve, God or the antichrist. For those who fear God will have respect for His word and tremble at His word. This is one of the major failings of mankind that he does not fear God, but is pompous and proud and full of himself and despises the things of God. The message of the eternal gospel calls on men and women to turn from these things and acknowledge God to be God. So that if God has said, and He has, that to be saved we must repent of sin and believe on His Son Jesus Christ, then that is what we must do. To fear God is to accept that what God says is sin, is sin and that is the end of the matter. To fear God is to live in obedience to His commands, and the first and greatest command is to love the Lord God with all your heart, soul and strength and to love your neighbor as yourself.

"Give glory to Him," the angel goes on to say. Men have glorified the sun, moon and stars of heaven, and not given glory to the one who made them. Today men glorify their own intellect and achievements, in the arts and science, technology and the construction of amazing buildings and machines, but do not give glory to the God who has so endowed them with such wonderful capabilities. We have been to the moon, we have shrunk the world through the ability to fly, we will make bigger and better and smaller more intricate things, we will be gods men say, but they do not give glory to God. We will eventually live forever, through the endless opportunities of stem cell therapy they say, or we will deep freeze ourselves so that when cures have been found for our diseases we can be revived and brought back to health. We will in the end be able to transplant any diseased organ of the body, or grow any organ of the body with stem cells. Having mapped the entire human genome we will be able eventually to find a cure to all genetic disorders, one day cancer will be beaten, Parkinson's disease will be cured, and so on. All these things are laudable, but where is the reliance on God that some of the pioneers of medicine had, and when cures are found do men give glory to God? Some men glorify terrorists and murderers, the purveyors of lies and deceit. Others glorify pop idols and entertainers, actors and prominent personalities, but do not give glory to the God who gives them their breath. In the context of this scripture, men will glorify the antichrist and worship him, saying, "Who is like this man, who can possibly overcome him?"

As well as the exhortation to repentance, which has always been in the eternal gospel, there is a strong note of warning. The warning is, "For the hour of His judgment has come." Time is fast running out for the peoples of the world. The Day of the Lord is fast approaching, when the last window of opportunity to repent and be saved, will have come and gone. God is gracious to the people of the world and gives them due warning of what is coming if they do not turn away from their sins. There will be no escape from the final judgments of God. They will be swift and decisive and bring about total destruction.

There is also a call to worship Him who made heaven and earth and the sea and springs of water. Worship is the most fundamental act of every human soul. Every one worships something or someone, because man has been created to worship. What a man worships is what he sets his heart on, and gives his affections to. It is a fact that the natural inclination of people from all around the world, is to worship anything but God. We have already looked at the multitude of things that men glorify, and the story is the same for the things man worships. The angelic preacher, sent from God, is making the final call for men to turn and bow down to, and set his heart on the God who either directly or indirectly has created all the things that he has ever worshipped. So the issue is the same as that which Paul addressed in his epistle to the Romans in chapter one. Should we worship the creature and the things that have been created, or worship the creator? The arguments over whether or not God exists and created everything, or whether all things exist by chance and random selection, will not be played out in the same context in these days as they are today. With the intervention of the trumpet judgments and the two witnesses and the angelic preacher, it will not be a case of where is the evidence for the existence of God, but more a case of here is the evidence but despite the evidence men will choose to worship Satan as they worship the antichrist.

Another angel follows the first one not with the message of the gospel, but with the message that Babylon is fallen. This is the first mention of Babylon in Revelation, and is the name given by God to the world empire of the antichrist. Babylon, originally, was the name of the capital of the Chaldean empire under king Nebuchadnezzar, but its roots go back to the tower of Babel written about in the book of Genesis. Pride was the thing that characterized both Babel and Babylon, and is certainly the overriding hallmark of the empire of the antichrist. After the universal flood, from which only Noah and his family emerged after being saved in the ark, God told them to be fruitful and multiply and fill the earth, but the founders of Babel decided that they were not going to fill the earth but build a city instead. They made bricks and built themselves a city and a tower, the top of which was in the heavens. They intended to make a name for themselves. It was because of the actions of these people that God confused their language and scattered them as had been His original purpose in order to populate the world. Much later Babylon was the world power that God used to discipline His people because of their sin, when Nebuchadnezzar came against Judah and ransacked Jerusalem. However God punished Nebuchadnezzar for his pride in thinking that he had acquired much wealth and power and prestige by his own power and resources. He was afflicted with a terrible disease that caused him to become like a wild beast and live in the fields and eat grass like cattle. This lasted for seven years until he came to realize that it was God that ruled in the kingdom of men and gives power to the one that He chooses. When he acknowledged God as the supreme ruler over the affairs of men he was restored to his throne. Nebuchadnezzar's son Belshazzar was also full of pride and God humbled him by giving his kingdom to the Medes and Persians. The kingdom of Babylon of the end times, will be even more overweening with pride, and will be in character just like its head the antichrist. The antichrist will of course be just like the one who empowers him, who is Satan, who fell because of pride from being the highest archangel, to being the arch enemy of God. The angel says that Babylon is fallen, "because she made all the nations drink of the wine of the wrath of her fornication."(Revelation Ch.14v8) The NIV says, "which made all the nations drink the maddening wine of her adulteries." The picture is that this end time Babylon will have intoxicated the whole of the world, and made the people of the world inflamed with a passion for evil things, just as strong as fierce anger. Those that have forsaken God will desire evil things just as an alcoholic craves for drink. Their lives will be full of evil passions, and evil practices that are characterized by lying, deceit, unfaithfulness, all kinds of lusts and evil desires and murder, and all the things that are commonly associated with sexual immorality. The fall of the kingdom of the beast is given in greater detail in Revelation Ch.17 which we will come to soon, although the fall has not actually happened when the angel delivers this message. As with other instances in Revelation, events are declared by God's messengers as if they have already happened, because nothing can stop them from happening.

Then a third angel followed and his message to the world is chilling in the extreme. He cries out, "If anyone worships the beast and his image, and receives his mark on his forehead or on his hand, he himself shall also drink of the wine of the wrath of God, which is poured out full strength into the cup of His indignation. He shall be tormented with fire and brimstone in the presence of the holy angels and in the presence of the Lamb. And the smoke of their torment ascends forever and ever; and they have no rest day or night, who worship the beast and his image, and whoever receives the mark of his name."(Revelation Ch.14v9-11) The same applies to this message as the one above. The doom of those who have committed themselves to the beast is here predicted, but not yet carried out. There is no hope at all for those who belong to the antichrist, who have drunk of his wine. Now they will also drink in full forever of the wine of God's wrath. It is very possible that many who read this book will be alive during this time, and the best way to escape from this awful eternal doom, is to turn to God NOW, if you have not already, and seek Him while he may be found and call on Him while he is near. Receive Jesus Christ as your savior from the eternal fires. Jesus the Lamb will not be absent from this lake of fire, but John tells us that those consigned to this awful fate will suffer forever in the presence of the one who they rejected as their savior. That will be like drowning forever within sight of a lifebelt, or like being in a burning house forever while seeing a fire engine outside the house. Only a fool will disregard the wrath of the Lamb, for those who reject His love, WILL face His wrath. The beast and Babylon are the end time manifestation of all that Satan has ever been all rolled into one high concentration of evil, but all those who have rejected Jesus in the past and now, will suffer the same awful fate which in the book of Revelation is also called the second death.

Again John writes, "Here is the patience of the saints."(Revelation Ch.14v12) John used this phrase once before when he talked about those who lead into captivity will go into captivity, and those who kill with the sword will be killed in the same way. God will take vengeance on behalf of His people, and the fall of Babylon and judgment on the wicked will come partly because of their treatment of the saints who will be killed. "Here are those who keep the commandments of God and the faith of Jesus." (Revelation Ch.14v12) The church will not be bowed or defeated, but will be faithful to God and to Jesus. Yes there is coming a time when the church will be a faithful church, and keep the commandments of God. The rise of the antichrist will sort out the wheat from the chaff in the church, and only those with the true faith of Jesus will remain in the church, the rest will be blown away by the strong winds of persecution.

A voice from heaven tells John to write, "Blessed are the dead who die in the Lord from now on." "Yes," says the Spirit, "that they may rest from their labours, and their works follow them."(Revelation Ch.14v13) The Holy Spirit is saying that those who die in the Lord will have left the toils and heat of the day behind them forever, and will enjoy the eternal rest that being with the Lord affords. This is true for all who have died in the Lord, but especially true for the saints who have faced the heat of the reign of the antichrist. What follows is in stark contrast, for John sees the reaping of two harvests. The imagery used for the first harvest is that of a field containing a dried, over ripe crop, which is harvested by one seated on a white cloud. It is not only necessary to the understanding of this vision, to note the condition of the crop being harvested, but also to seek to identify the one seated on the cloud. The older translations of the Bible such as the King James Authorized Version, and those that adhere to that translation; say it is One like the Son of Man. In that case there would be little doubt that the person in view is Jesus Christ. In favor of this translation is the fact that He is seen with a golden crown on His head. In later versions, such as the New International Version, the rendering is, one like a son of man, and this could reasonably be understood to be an angel. If it is Jesus then this could be a picture of Jesus reaping the harvest of the church, what has become commonly known as the rapture. Other scriptures indicate that the rapture would take place at around this juncture. However if it is an angel it would not be the rapture that is being depicted.

I personally favor the view that it is an angel, and is a son of man sitting on the cloud. The harvest of the church at the rapture could hardly be described as an over ripe, shriveled, dried up harvest. It would also be out of keeping with the order of things for an angel to be giving a command to Jesus the Lamb, who is in the midst of the throne. The harvest being reaped fits the condition of the enemies of God, that have faced the fierceness of His wrath. The once proud empire of the beast and false prophet, have been reduced to something like a dried up crop of wheat that is now only good for burning. This is one picture, I believe, of the end of the age reaping of what Jesus once described as the tares that have grown up in His field of the earth, which an enemy had sown. The other harvest is of grapes that are gathered and thrown into the winepress of the wrath of God. The first picture is of the state of God's enemies when He has finished with them, and the other is a picture of what He will actually do to them. An angel comes out of the temple in heaven, from the presence of God with a sharp sickle. Another angel comes out from the altar, who had power over fire. At the beginning of Revelation Ch.8 there is an angel who has a censer, and he offers incense to God with the prayers of the saints before filling the censer with fire and hurling it to the earth. It would appear that this same angel, who had power over the fire, cried out to the angel with the sickle to reap the clusters of the vine of the earth, for the grapes are now fully ripe. The angel obeyed and the grapes were gathered and they were trodden in the great winepress of God's wrath. If ever Gods enemies were under His feet it is now. These two harvests, like the prediction that Babylon is fallen, are yet to be reaped but the time is at hand. The only events to come, before the great day of God's vengeance, are the outpouring of the seven last plagues.

CHAPTER 20

PRELUDE TO THE END

It seems quite a while now since the seventh angel sounded his trumpet and the kingdoms of this world became the kingdoms of our Lord and of His Christ. This was the second time in Revelation that the time of the end had come. But then John's attention is drawn to some significant events that occur before the time of the end, so that they could be seen in detail. There was the woman clothed with the sun, with the moon at her feet and twelve stars around her head. The woman was persecuted by the fiery red dragon, Satan. Then John sees the two beasts, one rising out of the sea, the other coming out of the earth, these are the antichrist and the false prophet. After this came the vision of the one hundred and forty four thousand, now with Jesus in heaven before the throne of God, and then the angelic preachers and reapers. These things have been setting the scene in this epic drama for the final act, the outpouring of the seven last plagues, or as some versions of the Bible put it, the vials of the wrath of God.

However in Revelation Ch.15, before the plagues are poured out on the earth, John sees in heaven the sea of glass that he saw when the vision of the throne of God first came into view. When John first saw it, the sea of glass was clear as crystal, now it is reddish in color because it is mixed with fire. Standing on the sea of glass John again sees those one hundred and forty four thousand, who had the victory over the beast each one having a harp and they are singing the song of Moses and the Lamb. The song of Moses takes us back to the Old Testament, when the children of Israel were delivered from the Egyptians after crossing the red sea on dry land. It is recorded in Exodus Ch.15 and it is full of relevance to the context of Revelation Ch15. The victory that the Lord brought about for Israel coincides very much with the victory that He has brought about for the end time saints over the beast. It is a song about how the Lord has triumphed gloriously, that the Lord is a man of war. "Your right hand, O Lord, has become glorious in power; Your right hand, O Lord, has dashed the enemy in pieces. And in the greatness of Your excellence You have overthrown those who rose against You; You sent forth your wrath it consumed them like stubble."(Exodus Ch.15v6&7) In v13 the song says, "You in Your mercy have led forth the people whom You have redeemed; You have guided them in your strength to Your holy habitation." Finally v17 says, "You will bring them in and plant them in the mountain of your inheritance, in the place, O Lord, which You have made for Your own dwelling, the sanctuary, O Lord, which Your hands have established." Verse 18 is very pertinent to the whole context of Revelation when it says, "The Lord shall reign forever and ever."

This song of Moses has become the song of the Lamb also, because of all that He has done to bring deliverance to His people. By the grace of God they have, in these last days, escaped from the deception and fear of the beast that has gripped the rest of the world. They overcame him and did not receive his mark, or worship him. The Lamb has guided His people to His holy habitation, and now they stand before the throne of God and the Lamb, singing a similar song. It is a song extolling the marvelous works of God that are done in justice and truth. God is King of the saints and is to be feared for He alone is holy. They predict that all nations will come and worship before God, because of the manifestations of His judgments. The judgments that the earth is about to face are just and right, in view of how the saints, and the angels who preached, and how God himself has been rejected and hated and despised.

Because we are very near the return of Jesus to the earth in His second coming there is at this juncture, the need to deal with the whole question of what is commonly known as the rapture of the church. Some people may be surprised that it has not already been mentioned or discussed, but the reason for that is simply that in the book of Revelation, it is not an event that is featured. Nearly all evangelical Christians agree that the Lord will descend from heaven with a shout and with the voice of the archangel as Paul describes, and that it will occur before He comes to reign as King of Kings. But the purpose of the Revelation of Jesus Christ, is to reveal Him as King of Kings, and reveal His coming in glory with His saints. This is the message of this book from the beginning as can be seen from Ch.1v5. John is writing to the seven churches and greets them with grace from God the Father and the Holy Spirit, and when he extends the greeting from Jesus Christ to the churches he says, "and from Jesus Christ, the faithful witness, the firstborn from the dead, and the RULER OVER THE KINGS OF THE EARTH. To Him who loved us and washed us from our sins in His own blood, and has made US KINGS AND PRIESTS to His God and Father, TO HIM BE GLORY AND DOMINION FOREVER AND EVER. AMEN." No guesses as to where the emphasis lies there, it is the kingship of Jesus. So three times in the Revelation the second coming to the earth and the kingdoms of the world becoming His is recorded, at the end of Ch.6, Ch.11, and also Ch.16. The second to last verse in the whole book say, "Surely I am coming quickly" Amen. Even so, come Lord Jesus!" There are many similarities to the book of Daniel, where the theme is that the Lord rules in the kingdoms of men, and in the end will establish a universal kingdom that shall never be destroyed. Revelation is all about revealing to the seven churches and the church throughout the centuries since, that Jesus is the coming King.

Because Revelation is about the conflict between the kingdom of God and the kingdoms of this world, and Satan working behind them, it is consequently also about the involvement of the saints in this struggle. They are of course on God's side and hated by the world and Satan, therefore there is an emphasis on pictures of the saints being persecuted, and then rewarded in heaven. It may seem as if the ordinary Christian who goes through life without any particular tribulation or persecution, is not in view in this book. To a large extent this is true, but in every generation somewhere in the world Christians have been persecuted and killed for their faith, and have needed to draw comfort and strength from these scriptures. But what is very relevant to all the church of all the ages, is that Jesus is coming again to reign.

So when does Jesus come and take His church away in the event we call the rapture. As I said in the introduction to this book, I am not going to get involved in arguments about when this takes place, but I can present scriptures from other books in the Bible which give us some information on this subject. Starting in Paul's second letter to the Thessalonians Ch.2 it is clear that the antichrist will be holding sway before the Lord descends from heaven for His own. From the beginning of the chapter Paul writes, "Now brethren, concerning the coming of our Lord Jesus Christ and our gathering together to Him, we ask you, not to be soon shaken in mind or troubled, either by spirit or by word or by letter, as if from us, as though the day of Christ had come." It is very clear that what Paul is talking about is the coming of the Lord Jesus for His church, and he is reassuring the church that the day of His coming is still in the future and that they have not been left behind. This has been a fear for some believers, that Jesus has come in some kind of secret way, and they have been left. Paul says, "Let no one deceive you by any means; for that Day (the day of our gathering together unto Him) WILL NOT COME unless the falling away comes first, and the man of sin is revealed, the son of perdition, who opposes and exalts himself above all that is called God or that is worshiped, so that he sits as God in the temple of God, showing himself that he is God."(2Thessalonians Ch.2v3&4) The man of sin is clearly a reference to the antichrist, or beast, of Revelation, and Paul clearly says that we should not be deceived into thinking that our gathering together to Christ will happen until He is revealed. God is restraining the lawless one until it is His time for him to be revealed, although from the scripture that Paul wrote it is not at all clear who is the restraining agent on the earth.

In Paul's first letter to the Thessalonians in Ch.4v13-18, he talks about the resurrection of those who have died in Christ and of those who are alive and remain until the coming of the Lord. For when the time comes for our gathering together to Him, the dead in Christ will be raised to life, and all those who belong to Him will be changed and have immortal bodies, and rise to meet the Lord in the air, and be with Him forever. Paul wrote these things to the church as words of comfort, in times of mourning, when they had lost fellow believers who had died. In 1Thessalonians Ch.5 Paul writes that they are not ignorant of the times and seasons, and that the coming of the Lord will not catch them out as it will unbelievers. He then goes on to say that the day of the Lord will come to the kingdom of the antichrist, and those who have followed him, as when a thief comes to rob a house at night. The thief comes at night because he expects the occupants of the house to be asleep, so that he can carry out his operation without being seen or heard. But Paul says in v6-7, "Therefore let us not sleep, as others do, but let us watch and be sober. For those who sleep, sleep at night, and those who get drunk are drunk at night." The saints will be alert at the time of the rapture; they will be expecting the coming of Jesus to the air for His church, for they are children of the day. They will not be worshipping the beast and being intoxicated with his lies and deceit, they will be worshiping God and alert to the leading of the Holy Spirit. There is also the element of surprise, the thief will come when the owners of the house least expect him. "For when they say, "Peace and safety," Paul writes in v.3, then the Lord will return for His church in a very visible and glorious way, which will be followed by the total destruction of the world system of the beast and false prophet. But, Paul says in v.4, "but you, brethren, are not in darkness, so that this Day should overtake you as a thief." Also in v.8, "But let us who are of the day be sober, putting on the breastplate of faith and love, and as a helmet the hope of salvation." The next verse goes on to say that God has not appointed His children to suffer the fate of the antichrist and his followers, but to obtain salvation, the salvation that will be revealed when He comes to raise up those who have died and change those who are still alive, so that they can rise to meet him in the air.

Paul wrote to the Corinthian church about the raising of the saints in the last days when Jesus comes to the air, and His people will rise to meet Him. He explains that because of the sin of Adam death has come to all men, for in Adam all sinned. So in Ch.15v22-26 he writes, "For as in Adam all die, even so in Christ all shall be made alive. But each one in his own order: Christ the firstfruits, afterward those who are Christ's at his coming. Then comes the end, when He delivers the kingdom to God the Father, when He puts to an end all rule and all authority and power. For He must reign till He has put all enemies under His feet. The last enemy that will be destroyed is death." These verses make it clear that after Jesus comes for the church the next major event is the end when Jesus delivers the kingdom to the Father. Further to this in the same chapter Paul writes in v50-55, "Now this I say, brethren, that flesh and blood cannot inherit the kingdom of God; nor does corruption inherit incorruption. Behold, I tell you a mystery: We shall not all sleep, but we shall all be changed, in a moment, in the twinkling of an eye, at the last trumpet. For the trumpet will sound, and the dead will be raised incorruptible, and we shall be changed. For this corruptible must put on incorruption, and this mortal must put on immortality. So when this corruptible has put on incorruption, and this mortal has put on immortality, then shall be brought to pass the saying that is written: "Death is swallowed up in victory. O death where is your sting? O Hades where is your victory?" Paul has already stated that the last enemy that will be destroyed is death, and later as these last verses make clear, that victory comes about at the resurrection of the saints at the time of the rapture. This again places the rapture very near the end of time, before Jesus returns to reign.

In Romans Ch.8 from v18-23, Paul talks about the sufferings of this present time and says that the suffering is not worthy to be compared to the glory that will be revealed in us at the time when Jesus returns for His church. Then he explains that there is a strong expectation and longing on the part of the natural creation, the earth itself, for the time of the resurrection when the sons of God will be revealed.

Paul explains that at the time of the liberation of the sons of God, when they receive their immortal bodies, the creation itself will also be liberated from the bondage of corruption. There is going to be a new world. Paul speaks of the groaning in creation for this time, and also he says we ourselves groan in ourselves with a longing for the rapture, which Paul says is the redemption of our bodies. God is going to redeem not only His people from their corruptible bodies, but also creation from corruption too. The two events are closely linked and the new earth will follow closely on the tracks of the revealing of the sons of God. This again places the rapture near the end of time.

Peter echoes these truths in his second epistle Ch.3v10-18. A summery of what he wrote is that the day of the Lord will come as a thief in the night. Part of what will happen will be the passing away of the heavens and the earth which being on fire will be burned up. In the light of these things, Peter writes that we ought to be living holy lives of godly conduct. We should be looking for the day of God, and the new heavens and earth in which will dwell righteousness. To quote Peter from v14 he says, "Therefore, beloved, looking forward to these things, be diligent to be found by Him in peace, without spot and blameless:" There can be no doubt that Peter intends the people of God to be looking forward to these things and living their lives on earth in the light of them in holiness and the fear of God. In v17 he exhorts his readers, that since they now know these things they should always be steadfast and not be led away by the error of the wicked. But instead they should grow in grace and in the knowledge of the Lord and savior Jesus Christ. What a timely exhortation that is considering the fact that at least some of the church is going into these last days unprepared for what lies ahead.

We have heard from Paul and Peter; now let us hear from John. In 1John Ch. 2v18 he writes, "Little children it is the last hour; and as you have heard that the Antichrist is coming, even now many antichrists have come, by which we know that it is the last hour." Again in v20, "But you have an anointing from the Holy One, and you know all things." John like Paul warns the church of the coming of the antichrist, but says that those who belong to the Lord will not be deceived by the antichrist, because they have an anointing from God to discern between the truth of God and Satan's lies. This again would indicate that the church is on earth during the reign of the antichrist, and is in line with all the other scriptures, as we would expect it to be.

But the most important scriptures come from the lips of Jesus Himself. Matthew Ch.24 from beginning to end is full of vital information regarding the return of Jesus for His church and to the earth to reign. Jesus starts talking to the disciples about the destruction of the temple, which would take place in the year AD70 under Titus. The disciples quiz Jesus about when this would happen, but also ask Him about His coming and the end of the age. Some of the things that Jesus spoke about were fulfilled before and after AD70, and those who had eyes to see the signs of their times and who believed the words of Jesus, were able to escape the horrors of the Roman persecution of the Jews before they destroyed the temple and ransacked the city of Jerusalem. Jesus warned of wars and rumors of wars, of persecution and betrayal and false prophets and lawlessness. He warned of the abomination of desolation in the temple, the holy place, and He said when you see this flee to the mountains. When the Roman Cesar Gaius tried to set up a statue to himself in the temple in Jerusalem in AD38, Christians were alerted to the danger of the coming destruction. But many of the words of Jesus are to be fulfilled in the future.

As John the apostle warned, so did Jesus that many false prophets would come on the scene, and would deceive many. Jesus said that lawlessness would abound, and many would lose their love for Him. These are just the kind of conditions that will prevail in the last days, and then the arch deceiver the antichrist will come, who Paul describes as the lawless one. Jesus predicts the setting up, I believe, of some kind of idol to the antichrist in the holy place. Paul speaks of a similar thing in saying that he will set himself up in the temple of God, showing himself that he is God. Jesus said that these times will be times of unprecedented trouble, such as has not been since the beginning of the world, trouble the likes of which will never happen again. When all the troubles that are catalogued in the book of Revelation for this period are considered, it is no wonder that Jesus predicts great tribulation. He even goes as far as to say that if the days of trouble are not curtailed, then no flesh could survive. Jesus issues a further warning of false christs and lying wonders being performed by false prophets. He also warns us about those who claim to be Christ because of a supposed second coming. Jesus said that His coming will be as the lightning that flashes across the sky, visible, glorious, majestic, and with as much noise and fanfare as thunder that always accompanies lightning, not secret in some outlandish desert place or in a room somewhere hidden away.

To quote from Matthew Ch. 24v29-31 Jesus said, "Immediately after the tribulation of those days the sun will be darkened, and the moon will not give its light; the stars will fall from heaven, and the powers of the heavens will be shaken. Then the sign of the Son of Man will appear in heaven, and then all the tribes of the earth will mourn, and they will see the Son of Man coming on the clouds of heaven with power and great glory. And He will send His angels with a great sound of a trumpet, and they will gather together His elect from the four winds, from one end of heaven to the other." This is unmistakably the same event as Paul describes in 1Corinthians Ch15, when death is swallowed up in victory, when the trumpet sounds and the dead in Christ are raised.

In terms of what is revealed in Revelation, and considering all the above scriptures, I conclude that Jesus comes for His church and they rise to meet Him in the air, at the sounding of the last trumpet, the seventh trumpet of Revelation Ch 11v15. They rise to meet the Lord in the air and then the wrath of God is poured out on the earth in a very short period of time, bringing as we shall see total destruction. This renders the earth, and the kingdom of the beast described as Babylon the great city, unfit for further habitation, Satan and the beast and the false prophet are then destroyed and their armies, and are cast into the lake of fire along with all whose names are not written in the book of life. This is all described in detail from Revelation Ch.16 to the end of Ch.20.

The remainder of Revelation Ch15 from v5-8 is concerned with the preparations for the outpouring of the bowls of the wrath of God. Seven angels came out from the presence of God with the seven last plagues all dressed in white with gold bands round their chests. The plagues are added to seven golden bowls full of the wrath of God, that one of the four living creatures gives to the seven angels. The temple in heaven fills with smoke from the glory of God, and the whole temple area is barred to all who would enter, until the seven last plagues are poured out on the earth. The temple is a place of priestly service, of sacrifice and intercession, none of these things will now prevail for the earth, no prayer of intercession no sacrifice and no person can now intervene, the wrath of God will be poured out the day of grace is over. How far away is this fateful day? No one knows but it will come, and is your name written in the book of life? Will you be safe in the presence of Jesus or left on the earth to face the wrath of God? The words of Moses to the children of Israel of long ago are extremely pertinent, "Choose you this day who you will serve."

CHAPTER 21

THE SEVEN LAST PLAUGES

The seven seals have been opened, the seven trumpets blown, and now we have reached the point at which the seven last plagues are to be poured out. You will recall that the effect of the opening of the seals was to bring under the authority of the Lamb the major history shaping events from the time of His ascension to His second coming. The seven trumpet judgments are contained within the opening of the seventh seal, and coincide with the rise of the antichrist and it is reasonable to believe extend over a seven year period, before the second coming of Jesus to the earth. This book has covered these first two acts of the epic drama of the coming King, along with two interludes explaining things in detail that the angel wants John and us to see and hear. The third act is about to begin, and could cover a period of only a matter of weeks, as the bowls of the wrath of God containing the seven last plagues are loosed on the earth. They are certainly poured out in quick succession bringing about total destruction.

The first angel poured out his bowl and severe and malignant sores, which were foul and loathsome, came upon all those who had the mark of the beast and worshipped his image. Nothing on this scale has ever come upon men before, and no one left on the earth is excluded, for the beast had caused everyone both rich and poor high and low to receive the mark of his name. Only those who are now with the Lord in the heavens did not receive the mark or worship the image. Overnight this awful complaint has struck the whole of the earth's population. It might seem as if planet earth is under attack from aliens from outer space, as no one will think that this is an attack by one nation against another with some kind of deadly virus, because it will quickly become apparent that everyone is suffering. But by now I believe many people will know that this is the wrath of God, because they will have witnessed the resurrection of millions of those who died in Christ and seen others changed and rise to meet the Lord in the air. They will have heard the trumpet sound and the voice of the archangel and seen the sky all around the world light up with glory of the Lord. On top of the panic caused by the rapture of the church, imagine the consternation of people who make their way to their doctor or to the local hospital, covered with these malignant sores, only to find the doctors and consultants themselves in the same predicament. People everywhere will discover that there is no help available, and all of mankind on the earth is facing a horrible disease and an uncertain future. Even the beast himself, the man acclaimed as the savior of the world and who said that he was God, even he cannot help. The god that they worshipped is the cause of their downfall but worse, much much worse is to come, and will come very quickly.

Then the second angel poured his bowl out on the oceans of the world, and the world's oceans became blood and every thing that had been alive in the oceans died. The second trumpet judgment inflicted death and destruction on a third of the world's oceans, now the destruction is total. Men can no longer harvest the seas for food, those days are finished forever. However men may try to rationalize this event they will not be able to find any reasonable explanation for the oceans turning into blood. This churning mass of blood will dump thousands of tons of dead fish on the coasts of counties all around the world. The stench will be unbearable, but who will want to clear up this mess, when everyone is desperately trying to cope with painful malignant sores. Sea birds will go hungry, and only scavengers will benefit. This will be a great environmental disaster, but even worse is to come.

The third angel quickly followed by pouring out his bowl on the rivers and springs of water, and they also became blood. What can possibly be worse than this? Water is almost the most essential thing for the existence of man on this planet, nothing is more important, other than the air he breathes. The desalination of sea water is possible if no fresh water is available, but no water is available on earth, full stop. Springs and rivers, as well as reservoirs are the lifeblood of man's fresh water supply, and after this plague hits the planet the days of mankind's existence on earth are numbered. John hears the angel of the waters saying that the Lord is righteous in what He has done. He says that those who are on the earth have shed the blood of saints and prophets, and now they have only blood to drink, that is what they deserve. These are the days of the vengeance of our God. These are the days when mercy has to stand aside, just as vengeance has given way to mercy for so long. Another angel from the altar in heaven, possibly the one who cast the censer with fire from the altar to the earth before the trumpet judgments began, he also agreed with the angel of the waters. He said, "Even so, Lord God Almighty, true and righteous are Your judgments."(Revelation Ch.16v7) You may remember that these very people who are suffering used to say, "Who is like the beast, who is able to make war with him."(Revelation Ch.13v4) One can only wonder what they are saying now that God has declared total war, and with no terms of surrender, for surrender is not an option for the beast or the world, as they are facing eternal destruction.

The fourth angel poured out his bowl on the sun this time, and the angel was empowered to scorch men with fire. This indicates global warming on a scale never seen before; all around the world temperatures will soar to dangerous levels. Not only will men have to cope with terrible sores, but now scorching temperatures. Sun burn, sun stroke, unremitting thirst because of the total lack of water, men will be drinking blood as the only thing available to drink. The stench of rotting sea life will be multiplied when the sun begins to send out massive flames into space towards the earth. There will be no escape from the sun during the hours of daylight. John heard men blaspheming the name of God because of these plagues. They are now absolutely in no doubt at all who is inflicting such pain and misery on them. It will be impossible to find any atheists in these days because everyone will believe in the existence of God after what they have witnessed, and because of what they are suffering. But believing that God exists and turning to Him in repentance are poles apart. John tells us that the people on the earth did not repent or give God glory. Do you believe in the existence of God? That is a start, but only a start, for the devils believe and tremble. The day of salvation is now, if you have not believed on the Lord Jesus Christ and received Him as your Savior, if you have not repented and turned away from the practice of sinning, you may not face the wrath of God that John saw poured out on the earth, but you will end up in the same lake of fire that those alive on the earth then will.

The fifth angel then poured out his bowl of the wrath of God on the throne of the beast. "Who is able to fight against the beast," they said, well God is well able and the little Lamb in the midst of the throne. Just imagine this beast, with ten horns and seven heads that are crowned, being beaten by a little Lamb. But in fairness, the little Lamb is also the Lion of the tribe of Judah, and as such the beast is no match for Him. Also it has to be borne in mind that the power and authority that the beast has comes from the dragon, Satan, and he has already been defeated by the little Lamb, when the Lamb laid down His life, in order to take it up again. Through death He might destroy him who had the power of death, that is the devil. (Hebrews Ch.2v14) When this plague was inflicted on the throne of the beast, his kingdom became full of darkness, and because of the ongoing effect of the previous plagues, they gnawed their tongues because of the pain. Imagine if you can, being in such pain that you are constantly biting your own tongue. Darkness was a plague inflicted on the Egyptians before the children of Israel were released, and the Old Testament scripture speaks about it being a darkness that could be felt. God will inflict an absolute darkness on the centre of power of the beast, on his city Babylon. This will be a supernatural darkness, where every source of light will be extinguished. The beast may have thought himself invulnerable and untouchable by God's wrath, but he is mistaken. He himself will suffer like the rest of mankind who have followed and worshipped him. Sitting in total darkness, but strangely also in blistering heat, with thirst and now no doubt hunger taking its toll because of the inability to eat, not knowing how to cope with blisters and malignant sores, they continued in the same vein of blaspheming God because of their pain and did not repent of their evil deeds.

Then the sixth angel poured out his bowl on the great river Euphrates and the river was dried up to make way for the kings of the east. John then saw three unclean spirits that were like frogs coming out of the mouth of the dragon, the beast and the false prophet. They are, John tells us, spirits of demons who go out to the kings of the earth performing signs. We are not told what signs they perform, but I would suggest that they are empowered to reverse the effects of the judgments that have come upon the people of the earth. They go out to the kings of the earth in order to gather them to the battle of the great day of God Almighty. This would have the effect of enabling the armies of the world to gather strength and mobilize, and also give the illusion that the beast and the false prophet have the power to overcome God in battle, because they have alleviated the effects of the wrath of God. Deception is the name of the game, and God makes sure that the world will be deceived. Not that God is playing games, but as on other occasions, He uses the deceptive power of Satan to bring about His own purposes. It is the purpose of God to bring together the nations who have rejected Him and blasphemed His holy name, in order to defeat them once and for all and then consign them to the lake of fire. But Jesus is about to return and destroy the kingdom of the beast and his armies, and the three demons will bring the kings of the earth and their armies to the place called Armageddon, where the great conflict will take place. Jesus says, "Behold, I am coming as a thief. Blessed is he who watches, and keeps his garments, lest he walk naked and they see his shame."(Revelation Ch.16v15) Having seen the sign of the Son of Man in heaven, and all the elect gathered to Him, and having suffered so much at the hands of God, is it possible that men could again be deceived into thinking that they can fight against God and win? From what we read here it would definitely seem so. But Jesus will come upon them suddenly, and without warning, like a thief in the night and they will not escape.

The seventh angel poured out his bowl into the air and then John heard, coming from the throne in heaven a loud voice saying "It is done!" The work of redemption is accomplished and what began with the opening of the first seal centuries before is now done. Jesus has been in the midst of the throne in heaven at the Fathers right hand, and as Paul wrote, "For He must reign till He has put all enemies under His feet."(1Corinthians Ch.15v25) John again sees and hears very similar things to when the seventh trumpet was blown and he had a vision of the end. John hears noises and thunderings and lightnings and there was a great earthquake. The consequence of which was Babylon being divided into three parts and the cities of the nations fell. Imagine the earth's crust convulsing in such a way as to destroy the cities of the world. New York a massive heap of rubble as well as Chicago and San Francisco. London, Paris, Berlin, Rome, Cape Town, New Delhi, Shanghi, Manila, Sydney, and a host of other major cities all around the world destroyed in a matter of hours. It would seem that the epicenter of this truly earth shattering event will be Babylon, the city of the beast. God particularly remembers Babylon, to vent upon it the fierceness of His wrath. In the earthquake the islands of the earth are submerged in the sea, and the great mountain ranges disappear as the earth's crust is pulled and stretched. This is the birth pangs, or as some scriptures put it, the earth in labour pains, bringing to birth a new earth. Jesus in Matthew Ch.24v8 speaks of the beginning of sorrows; the word translated sorrows meaning labor pains, and includes in these sorrows earthquakes. In this final great earthquake a new earth is about to be born, that will almost be unrecognizable, compared to the old one. The earth is finally subjected to a tremendous volley of hailstones, each one weighing about a talent. Unrepentant to the end men continued to blaspheme the name of God, before they are finally consigned to the lake of fire, with Satan and the beast and false prophet.

The rest of the book of Revelation is taken up with a detailed look at the fall of Babylon, the second coming of Jesus to the earth, the final demise of Satan, the great white throne judgment and finally the new heavens and earth. This is consistent with the whole pattern of how John has received this revelation of the future. The opening of the seals and then a look in detail at some events, then the trumpet judgments and a closer look at various things that happen during that time. After that the pouring out of the bowls of wrath and the final interlude. Then in case we have forgotten, almost the last words of Jesus himself to John are, "I Jesus have sent my angel to testify to you these things in the churches. I am the root and the offspring of David, the Bright and Morning Star."

CHAPTER 22

MYSTERY, BABYLON THE GREAT

The three acts of the epic drama that is the book of Revelation have been played out and seen by John, not that it is a mere play, for it is the reality of the past, present and future for the earth. I have used the illustration of a play of three acts to help in seeing the structure of the book. John has had exclusive access to the preview, which he is told to write in a book to the seven churches of Asia. The beginning of Ch.17 marks the beginning of the third and final interlude, but it is an interlude between the end of time and eternity. The angel that Jesus sent to show John these things wants him to have a detailed look first of all at Mystery Babylon the Great, and it is one of the angels who had the seven last bowls of the wrath of God who shows him Mystery Babylon.

"Come, I will show you the judgment of the great harlot who sits on many waters," (Revelation Ch.17v1) he said to John. Mystery Babylon is the hidden Babylon behind the empire of the beast. The beast himself will appear to the world as a wily politician, able to negotiate, browbeat, and deceive the nations to follow him, and even to worship and adulate him. But there is a spiritual side to this man, which should not surprise us, since he is empowered and energized by Satan himself. The spiritual side is occultist in nature, and is dominated by witchcraft and sorcery. Hence his ability to deceive and mesmerize the world. He will do what no other man has ever been able to do, and that is to unite the world under his leadership, all shades of political opinion and all religions, sects and cults. After all, except for the members of the true church of God whose names are written in the Lambs book of life, the rest of the world has been deceived into believing a concoction of lies spun by Satan. Satan will, through the beast and false prophet, be able to unite those he has deceived. Mystery Babylon is the spiritual power behind the outward material and political power of the beast. This great harlot, as she is described, has so to speak plied her wares among the kings of the earth. They have all been to bed with her, and committed sexual immorality in a spiritual sense, with her. They have sold themselves to the antichrist, and fully committed themselves to work the works of evil and darkness. They are united with spiritual powers of darkness, and in fact are in league with the devil. The people of the nations around the world follow their leaders. So John says, "the inhabitants of the earth were made drunk with the wine of her fornication."(Revelation Ch.17v2) The peoples of the earth are absolutely intoxicated under the influence of the powers of darkness. They crave for the hidden things of darkness and evil, and indulge themselves in all the practices of the occult. It is significant that there is in our day a build up to the coming of these days, when Satan truly will have come down to the earth. There are a growing number of people who would not in any way want to be associated with God or Jesus Christ or the Bible or the saints of God, but say they are spiritual. That is they have a strong spiritual element in their lives which is important to them. They may be followers of the new age movement in a general sense, since this movement covers a multitude of beliefs. There is also a growing interest in the things of the occult and witchcraft, in paganism and pre-Christian religions in general. The interest in UFOs is fundamentally a spiritual thing, and fostered behind the scenes by demonic powers. It is all Satan's strategy in preparation for the coming of the antichrist and the full manifestation of Mystery Babylon.

John is carried away in the Spirit into the wilderness, to see the great harlot. What John saw he describes in v3 of Ch.17, "And I saw a woman sitting on a scarlet beast which was full of names of blasphemy, having seven heads and ten horns." We have certainly met this beast before, it is the beast who rose out of the sea and is identified as the antichrist. This harlot sits on him, showing that there is a close association between the beast and the harlot for the time being, and that she needs the beast and the beast is content to carry her. This is no poor prostitute trying to scrape a living, but this harlot is dressed in purple and scarlet. For anyone to be dressed like this in John's day, would denote that they were either extremely rich, or were royalty. She also wore gold and precious stones and pearls and held in her hand a golden cup. This harlot is a high class whore, whose representatives on the earth will sit in high places, among the rich and powerful. To the lust filled eye this woman would seem irresistible, and so she had proved to the world leaders of her day, who had all fallen for her evil charms. But although the cup she held was gold and probably appeared beautiful, in the cup were abominations and the filthiness of her fornication. The things that filled her cup were of course the things that are filthy and abominable as far as God is concerned. As for the great harlot they were her meat and drink. On her forehead a name was written, "MYSTERY, BABYLON THE GREAT, THE MOTHER OF HARLOTS, AND OF THE ABOMINATIONS OF THE EARTH." This is her title and she is proud of it. She is the one who the children of Israel were led astray by as on numerous occasions they were unfaithful to the Lord. This spiritual power of darkness often lured them away to worship Baal and countless other gods. This mother of harlots is the same spirit that has plagued the church over the centuries also, causing the church to go seriously astray from the truth of God's word and into countless heresies and evil practices. At the beginning of Revelation in the messages to the churches, Jesus exposed the spirit of the mother of harlots in several of the churches, and called on them to repent.

As a number of the churches that John wrote to were affected by this evil spirit, there was a manifestation of this spirit in the lives of people, and also the organizations they belonged to. So this harlot is not just a spiritual entity, but also an organization with spiritual overtones that real people belong to. John saw the woman drunk with the blood of the saints and with the blood of the martyrs of Jesus. The spirit of this harlot has been around for a long time, and has been the spirit that has controlled the persecution and killing of God's people throughout time. No wonder she is drunk, for she is responsible for the deaths of millions. She is the spirit that motivated the Romans to torture and kill Christians in the early days of the church. She has over the centuries infused Muslims with hatred to kill Christians and Jews, because of writings in the Koran. That situation still exists today in some parts of the world, where fanatical Muslims seek to wipe out all Christians in their area, not that the majority of Muslims behave like this. Not that all who were killed in these persecutions were true children of God, some have called themselves Christians for political reasons. The killing of thousands of the saints of God by the Roman Catholic Church, was inspired by this harlot. But when the antichrist holds sway on the earth, the blood of the martyrs of Jesus will flow more than ever at the hands of this vile harlot. When John saw her he was totally and utterly amazed and filled with astonishment.

The mystery of the woman and the beast is then explained to John by the angel. The angel repeats what had been previously revealed to John, that the beast was, and is not and will ascend out of the bottomless pit. This is essentially the same as what we have seen previously when John wrote that the beast received a deadly wound that was healed, and all the world marveled and followed the beast. The reaction of the world to the beast after his miraculous recovery is again repeated by the angel. But then the angel gives John some information that is new. The seven heads, he says, are seven mountains on which the woman sits. In John's day the seven mountains would be easily identified with Rome, as it was the centre at that time of the world power that opposed and persecuted the church, and the head of Rome was Caesar who claimed to be god and demanded that his subjects worship him. But this idolatrous system developed into another idolatrous system of worship, the Roman Catholic Church. The popes have always laid claim to names and titles that are blasphemous, and also have tried to stamp out all opposition to their claim that they are the Vicar of Christ and that only the Roman Catholic Church is the true church. Popes have always claimed to be infallible, when it comes to matters of doctrine. Down through the centuries the Roman Catholic Church has been guilty of the worst corruption and vileness, is decked out in the finest clothing and has accumulated untold wealth, while her subjects have lived and died in abject poverty. She has shed the blood of countless true saints of God, and certainly fits the bill and description of the great harlot. Like the harlot seen by John, this church has also sought to weald political power and for many centuries did. Unfaithfulness to God and His word has been the characteristic of this church, as she has preferred to blind the eyes of her followers with church traditions that contradict the scriptures, and has mixed all this in with pagan practices from around the world in order to gain adherents. But whether or not the antichrist will arise from Rome or somewhere else time will tell.

John is then told that there are also seven kings. It may be that the seven heads also represent seven kings. Attempts have been made to identify these kings with Roman Caesars of the past, and also with past empires, but be that as it may it could be that future rulers will fit the bill. What John is told is that, "There are also seven kings. Five have fallen, one is, and the other has not yet come. And when he comes, he must continue a short time." Then John is told, "The beast that was, and is not, is himself also the eighth, and is of the seven, and is going to perdition."(Revelation Ch.17v10-11) It seems clear from these two verses that the antichrist has his roots in these seven kings, because he is counted as the eighth and is of the seven. This seems to indicate that he will be similar in character and behavior to the seven that preceded him. This is now the second time that John has repeated that he, the beast, is going to perdition. His origins may be obscure to us from the information we have been given, but his end is certain, he is heading for perdition. The ten horns of the beast are also ten kings. The seven kings speak of his origin and the ten speak of ten kings that are ruling at the time of the reign of the antichrist, and submit themselves to him. They are said to reign for one hour, which would denote a very short period, and the inference is that they receive their authority from the antichrist and rule as his vassals. "They are of one mind, and they will give their power and authority to the beast." (Revelation Ch.17 v13) It is possible that these kings are the same as the ones referred to in Ch.16 v14, where the evil spirits that have the appearance of frogs go out to deceive the kings of the earth to gather them to the battle of Armageddon. It is even possible that the world has divided into ten power blocks, similar to the European Union, and will be ruled by ten kings, and these kings are the ten horns.

We are told in Ch.17 v14 that these make war with the Lamb. This is a reference, I believe, to the battle of Armageddon. For we are told, the Lamb will overcome them because of who He is, He is Lord of lords and King of kings. Notice who starts the war; it is the kings of the earth under the leadership of the beast. As I have written in the previous chapter, they actually believe that they can fight against God and the Lamb and win. How deceived can people be? How reckless and stupid, and yet it is God's judgment on them. How true the scriptures are, when as it is written, "Do not be deceived, God is not mocked; for whatever a man sows, that he will also reap."(Galatians Ch.6v7) These kings, their leader and their subjects have blasphemed the name of God, have mocked at His mercy and refused His warnings and have witnessed His superior power, and yet they still go to war against Him. The scripture in Proverbs Ch6v15 will be true of these men which says, "Therefore his calamity shall come suddenly; suddenly he shall be broken without remedy." Jesus has already said that He will come upon them as a thief in the night. This will now be the second time that they are caught out in this way, as when Jesus came for His church just prior to the outpouring of the wrath of God, they believed that they had overcome the Lamb by killing His people. They were saying peace and safety and who can fight against the beast. But Jesus came to the air and took all of His people, and they are in the heavens waiting to return to earth with Him, to destroy the armies of the beast. It is amazing how those deceived by Satan and sin fall for the same deceptions time and time again. But all these things will come to pass because Jesus the Lamb reigns and He overrules in the affairs of men and devils and Satan himself.

We are further told that when the Lamb comes and defeats the kings and the beast, that those who will come with Him are called, chosen and faithful. It is necessary to refer back to the seven churches from time to time, because this book was written to them. The message of this book is that Jesus is the Lamb and He will overcome all the power of evil in the earth that all authority and power belong to Him. The great conflict at the end of time is featured prominently because this is when Satan will finally be defeated forever. The main characters on the earth right at the end will be the beast, the false prophet and these ten kings, and they will be defeated. Jesus has called for the churches to be faithful to Him, because he has called them and chosen them out of the world to be His people, and those who are faithful to Him will be with Him on that great day of triumph. He calls the church today to be faithful to Him, and to put all other allegiances aside.

At the beginning of Ch.17, John is told that the harlot, who rides on the beast, also sits on many waters. John is now told by the angel that the waters she sits on represent peoples, multitudes, nations and tongues. This indicates that her influence and power extent throughout the earth, as we have seen previously, John says that the inhabitants of the earth were made drunk with the wine of her fornication. But the ten kings, who are the ten horns on the beast, will come to hate the harlot. They will see her as not one with the beast but just something along for the ride. The harlot, as far as the beast is concerned will have outlived her usefulness, for John is told that the ten kings "will hate the harlot, make her desolate and naked, eat her flesh and burn her with fire."(Revelation Ch.17v16) She had been useful in order to bring the religious types and the spiritual people into the grip of the beast, but now she can be dispensed with. This indicates that at some time towards the end of the reign of the antichrist, all religions and spiritual organizations will be done away with and only the ideas of the antichrist will be tolerated.

But the thing that is of most interest in this turn of events is the fact that it is God who has put it into the hearts of these kings to destroy the harlot. The harlot has been responsible for the deaths of many of God's children, and now her time of judgment has come, and God uses the ten kings who are under the control of the beast to destroy her. The uniting of all religions under one umbrella, in the harlot, is at an end for she will rise no more. How interesting, that it is the false religions of the world that have been responsible for shedding the blood of the saints. But it has always been so. Jesus spoke of the religious scribes and Pharisees of His day in the following terms, "Serpents, brood of vipers! How can you escape the condemnation of hell? Therefore, indeed, I send you prophets, wise men and scribes: some of them you will kill and crucify, and some of them you will scourge in your synagogues and persecute from city to city, that on you may come all the righteous blood shed on the earth, from the blood of righteous Abel to the blood of Zechariah, son of Berechiah, whom you murdered between the temple and the altar." (Matthew Ch.23v33-35) The organizations that represent corrupted and pseudo Christianity, as well as those religions that are based on the doctrines of demons, have always down through the centuries of the existence of the church been at the forefront of the persecution of the saints of God. But no doubt the beast has always viewed the harlot with suspicion, for he considers that he is God, and he cannot even tolerate the existence of a corrupt and unfaithful pseudo church, even though she is full of evil and hatred for God and His children.

The earthly organization of the harlot spirit is now gone, but John is also told that the woman you saw is the great city Babylon. The spirit behind the harlot has a number of faces, and this is one more. The harlot spirit is mystery Babylon, the mother of harlots, the one behind all unfaithfulness to God. This spirit is also manifested in the city of Babylon, the city of the beast and it continues for a little while longer, before it also is destroyed by God.

CHAPTER 23

THE FALL OF THAT GREAT CITY BABYLON

After John had seen the demise of mystery Babylon, he sees another angel coming down from heaven, who had great authority and glory. The earth was lit up with the glory and splendour of the mighty angel. He cried out with a very loud voice and said that Babylon the great is fallen is fallen and has become a place for demons and foul spirits and unclean birds. This would be a reference to the vultures that are invited to come and devour the flesh of those who have fallen in their futile war with God.

Babylon had been the centre of all that was opposed to God, and it had exported around the world evil and wickedness. So not only is Babylon fallen, but all the nations have drunk of the wine of the wrath of her fornication. Wrath from God has come upon all the nations because they shared in the evil deeds of Babylon. John uses the expression, "The kings of the earth have committed fornication with her,"(Revelation Ch.18v3) to denote that these ten kings that have given their authority to the beast, have become one with the beast in his opposition to God. Then John adds that the merchants of the earth have become rich because of trading with Babylon. In the prosperous western world economic prosperity has become a god in these days, and will be much more in the days of the beast. Because he will hold all the economic strings, and control who can buy and sell around the world, Babylon will be rich beyond anything previously seen in the earth. John talks about the abundance of her luxury. Dictators have often decked themselves out in an extravagantly luxurious way, Chouchesku of Rumania, and Saddam Hussein of Iraq are two recent notable examples, but they will seem as paupers compared to the antichrist who will have the wealth of the world at his disposal.

We have to bear in mind that John is looking in detail at things that have been written about three times already, because three times John has seen the vision of the return of Jesus and the defeat of all His enemies. Regarding Babylon and the kings of the earth, this is clearly seen in the following verses. Revelation Ch.6v15, "And the kings of the earth, the great men, the rich men, the commanders, the mighty men, every slave and every free man, hid themselves in the caves and rocks of the mountains, and said to the mountains and rocks, "Fall on us and hide us from the face of Him who sits on the throne and from the wrath of the Lamb!" For the great day of His wrath has come, and who is able to stand?" Then again in Ch.11v15, "Then the seventh angel sounded: And there were loud voices in heaven, saying, 'The kingdoms of this world have become the kingdoms of our Lord and of His Christ, and He shall reign forever and ever!" Finally in Ch16v19, "Now the great city was divided into three parts, and the cities of the nations fell. And great Babylon was remembered before God, to give her the cup of the wine of the fierceness of His wrath." So when we read in Ch18v4 that a voice comes from heaven saying, "Come out of her, my people, lest you share in her sins, and lest you receive of her plagues," it has to be borne in mind that what John is writing in Ch.17 and Ch.18, is a review in detail of things that have already been written about as having happened. God in this warning to His people is telling them to come out of Babylon, just as Jesus warned His people to get out of Jerusalem before the Romans came and destroyed it, in the judgment of God in their day. For the seven churches in Asia some of which had become involved in what could be described as Babylonian practices, it would be a warning to them also not to associate themselves with such things, and be in danger of facing the judgment of God. This is a warning also to the church today to separate itself and sever all ties with the Babylonian system of the world and the mystery Babylon of what is a corrupted and unfaithful harlot comprised of organized world religions. "For her sins have reached to heaven, and God has remembered her iniquities." (Rev. Ch.18v5)

The voice from heaven continues to say that Babylon should receive double for all her sins, and in what she did to God's children she should receive double in recompense. To the same measure that she exalted and made herself glorious in the same measure may she be tormented and made sorrowful. I sit as a queen and I am not a widow, I will not know the sorrow of bereavement, Babylon had said in her heart. Boastful as ever and proud of heart, just as Ancient Babylon had been when Nebuchadnezzar was king, but God knows how to humble the proud and bring them down. Isaiah Ch47 predicts the fall of Babylon, in ancient Israel's day, but when one reads that chapter it becomes very apparent how relevant it is to the last days of the Babylon to come. In one day she will be destroyed. She will be burned with fire, for the Lord who judges her is strong. There will be weeping on the part of the kings of the earth, who were committed to her in heart and soul, and shared in her sensuous lifestyle. When they see the smoke rising up to heaven from her destruction, they will keep their distance, wondering that in one hour such a great city is destroyed. The merchants of the earth who grew fat and rich through trading with her will be in mourning. Everything from gold and silver and precious stones, to every other conceivable commodity including the bodies and souls of men, were the merchandise she traded in but God has destroyed it forever. So great is the shock of Babylon's destruction that John repeats almost word for word the lamentation and mourning of the merchants and the merchant seamen and sees them crying out, weeping, wailing, heart broken and shattered, for in one hour she is made desolate. How are the might fallen!

In Revelation Ch.18v20 however, there are words in stark contrast. "Rejoice over her, O heaven, and you holy apostles and prophets, for God has avenged you on her!" The heavenly hosts are rejoicing along with the saints in heaven and those with the Lord in the heavens. This is not an unchristian sentiment that does not belong in the New Testament, but a rejoicing over the justice and judgment of God being executed on the earth. Romans Ch.12v19 says "Vengeance is Mine I will repay, says the Lord," and it is a thoroughly New Testament truth and concept. So is the truth that the wrath of God is poured out on all ungodliness and wickedness of men. God's people should rejoice when evil and evil men are overthrown in the judgments of God.

In prospect of what will shortly come to pass, John sees a mighty angel cast a great millstone into the sea. One can imagine the effect on the sea, how the sea would be churned up. In the same way the angel said that the overthrow of Babylon would be a violent overthrow and it would, like the millstone sinking to the bottom of the ocean, be found no more. No more would the ordinary, everyday things of life occur in Babylon. The sound of music, the noises of industry, the light of a lamp or the rejoicing at a wedding, all would be gone forever. For it had been by sorcery that all the nations were deceived by her and in her was found the blood of the righteous, the prophets and the saints of God who lived on the earth. What an evil and corrupt history Babylon has had from the days of its inception at the tower of Babel, through all its different guises and earthly kingdoms culminating as it does in the kingdom of the antichrist, Babylon has been both in its spiritual source and outward manifestations the great implacable enemy of God but is no more. John has more to say about the defeat of the beast and the false prophet and Satan himself, but that comes after another look at the second coming of Jesus to the earth with the hosts of heaven, the angels and saints.

CHAPTER 24

THE KING IS COMING

Chapter 19 of Revelation starts with echoes of the rejoicing over the fall of Babylon that John recorded in the previous chapter. A multitude in heaven is crying out "Alleluia! Salvation and glory and honor and power belong to the Lord our God!"(Revelation Ch.19v1) They continue to cry out that the Lord is right to have judged the great harlot because she had corrupted the earth with her immorality. In dealing with Babylon God has dealt with the manifestation of evil in the earth, as it was a creation of the fallen one Satan. The heavenly host also praises God because He has taken His revenge on Babylon for the blood of the saints that she shed. Again they say, "Alleluia." The smoke of her destruction rises up to heaven forever, so great is her fall and her punishment. All of heaven is agreed on the fate of the great city that corrupted the earth. This includes the twenty four elders and the four living creatures, who are constantly praising and worshipping God. They fell down before the throne of God saying, "Amen! Alleluia!." Then John hears a voice from the throne which said, "Praise our God, all you His servants and those who fear Him, both small and great!"(Revelation Ch.19v5) This is the signal for the greatest anthem of praise to God that has ever been heard. Like the sound of the Victoria Falls, Niagara Falls and the sound of great thunder all combined, John hears the sound of a great multitude all saying, "Alleluia! For the Lord God Omnipotent reigns!"(Revelation Ch.19v6) This is one of the greatest climaxes of this book, when all of heaven praises God because in actual reality and at that moment there is no longer any more challenge to the absolute authority of God on the earth. God has always been in charge of the affairs on the earth, but now with the fall of Babylon, there is not even any opposition to His rule. This is the moment when what happened in the Garden of Eden, with the fall of man and Satan's temporary victory, is fully and completely reversed forever. No wonder all of heaven is ecstatic with praise to the Lord God Almighty, who reigns forever and ever.

Let us rejoice and be glad, John hears the heavenly host saying, and give God glory for the marriage of the Lamb has come and His wife has made herself ready. In this final interlude, between the end of time and eternity, John is reviewing all the major events that have taken place surrounding the second coming of Jesus, and the marriage of the Lamb is now reviewed. The relationship between Jesus and His redeemed people the church is described in the New Testament in a number of ways, and one of them is as a bride. The church is regarded as the wife of the Lamb even before the marriage takes place. This is in line with Jewish tradition, where a woman was regarded as a man's wife when they became engaged to be married. This is clearly seen in the case of Mary and Joseph, the earthly parents of Jesus. Matthew records in the Ch.1v18 of his gospel, "Now the birth of Jesus Christ was as follows: After His mother Mary was betrothed to Joseph, before they came together, she was found with child of the Holy Spirit. Then Joseph her husband, being a just man, and not wanting to make her a public example, was minded to put her away secretly." Mary and Joseph were regarded as husband and wife even though they had not come together in sexual union. This underpins the fact that Jesus was conceived of the Holy Spirit, and is the Son of God. So the church is already the wife of the Lamb, because she is betrothed to Him. She has got an engagement ring to prove it. Ephesians Ch.1v14 speaks about the Holy Spirit being the guarantee of our inheritance, until the redemption of the purchased possession. The word guarantee is the Greek word 'arrabon' and came to mean a pledge or earnest in modern Greek the word 'arrabona' means engagement ring, so the verse is saying in effect that the indwelling of the Holy Spirit, is the engagement ring that Jesus has given to His bride, guaranteeing that the marriage will take place. What is meant by the marriage of Jesus the Lamb and His bride the church? We understand marriage as a union of two people, a man and a woman. Marriage in the context of the Old Testament often involved the father and mother of the bride choosing a husband for their daughter. But it does not seem that this is always the case. However in the prayer of Jesus that is recorded in John Ch.17v2 Jesus prays, "As you have given Him authority over all flesh, that He should give eternal life to as many as You have given Him." Then in v6, "I have manifested Your name to the men whom You have given Me out of the world. They were Yours, You gave them to Me, and they have kept Your word." It is clear from these verses that Jesus acknowledges that the Father has chosen His bride for Him, they are the men and women that the Father has chosen out from the world.

The marriage of Christ and the church is obviously not a marriage in any earthly sense. It is not a physical union, but a spiritual union, which will be consummated when Jesus returns and His bride shares in the immortality that as a man in glory Jesus has had for nearly two millennia. John says His wife has made herself ready. The church will be ready to be the wife of the Lamb when she is as Paul described in Ephesians Ch.5v27, "That He might present her to Himself a glorious church, not having spot or wrinkle or any such thing, but that she should be holy and without blemish." Paul when he spoke to the Ephesians about the Holy Spirit being the engagement ring that betroths them to Christ, said that it was until the redemption of the purchased possession. The purchased possession is the church, and the redemption takes place at the rapture of the church when the church is perfected and becomes one with Christ. This is the closest that the book of Revelation comes to in referring to the rapture of the church. Another of the Jewish traditions surrounding marriage that also applies to the church is that the bride was veiled until the marriage was consummated. Peter wrote in his first epistle Ch.1

about the salvation ready to be revealed in the last time, and in that context said in v8, "Whom having not seen you love. Though now you do not see Him, yet believing, you rejoice with joy inexpressible and full of glory." Although we do not yet see Him, there is coming a time when we will. John wrote in his first epistle Ch.3v2, "Beloved, now we are the children of God; and it has not yet been revealed what we shall be, but we know when He is revealed, we shall be like Him, for we shall see Him as He is." Revelation Ch.22v4 says of the church, "They shall see His face, and His name shall be on their foreheads." At the marriage of the Lamb, the church will see the face of Jesus, the veil that has hidden Him from view will be removed.

The church will be clothed in fine linen, that is perfectly clean and white and glowing with the glory of God. No bride will have ever looked so beautiful, so perfect without any blemish. Right throughout the book of Revelation the saints are always portrayed as wearing white, speaking of the purity that comes from being washed in the blood of the Lamb. Despite what some versions of the Bible say, the word righteousness in this context, is referring to the righteousness that comes from the saints of God being justified by faith in the atoning blood of Jesus that he shed for them on the cross.

Then the angel said to John, "Write: Blessed are those who are called to the marriage supper of the Lamb!" Then the angel went on to say that, "These are the true sayings of God."(Revelation Ch.19v9) Maybe some have imagined a great feast in heaven with every kind of delicious food set out on endless rows of tables. Just as some perhaps have imagined a kind of wedding where Jesus says, "I do," and the church responds similarly. There will no doubt be great celebration at the time of the rapture of the church, and all who are at the wedding will rejoice as Jesus looks at the fruit of the travail of His soul and is satisfied. For as Paul wrote, "Husbands, love your wives, just as Christ also loved the church and gave Himself for her."(Ephesians Ch.5v25) Jesus has given everything in order to obtain His bride, in all the long history of men paying a dowry in order to obtain a wife, never was such a price paid than was paid by Jesus.

John has no doubt been overwhelmed by what he has seen, and he falls at the feet of the glorious angel that has been revealing these wonderful things, and starts to worship him. But John is rebuked as the angel assures him that he is just a fellow servant of Jesus, like all of John's brothers in suffering, who have the testimony of Jesus. "Worship God!" John is told in no uncertain terms. "For the testimony of Jesus is the spirit of prophecy."(Revelation Ch.19v10) The message not the messenger is of vital importance. The messenger is merely a servant just like John, but the testimony of Jesus, which is what the angel has been conveying to John is the spirit of prophecy. So worship God who is the originator of the message, who has given us His Son, in order to reveal Himself.

What John sees next is the most graphic view he has seen yet of the second coming of Jesus to the earth as King of Kings and Lord of Lords. Consistent with the preceding interludes that have described in detail things that have already happened, so John now sees the climax of the Lord's victory over his enemies. He sees heaven opened and a white horse. It is significant that a white horse is seen first. This sets the scene for what is to follow. For the most part, in the book of Revelation, the horse is associated with war, so we will not be surprised to discover that the Son of God is coming to wage war. The one sitting on the horse is called Faithful and True. There can be no question as to who this is. He is the faithful and true witness, the firstborn from the dead and ruler of the kings of the earth. We are told here that in righteousness He judges and makes war. Some men in the past have described their wars as holy wars, or just wars. Some wars, no doubt, have been more justified than others, and some wars in the Old Testament were instigated by God, in order to reveal His wrath against the ungodliness and wickedness of men. But there is only one who can be said to be able to wage war justly and in righteousness, and that is God. For all men are sinners and there is none righteous, no not one. So when men have waged war on each other, it has always been one army of sinners fighting another army of sinners. But when God wages war it is a just and holy and sinless God waging war on sinners who deserve to die.

His eyes were as a flame of fire, and on His head he had many crowns. On His head were many diadems, kingly crowns, not the stephanos crowns, that the athletes won at the Olympic games. Jesus has not won these crowns, but they are His by right, because He is the King of kings and Lord of lords, and always has been. Because of who He is, no foe has been able to withstand Him or successfully fight against Him. He also had a name that no one knew except Himself. Not everything has been revealed, or ever will be revealed to us, let us be content that God and Jesus have some secrets.

His clothing was dipped in blood, and He has the name, The Word of God. He is coming to wage war, but He is still the Lamb of God who shed His blood for the sins of the world, that He might purchase out from the world a people, a bride, for Himself. In this book of Revelation we are never far from the truth that He was led as a lamb to the slaughter, and like a sheep that is dumb before the shearers, so He did not open His mouth to defend Himself. He is constantly referred to as the Lamb, and the Lamb who shed His blood. The revelation that Jesus is the Word of God is certainly not new to John. Some of the best known scriptures in the whole of the Bible are found right at the beginning of John's gospel. "In the beginning was the Word, and the Word was with God, and the Word was God." To emphasize that John is referring to a person when he speaks of the Word being with God, in v2 he says, "He was in the beginning with God." The One who was in the beginning is the One who will be at the ending of all things as well, for He is the Alpha and Omega, the Beginning and the Ending.

Following Jesus on His white horse are the armies of heaven. They are obviously the church, His bride who will be at His side now forever, and they are also on white horses. The church has come to make war on the enemies of God also, and will be victorious in their Lord and Savior. They are seen as being dressed in the white robes of the saints. What a majestic sight this must have been for John. He has seen in previous visions, armies of men going to war, armies of locusts tormenting those who did not have the seal of the living God, armies from the east numbering two hundred million that killed a third of mankind, armies of angels warring against each other in the heavens when Satan was cast down to the earth, but nothing that could remotely be compared to this. No army was ever so vast, with regiment after regiment parading past him, following Jesus to the battle of Armageddon.

Some of the things that John saw when he first saw Jesus he now sees again as Jesus comes from heaven with His mighty army. His eyes as a flame of fire, and now out of His mouth goes a sharp sword. This sword is the sword of His word which is powerful and with it He will strike the nations. He will rule them, or as the Greek infers He will shepherd them. Jesus Himself refers to this when in Matthew Ch.25v32 He says to the disciples, "All the nations will be gathered before Him, and He will separate them one from another, as a shepherd divides his sheep from the goats." The separation occurs on the basis of those who have shown kindness and love to Him, by showing kindness and love to His brothers when they were in prison and hungry. He will shepherd them with a rod of iron, there will be a firm hand and settled judgment of the nations on that day which cannot be reversed. The judgment on those who are separated from Him is everlasting punishment.

He Himself will tread the winepress of the fierceness and wrath of Almighty God. This will not be left to angels, but the Lamb himself will execute judgment on the nations that have followed the antichrist and the false prophet. He has been the one who as the Lamb in the midst of the throne, has through the agency of man, demons and the angels of heaven brought judgments and punishments on the world of rebellious men, and now comes to destroy once and for all those who have shaken their fists at Him and blasphemed His name. Some may argue that this is not like our God or Jesus at all. That God is always eternally forgiving, loving and kind even to His enemies. But God is not mocked and whatever men sow they shall reap. They have sown blasphemy, hatred of God, shedding the blood of the saints of God, the worship of Satan himself and the practice of every evil and abominable thing, and now as God is just He is giving them what they deserve. Those who think otherwise do not have a Biblical understanding of God, but only an understanding of a god of their own invention.

He has on His clothes and on His thigh the name of, "KING OF KINGS AND LORD OF LORDS," because that is who He is. There has never been any question that this day would eventually come. It is the inevitable consequence of Satan's actions and the rebellion of man. God is not a distant absentee landlord who has started things on the earth and then left it to its own devices. God has intervened in the affairs of men on a number of occasions. Jesus said, "But as the days of Noah were, so also will the coming of the Son of Man be." (Matthew Ch.24v37.) God intervened to bring to an end all that had the breath of life in a universal flood in the days of Noah. The only ones who were saved were those in the ark, because Noah found grace in the sight of the Lord. Now the end has come again for all flesh on the earth, but this time there will be no ark of salvation, only a looking forward to judgment. God's people have already been saved and will not face the judgment of the wicked.

Then John saw an angel standing with the sun to his back, and he cried out loudly to all the birds that were flying in the sky, and invited them to gather together for the supper of the Great God. The next verse makes it clear that the whole world is against God in this final great battle, the battle of Armageddon. The birds are told that they can gorge themselves on the flesh of kings, captains, mighty men, horses, and their riders and the flesh of all people small and great, free and slave. John saw the beast, who had led the world in their fight against God, and the armies with him together to make war with the King of kings and Lord of lords. We saw this scene before in Ch.16v13-16, where this vast army of men comes to fight against God. This actually turns out to be not so much a fight, as a rout. The army of the beast may have the latest weapons, whatever they may be. I am sure that even today the rich and powerful nations have weapons that the general public are not aware of, that are very advanced technologically and powerful weapons of mass destruction. But with all the power and wealth that the beast accumulates, the weapons that his armies go to fight against God with, will I imagine, be far more advanced than anything nations possess today. But whatever he possesses in terms of weaponry on that day, what earthly use will they be against the one with the sharp sword that comes from His mouth. One word from the Lord of Lords and King of Kings, and the whole of the universe could disintegrate.

John sees that the beast is captured, and also the false prophet who in former times had been able to work miraculous signs, as he was empowered by the beast. So much for, who is like the beast, who is able to make war with him. That question has been answered, and ironically it did not even take a fight to see him captured. He was just taken, because he is just a man. The number of his name is 666, the number of a man, and as such he is no match for Jesus. These two, the beast and false prophet are taken and summarily cast alive into the lake of fire. They are not annihilated, but cast alive into the lake of fire that will be their place of torment forever and ever. They are war criminals of the worst kind, but there is no trial for them. They waged war against the saints and prevailed against them on the earth, but now in Jesus Christ the Lord and King, the saints war against him and prevail. The rest of mankind were killed with the sword that came from the mouth of Him who sat on the horse, and the birds that were invited to the supper of God were filled with their flesh What a sight this must have been for John to see, how truly awful, how horrendous. The sights and sounds of the First World War trenches have been preserved for us to see in old films taken at the time, as well as scenes from the holocaust, the gas chambers, and the concentration camps. Battles fought in the far east and in Europe, the devastations caused by area bombing, in both England and Germany in the Second World War, as well as all the other wars that have carried on unabated ever since, if we were able to combine them all into one graphic scene of pain, horror and destruction, with all due respect to those who suffered so much, the aftermath of this war that will end all wars will exceed all these other horrors by far. Such is the fate of all those who foolishly think that they can fight against God and win.

CHAPTER 25

THE DEVIL'S DOWNFALL

In this third and final prelude to the beginning of eternity, when Satan and the beast and false prophet, along with all those whose names are not written in the book of life will be cast into the lake of fire forever, special attention is paid to the downfall of Satan. In Revelation Ch.12, which is part of the second interlude, John sees things which relate to Israel and the birth of Jesus and Satan's attempts to destroy Jesus through King Herod. Also Satan's attempts to destroy the nation of Israel, and persecute the church are featured, but in all these efforts Satan is frustrated, and he looses his place in heaven and is cast down to the earth. Now also in Revelation Ch.20 John sees things that relate to the past, but this time it does not concern Satan and Israel and the church, but Satan and the nations.

John saw an angel coming down from heaven, and the angel had the key to the bottomless pit and a great chain in his hand. This is the pit out of which locusts came to torment the men and women who did not have the seal of the living God. This pit would seem to be the place where demons are imprisoned, awaiting final judgment, but in God's purposes they were released to do His bidding. This powerful angel took hold of Satan and bound him for a thousand years. In v2 of Ch.20 the evil one is called, "the dragon, that serpent of old, who is the Devil and Satan." The old serpent was the guise that he had in the Garden of Eden, the dragon seems to be the way he is described when he is persecuting the people of God. The name Devil means accuser, as he is the accuser of the saints of God, Satan has the meaning of adversary, he being the great adversary of God. This mighty angel who fell from his original high estate in heaven has these names because they describe his character and activities. It would also appear that these names are mentioned at this time because Satan is going to be bound in respect of certain of his activities relating to these names. It was as the serpent that he tempted and deceived Eve in the Garden of Eden. As the accuser he accused Job before God and persecuted him as severely as he could without taking his life. As the adversary he opposed God by seeking to hold the nations in total spiritual darkness, and did his level best to infect Israel, God's chosen people, with that darkness also. John describes how he is cast into the bottomless pit for a thousand years. It is most important at this juncture to take note of the result of this binding and imprisoning, and also to take into account that Satan is a spiritual being who does not have a physical body. Although what John sees appears to be the physical binding and casting of Satan into the bottomless pit, we should not imagine that it is a physical binding that takes place, but a binding in the sense of putting a restriction on Satan's activities, and movements. We are told specifically that he is bound so that he should deceive the nations no more till the thousand years are finished, and that afterwards he must be released for a little while.

What should we make of this binding, and when does it take place? Satan is bound so that he cannot deceive the nations. The nations are the Gentile nations of the world, so we need to ask ourselves a question. When have the Gentile nations of the world been held in spiritual darkness and the deceptions of Satan, and when were they not so bound? The answer to that question would appear to me to be fairly easy to answer. After the death of Jesus and His resurrection and ascension to the throne in heaven, He commenced to reign as the Lamb in the midst of the throne. The Holy Spirit was sent to the earth with the specific role of being the Comforter and giving the church the enabling power to be witnesses to Jesus and of sanctifying the church so that it would be a holy temple to the Lord. In His role as the enabling power in the lives of the believers, so that they would be witnesses to Jesus, The Holy Spirit was poured out on the Day of Pentecost. In Acts Ch.1v8 Jesus told His disciples, "But you shall receive power when the Holy Spirit has come upon you; and you shall be witnesses to Me in Jerusalem, and in all Judea and Samaria, and to the end of the earth." Jesus is forecasting the inclusion of the Gentile nations in the church. Jesus had spoken of the inclusion of the Gentile nations in John Ch.10v16 when He said, "And other sheep I have which are not of this fold; them also I must bring, and they will hear My voice; and there will be one flock and one shepherd." Those that were not of this fold, were those from the Gentile nations that would hear His voice and follow Him as their shepherd. A very significant event took place five days before the Passover feast, after which Jesus would go to the cross and be crucified. There were some Greeks who had come to worship at the feast and asked to see Jesus. When Jesus heard of their enquiry to see Him He said, "The hour has come that the Son of Man should be glorified." (John Ch.12v23) Jesus then went on to talk about His death in terms of a corn of wheat falling into the ground to die, so that it can reproduce itself many times over. Jesus said then that those who follow Him should live by the same principal, and lay down their lives. Jesus is troubled by the prospect of what He will suffer, but does not seek to evade the suffering. But instead He says, "Father, glorify Your name." (v28) Then a voice came from heaven which said, "I have both glorified it and will glorify it again." Jesus then told the disciples, when some around had thought it had thundered, that the voice came from heaven for their sake. Jesus then said, "Now is the judgment of this world; now the ruler of this world will be cast out. And I, if I am lifted up from the earth, will draw all peoples to myself." Jesus is predicting that through His death he will draw all peoples to Himself, and that is in the context of the ruler of this world being judged and cast out. This all took place starting with the great victory of the death of Jesus which achieved among other things the grip of

Satan over the Gentile nations being broken. This was evidenced first of all in the conversion of Cornelius, the Roman centurion, and the outpouring of the Holy Spirit on him and his household. Then in an ever increasing way through the ministry of Paul the apostle to the Gentiles. Paul approaches this whole subject, from a theological point of view, in Romans Ch.9,10 and 11, and speaks about blindness in part happening to Israel, so that the Gentiles would be grafted into the olive tree of which Christ is the root. This has all happened over the last twenty centuries, and will continue until Satan is released again after the rapture of the church, in order to deceive the nations again and bring them together to the battle of Armageddon. For those who query this interpretation of the binding of Satan, because he is said to be bound for a thousand years, I would simply say that this is not the first time that the number one thousand has been used in the symbolic sense of completeness in Revelation, and will not be the last. This I believe was the case with the one hundred and forty four thousand, where there were a complete number of people, the whole house of Israel. Here we have a complete period of time, in which Satan's power is restricted, so that during that time he cannot deceive the nations any more. God has set the time of his release, till then the gospel will continue to be preached, by Gentiles, then more particularly during the times of great tribulation by Jews, and also by an angel who will finish the great task.

John next saw thrones and they sat on them and judgment was committed to them. It is not at all clear who they are who are being referred to, or how many there are of them. But what we do know is that judgment is committed to them by God. In the context of what John has seen previously we can also say that Satan is being restricted before being released only to face his eternal doom, and others are being given authority to judge as kings. This could be a reference to what Paul spoke about in 1Corinthians Ch. 6v2&3, "Do you not know that the saints will judge the world? And if the world will be judged by you, are you unworthy to judge the smallest matters? Do you not know that we shall judge angels? How much more the things that pertain to this life." After the final defeat of Satan and his hosts, the saints will have a role in the judgment of the world and fallen angels. This is also indicated by verses from Daniel Ch.7v9&10 where we read, "I watched till thrones were put in place, and the Ancient of Days was seated: His garment was white as snow, and the hair of His head was like pure wool. His throne was a fiery flame, its wheels a burning fire: A fiery stream issued and came forth from before Him. A thousand thousands ministered to Him; ten thousand times ten thousand stood before Him. The court was seated, and the books were opened." This is a court scene where not only is God sitting in judgment, but there are also other thrones which are set in place for others also to sit and judge. A promise is given to the saints of the church in Thyatira, that to him who overcomes and keeps the works of Jesus to the end, then he shall have power over the nations, and to the saints in Laodicea that those who overcome will sit with Jesus on His throne. At the end of the day it will be the saints who will rule with Christ and sit in judgment on the nations and fallen angels. What a prospect, what a responsibility and what a privilege for those who overcome and remain faithful.

Then John saw the souls of those who had been beheaded because of their witness to Jesus and because they would not deny their allegiance to the word of God. They are the ones who refused to worship the beast or his image, nor had they received the mark of his name on their foreheads or their hand. These are the heroic saints of the terrible period of the reign of the antichrist, but also I believe include martyrs of all the past centuries who have not bowed the knee to Satan and his many antichrists. They lived and reigned with Christ for a thousand years. John saw the souls of those who had been beheaded, so he is obviously seeing those who were martyred for their testimony and are now with the Lamb in heaven. They were hated and despised on earth by the enemies of God, and special mention is made of those who died at the hands of the antichrist, but now in heaven they reign as kings and priests to God and His Christ. Again they are said to live and reign with Christ for a thousand years, which is the allotted time that God has set, before the rest of the dead are raised to face the great white throne judgment.

Those who participate in the first resurrection are those who are blessed and holy, and over whom the second death has no power.

The second death is to be cast into the lake of fire forever. They are priests to God and reign with Him in heaven, where those who are representatives of the redeemed, the twenty four elders sit on thrones around the throne of God. John has heard the four living creatures and the twenty four elders singing of these souls in heaven in Revelation Ch.5v9&10, and again in Revelation Ch.7v9 after the fifth seal is opened he sees them under the altar. Ever since Jesus has held the keys of death and Hades, death has had no hold on His saints, even though death has claimed their mortal bodies, death has had no claim on their souls, but they have after death been with the Lord. Paul wrote to the Corinthians, that to be absent from the body is to be present with the Lord. Just as Jesus has been reigning in heaven since His resurrection and ascension, so the saints are reigning with Him in heaven. After all, the status of the saints on earth as kings and priests is a continuing status which sees them as kings and priests in heaven. It is because the saints while still on earth have been raised to life with Christ from being dead in sins, and also have been raised with Christ to sit with Him in the heavenly places, they can assume this position in reality when they die and go to be with the Lord. It is while the saints are still on the earth that they have eternal life and will not come into condemnation, but have passed from death to life. The great escape from the second death takes place on earth for the saints, just as does the reigning with Christ.

In the Greek Revelation Ch.20v7 says, now whenever the thousand years have finished Satan will be released. This would indicate that this period of a thousand years should be understood as an allotted time that has been determined by God for the curtailing of Satan's freedom to deceive the nations. When God decides to release him Satan will be free to deceive the nations again. Revelation Ch.20v8-9 says, "And will go out to deceive the nations which are in the four corners of the earth, Gog and Magog, to gather them together to battle, whose number is as the sand of the sea." Then the next verse says, "They went up on the breath of the earth and surrounded the camp of the saints and the beloved city. And fire came down from God out of heaven and devoured them." These things are predicted in the 38th and 39th chapters of Ezekiel. We have come across this event in previous chapters, where certain other details of this time are recorded. You will remember that John saw three unclean spirits coming out of the mouth of the dragon, the beast and the false prophet in order to gather the nations to do battle with God. (Revelation Ch.16v14.) This is just before the seventh angel poured out his bowl and a loud voice was heard from heaven saying "IT IS DONE." Not only is the beast and false prophet taken and cast into the lake of fire at this great battle, but Satan himself is also cast into that place of eternal fiery torment. John deals with Satan's downfall in a separate chapter because the beast and false prophet were merely men, but with Satan he traces some of the long history of his defeat, which started when Jesus died and rose from the dead and ascended to the throne, and he could deceive the nations no more. We are told in this chapter how the vast army is killed, John says that fire comes down out of heaven and devoured them. The devil joins the two other deceivers who were empowered by him and they are tormented forever and ever.

What is so striking about all that John writes is the absolute control that God and the Lamb have over Satan, and the world that has rebelled against Him, so that He is able to fulfill all His plans and purposes to the letter as predicted, and to His own timetable. This is the wonderful message of this book, that our God and the Lamb reign, and this is the great revelation concerning Jesus Christ that the church needs to grasp. If these things that John has seen and heard are not literally going to take place then the victory over Satan is only symbolic and so is the reign of Christ. But these things will take place and the whole of the scriptures testify to it.

CHAPTER 26

THE FINAL JUDGMENT

After John had seen the purpose of God carried out in respect of Satan and his two henchmen, the next thing that John sees is a great white throne and Him who sat on it. He saw that the earth and the heaven fled away from the face of the One on the throne and there was no place for them before the throne of God. The heaven and the earth are going to pass away and be rolled up as a scroll, and as a garment no longer required they will be folded up. Satan's old sphere of influence will be done away with just as he has been done away with. Things will never be the same again.

Next John saw the dead small and great standing before God. The dead are those who were not raised to life until the thousand years were finished. They are those whose names are not written in the book of life. They are those who were not raised when Jesus came to the sky for His redeemed people, for they died still dead in their sins. They were never washed in the blood of the Lamb, so are still polluted by sin. So much has been written and imagined about this truly awful day, about how those who are described as the dead will feel as they stand before the throne of God. How all the arguments that they based their sin and rebellion against God on will mean nothing then, simply because they are now face to face with Almighty God. How lonely everyone will feel despite the fact that billions of men and women will be there. Lonely because there will be no conversation, no companionship, no sense of comradeship, no mother or father to bring reassurance or comfort no friendly smile to warm the chill that everyone will feel because this is the day of reckoning. No one will be able to strengthen the heart of another, for all will have lost all hope of escaping the inevitable doom of the lake of fire forever and ever.

The books were opened, and one other book was opened and that is the book of life. The dead were judged according to their works. How would you like to be judged according to your works before Almighty God? How would you like to have all your actions scrutinized and examined by the God who is all knowing, all seeing and all powerful. To help us understand the extent of God's knowledge about us all, we could do no better than look at Psalm 139. David the psalmist first of all says that God has searched him and known him. He says that God knows all his actions, his sitting down and rising up. God knows his thoughts and also understands them long before he ever thinks them. God knows him so well because He is always there with him, so that God is well acquainted with all his ways. David says that God knows all the things that he speaks, nothing is hidden from Him. The question is asked, "Where can I go from your Spirit?", and the answer is nowhere! In v13-14 we read, "For you formed my inward parts; You covered me in my mother's womb. I will praise You, for I am fearfully and wonderfully made; marvelous are Your works, and that my soul knows very well." God is our creator and knows all about us from conception to death, so with this understanding I ask the question again, how would you like to stand before God and be judged on your works, and let your works determine whether or not you are cast into the lake of fire? There is a way of escape from this predicament. It is the way that Jesus spoke about when He said "I am the way, the truth and the life." (John Ch.14v6) Those who have put their trust in Jesus, believing in their hearts that He died in their place and for their sins, have their sins forgiven by God so that they will not have to answer for their sins on the great Day of Judgment. But for everyone whose sins remain unforgiven in this life who ends up before God's throne on that day there is no hope, because the time in which they could have turned from sin and put their faith in Jesus has gone forever. The time to repent of sin and trust in Jesus Christ as the savior is NOW!

The dead were judged according to their works by the things that were found written in the books. The dead that had died in the sea were before the throne, Death and Hades, the place of the dead gave up their dead, there will be no escaping that day. Cremation will not be a means of escape, or however anyone died, all will stand before God on that day who are not already with Jesus as His bride. Death and Hades were cast into the lake of fire, and so were all those whose names were not found written in the book of life.

This is not the first mention of this terrible second death sentence that is passed on those whose names are not in the book of life. You will recall, that before the final outpouring of the wrath of God that brings destruction and death to God's enemies, there is an angel that preaches the everlasting gospel to the whole world. Then there is another angel that proclaims the fall of Babylon, and finally a third angel that makes the proclamation that anyone who worships the beast or has his mark will face the wrath of God. That wrath will not only be experienced at the battle of Armageddon, but also forever in the lake of fire. Revelation Ch.14v10&11 says, "He himself shall also drink of the wine of the wrath of God, which is poured out full strength into the cup of His indignation. He shall be tormented with fire and brimstone in the presence of the holy angels and IN THE PRESENCE OF THE LAMB. And the smoke of their torment ascends forever and ever; and they have no rest day or night, who worship the beast and his image, and whoever receives the mark of his name." Who will be in charge of the lake of fire? Who will be ruling over that place? It will be the Lamb, for He is Lord over all. He shall strike the nations, of them that forget God and rebel against Him, and He Himself will rule them with a rod of iron, He Himself treads the winepress of the wrath of Almighty God.

People on that day will be judged according to their works, according to the things written in the books in heaven. This means that God has a record of everything that everyone has ever done. But by what standard are the works of men and women going to be judged to have been so evil that they are cast into the lake of fire? Paul sheds light on the answer to this most important question. When Paul was at Athens he was stirred in his heart because the city was so full of idols to many different gods. There was even an altar to the unknown god, and when Paul saw this altar he also saw an opportunity to preach to the Athenians about the God that they did not know. He started by stating the obvious, that it was God who had created everything, and that He does not need temples or idols to represent Him since He is the one who gives life and breath to everything. The next important fact that Paul preached was that God has made all men from one blood, and has made ways for men to seek and find Him and appointed to every race its place in the earth. For in Him we live and move, he said, and as He created us we are His offspring. Logically from this it is not rocket science to deduce, that as we are living, moving, functional, responsible and intelligent beings made in the image of God, that we should not think of God as something that can be represented by anything made out of gold or silver. Paul said that God overlooked the past times of ignorance, but because of the coming of Jesus who is God revealed as a man, it was no longer possible for God to overlook idolatry anymore. Acts Ch.17v30&31 says, "Truly, these times of ignorance God overlooked, but now commands all men everywhere to repent, because He has appointed a day on which He will judge the world in righteousness by the Man whom He has ordained. He has given assurance of this to all by raising Him from the dead." God is going to judge each individual person of all the nations who reject Him, by the standard of the life of Jesus Christ. Jesus Christ will be the benchmark of judgment on that day. Every man and woman that has lived on this earth will either have found refuge in Jesus and be covered by His righteousness and showing by their lives that they are children of God, or they will stand before God naked on that day to be judged by that standard of righteousness.

Jesus spoke about this very thing in Matthew Ch.25v31-46. All the nations on that day will be gathered before Him, and the sheep will be separated from the goats. The sheep are those whose works have demonstrated that they have the Spirit of God living in them and they have behaved as Jesus Christ would have done. The goats on the other hand have behaved like their father the devil. Jesus the King will say to His sheep, "Come, you blessed of My Father, inherit the kingdom prepared for you from the foundation of the world." (v34) Then the King tells them that when they looked after even the least of His brothers, by feeding them, or giving them drink and taking them into their homes, they did it to Him. Or when they clothed the naked and visited the sick of His brothers, or came to them in prison, they did it to Him. Jesus and His body are inseparable so whatever we do to His brothers we do to Him. The King will say to the goats that are on His left, that as they willfully neglected to do any of these things when they saw the naked and hungry and imprisoned children of God, they did not do it to Him. This is the standard of Jesus Christ that they have failed to reach. Many people think that they are not evil enough to be cast into the lake of fire, but those who go there will go there not only because of their evil works but also because of what they neglected to do. For Jesus came to earth and left the glory of heaven, He came and ministered to the needs of His children, even to giving His life to purchase eternal salvation for them. The King will say to those on His left, "Depart from Me, you cursed, into everlasting fire prepared for the devil and his angels." (v41) Also in v46, "And these will go away into everlasting punishment, but the righteous into eternal life."

CHAPTER 27

ALL THINGS NEW

Finally John saw all the things that are going to be new. At last we have come to the time in the visions that John sees when the old order of things is done away with and what will last forever comes into view. Just as the old covenant that God instituted under the Law of Moses passed away forever when Jesus inaugurated a new covenant in His blood, so now the old earth and heavens have passed away forever. The old covenant, like an old wine skin needed to be discarded because it could not contain the new wine of the Spirit, as opposed to the old wine of the letter of the law, so the immortal new creation of God needs a new earth and heavens. Satan is forever confined to the lake of fire along with all those who have worshipped and followed him, so he will never be able to spoil God's new creation. Now the full effectiveness of the life, death, resurrection and ascension of Jesus has come to fruition. For this is what Jesus died to bring about, everything new. There are some surprises in store for us as we look at what changes God will bring about in the new heavens and earth. By the way, for anyone who believes in theistic evolution, do you honestly think that it is going to take God countless millions of years to bring about the new heavens and earth? Of course it won't take God any time at all to bring about this totally new environment, just as it only took Him six days to create the first heaven and earth. None of the New Testament writers tell us how long it will take, simply because Almighty God doesn't need any time at all to do what He wants to do, He just speaks and it is done. That is how He did it the first time, and He doesn't need anyone to theorize about how He does things, but He is pleased when His children simply believe His word.

We have previously looked at other scriptures that speak about the old spiritual and material order of things passing away, so I will not repeat them here. One very interesting thing about the new earth is that there will be no more sea. This is very different from the first earth which was first of all covered in water. The old earth needed water in abundance to sustain the life that God was going to create on it, but that will not be the case for those who have spiritual, immortal bodies. There will be a river, the river of the water of life that flows from the throne of God. There will be no vast oceans; earth will no longer be the blue planet. The sea plays a vital role in the weather of the earth at present, but God will install a totally new watering system in the new earth. There will be no marine life as on the earth at the present time, the environment will be completely different.

After a look at the form of the new earth, John sees something else that is new. Coming down from out of heaven from God, he saw the New Jerusalem, prepared as a bride ready for her husband, We have already seen in a previous chapter that John said, "the marriage of the Lamb is come and His wife has made herself ready."(Revelation Ch.19v7) The marriage has taken place, the church being united with Christ at the rapture, and now John sees the bride after the marriage descending from heaven to her eternal home where she will live with her Husband who is Jesus the Lamb. I suppose one could say that the Lamb has presented His bride to the Father and now they have come to set up house on the new earth that the Father has provided for the bride and groom. Jude speaks about this in v24 of his epistle when he wrote, "Now to Him who is able to keep you from stumbling, and to present you faultless before the presence of His glory with exceeding joy."

Having seen the bride descend from heaven John hears a voice from heaven saying that God himself is also going to live with men on the new earth. This I believe has always been what God wanted, to live with men. This had been temporarily delayed by some thousands of years, since Adam fell into sin, but God has righteously and justly dealt with all the issues surrounding sin so now God can be among His people on the new earth. Truly this is the family of God, living together, God with His Son the Lord Jesus and the bride, those redeemed by the blood of the Lamb. The Holy Spirit is not of course left out for He is the one who introduced the bride to the bridegroom and stays close to the bride and indwells the bride. But God is still God among His people. There is no change in the relationship that the church has with the Father now. It will just be a change in location for both God and His people, because now that His people have been made like Jesus, with immortal bodies and totally free from all sin and pollution, they can live in the presence of God as Jesus does now.

Some other things that will be new are that God will wipe away all tears from the eyes of His people. There has been such a strong emphasis in the book of Revelation on the people of God who have suffered persecution and been killed for their testimony, that now John says that all suffering and pain is at an end. There will be no more death, nor sorrow nor crying. It has been the norm for sorrow and crying to be caused by the departure of those we loved, while still living in the old earth. There will be no more death because death is associated with sin and in God's new earth there will be no more sin. In any case God's people will have bodies that cannot die, but so will those who are tormented in the presence of the Lamb in the lake of fire. But there the conditions are the exact opposite to those on God's new earth. For there will be nothing but sorrow and crying and gnashing of teeth forever. There shall be no more pain, because the things that used to be are no more. Pain had been caused by sin as well as death. Pain in our mortal bodies constantly reminds us that we are mortal and that our bodies are decaying and growing old and malfunctioning. The new bodies that the bride of Christ will enjoy will never grow old or decay, God is the provider for His people of the elixir of life and eternal youth. Some people dream of being able, through stem cell research, to obtain eternal life, but they are doomed to fail because of sin. But God offers eternal life through Jesus Christ to all who will put their trust in Him. Anyway who in their right mind would want to spend forever on an old earth that is sin and sorrow ridden? God will not allow it to happen for as we have seen through this revelation of the future the old earth is going to be burned up.

It is official, for the One who sits on the throne has made the proclamation, "Behold, I make all things new!"(Revelation Ch.21v5) John is told to write these words because they are true and faithful words. All of Gods children should believe them because they are equal in truth and weight to the rest of God's words that are faithful and true. We talk about God's children going to heaven, but actually they will spend eternity with Him on the new earth. The new earth will share one thing in common with the old one; it will be the centre of the universe, it will be God's home. I believe that this old earth is the centre of all that God has created in the material world, and that man is the pinnacle of His creation. God has chosen this tiny planet on which to work out His great purposes, He sent His only begotten Son to die for our sins on this little planet. Satan knows the importance of this earth, because he has concentrated all his efforts here in order to try and frustrate God's purposes. I believe this earth is totally unique in the whole of the universe, and that evolutionary theorists are wasting their time and money that could be put to a far better use, looking for earth like planets and trying to discover some kind of life elsewhere. It is all a futile waste of time.

Then the one who sat on the throne said to John, "It is done! I am the Alpha and the Omega, the Beginning and the End."(Revelation Ch.21v6) We have come across this phrase before when the seventh angel had poured out his bowl into the air, and a loud voice was heard coming from heaven which said, "It is done!" On the latter occasion it heralded the end of the old earth, and on the former occasion God is proclaiming the accomplishment of the new earth. It has all been accomplished because God is the Beginning and the End; He spans all the events of time. He knows the end from the beginning, and He is able to fashion everything to conform to His will. Even the rebellion of Satan, demons and men are worked to fulfill His purposes. All should stand in awe at the greatness of Almighty God.

God issues an invitation to those who read this prophecy and are thirsty. Thirsty for what you may ask? The answer is, thirsty for the water of life. God says, "I will give of the fountain of the water of life freely to him who thirsts"(Revelation Ch21v6) Naturally speaking all water is the water of life. We are 90% water and need a constant supply of water to stay alive and healthy. But is this all that God is talking about? I rather think it isn't. The water of life is the Spirit of life that God gives to those who ask Him. The Holy Spirit is the source of life who lives in every one who receives Jesus Christ as their Lord and Savior. To everyone who is thirsty for God, He gives the Holy Spirit freely. To all who desire God as the psalmist did the Lord meets their need freely. He wrote, "As the deer pants for the water brooks, so pants my soul for You, O God. My soul thirsts for God, for the living God."(Psalm 42v1) Jesus said to the Samaritan woman that he met at Jacob's well, "If you knew the gift of God, and who it is that says to you, "Give me a drink," you would have asked Him, and He would have given you living water."(John Ch.4v10) Again Jesus said to the woman in v13-14, "Whoever drinks of this water shall thirst again, but whoever drinks of the water that I shall give him will never thirst. But the water that I shall give him will become in him a fountain of water springing up into everlasting life." Again on the same subject of the water of life Jesus said in John Ch.7v37-38, "On the last day, that great day of the feast, Jesus stood and cried out, saying, "If anyone thirsts, let him come to Me and drink. He who believes in Me, as the scripture has said, out of his heart will flow rivers of living water." After the words of Jesus John comments that Jesus was speaking of the Holy Spirit who was not yet given because Jesus had not yet died and risen and ascended to sit at His Father's right hand. Almost at the very end of the scriptures the same invitation goes out to all who are thirsty to come and drink of the water of life freely. The invitation is to you if you are thirsty, to drink of the Holy Spirit now, and for the rest of eternity on God's new earth.

What John writes next again reminds us that he is writing to the seven churches in Asia. It is vital to remember that John is writing to the churches and consequently to the church throughout the following centuries. God says, "He who overcomes shall inherit all things, and I will be his God and he shall be My son."(Revelation Ch.21v7) Jesus promised many things to those who overcome when He wrote to the seven churches. Here He says that those who overcome will inherit all those things that are promised, but best of all, there is the Father son relationship between God and His children. A contrast is drawn between those who inherit all things and those who loose everything in the lake of fire and are condemned to experience the second death. God specifies the categories of people who are cast into the lake of fire. Firstly the cowardly, those who sided with the beast and false prophet, or were afraid to take a stand for righteousness and truth. There have always been those who choose to take the broad way to destruction and go with the flow. Secondly the unbelieving will go to the lake of fire. The unbelieving are not those who have genuine doubts, but are those who have chosen not to believe and refused the voice of the Holy Spirit speaking to them, who would have brought them to faith in Jesus as their Savior. Many people have refused to listen to the Holy Spirit because they had their own agenda and did not want God interfering with their life. The abominable are those who practice those things that are an abomination to God. Idolatry, for instance is an abomination to God, and those who practice it will face the fiery wrath of God. Murderers will go to the lake of fire forever. But beware, for Jesus said that anyone who hates his brother in his heart, is a murderer and is in danger of hell fire. The sexually immoral face a future in the flames of torment, and this includes those who are practicing adulterers, fornicators, homosexuals and lesbians, those who practice bestiality, cross dressing, abuse of children, prostitution and every other kind of sexual practice that deviates from the holy and pure sexual relationship that should exist between a man and a woman who love each other, and have made a lifelong commitment to each other in marriage. Sorcerers will be tormented in the flames and the meaning behind the word is most interesting. It does include those who are involved in occultist activities but also those who meddle in drugs. There have always been those who use drugs to enhance their ability to dabble in the occult and the demonic but in these days there has been an explosion of such activity. All who have given their hearts affection to any other god or thing that is worshipped will have their place with those listed above. Lastly John says that all liars will be there in the flames. All those who contradict the Word of God are liars, for to contradict the Word of God is to call Him a liar and those who deny the truth and side with the devil who is the father of lies will be with the devil in the flames. Where will you be, is your lifestyle included in any of the above? If so you have only the lake of fire to look forward to unless by the grace of God you repent, confessing your sin and live according to righteousness.

And now for something completely different. One of the seven angels who had the seven last plagues came to John and said, "Come I will show you the bride, the Lamb's wife."(Revelation Ch.21v9) At a wedding the bride is normally the centre of attention, although at this wedding it will be the bridegroom, for He is the Lamb of God the Lord Jesus Christ, and He will always be at the centre. But even so God the Father is proud to present the bride he has got for His Son. John is then carried away in the Spirit to a great and high mountain, and then the angel shows him the great city, the holy Jerusalem, coming down out of heaven from God. That sounds familiar doesn't it, for in v2 of Ch.21 John records that he saw the New Jerusalem coming down out of heaven from God prepared as a bride adorned for her husband. So here twice in this chapter the New Jerusalem is identified as being the bride of Christ, the church. The angel said to John I will show you the bride, and he showed him the city. We should not be at all surprised at this, because the bride of Christ, the church, is also said to be a holy temple a building in which Jesus is the chief corner stone. This city that John goes on to see is a marvelous representation of the bride of Christ.

The first thing that John says about this city is that it has the glory of God. In John Ch.17v20-24 Jesus prays for His bride to the Father and says these words, "I do not pray for these alone, but also for those who will believe in Me through their word; that they all may be one, as You, Father are in Me, and I am in You; that they also may be one in Us, that the world may believe that You sent Me. And the glory which You gave Me I have given them, that they may be one just as We are one. I in them, and You in Me; that they may be made perfect in one, and that the world may know that You have sent Me, and have loved them as You have loved Me. Father I desire that they also whom You gave Me may be with Me where I am, that they may behold My glory which You have given Me; for You have loved Me before the foundation of the world." Jesus is asking the Father that the church who is one with Him may be with Him beholding His glory and sharing His glory. This is all fully fulfilled when the marriage of the Lamb takes place and the bride shares in the glory of God. That full and complete unity that Jesus prays for comes to pass when His bride is made like Him when He comes to collect her at the rapture and she is glorified.

"Her light was like a most precious stone, like a jasper stone, clear as crystal." (Revelation Ch.21v11) Notice that John describes the city as her and in the next verse as she. This wonderful bride sparkles like a precious stone, as she emanates the glory of God. There is no flaw in this precious stone, and there is no blemish or contamination from anything that would discolor it for it is like the perfect, flawless, pure and holy bride that will be the wife of the Lamb. How amazing that those who were once enemies of God and sinners, are so transformed into such a beautiful bride. By the way, for those who have heard or read in various books fanciful ideas about this city, such as the city is a massive cube hovering over the earth, of a gigantic pyramid sticking out thousands of miles from the new earth into space in which the millions of the redeemed will have their own home, taking God's word literally and sensibly for what it says eliminates all such speculations. Clearly the city is the bride.

The next verse describes the gates of the city, and John saw that there were twelve of them. On the gates were written the names of the twelve tribes of the children of Israel. It is so fitting that this wonderful representation of the church should have the names of the twelve tribes on the gates. After all it was the people of Israel that brought the gospel to the world, they were the initial heralds that sounded out the gospel message that brought the entire world, every kindred, tongue, tribe and nation into being part of the city. It is also an indication to me that as the church are the sons of Abraham, who is the Father of us all, so all who are of the faith of Abraham, including Abraham himself, is part of the city. Hebrews Ch.11v39-40 says, "And all these, having obtained a good testimony through faith, did not receive the promise, God having provided something better for us, that they should not be made perfect apart from us." Those that the writer to the Hebrews is talking about are those who through faith obtained a good report, and he lists a few of them by name in Ch.11. He says that they died without receiving the things that God had promised, in contrast we have already received the promise of eternal life, because we now live after Jesus has finished His work of salvation, and not beforehand. But these scriptures are very clear that they without us would not be made perfect. The Greek word perfect means to be complete, in other words it is the church that completes the body of believers who lived before Christ, and we are all one bride of Christ. It was Jesus who said in effect, that those in Old Testament times who were men and women of faith were born again of the Spirit of God just as we are now, when He said to Nicodemus regarding being born again, Are you the teacher in Israel, and do not know these things? You should be aware of these things Jesus said to him, from your reading and understanding of the scriptures. God has dealt with the sins of the world, whether they were committed before Jesus came or after Jesus came, in exactly the same way. Sins can only be atoned for by the blood of Jesus, and this is the teaching of the scripture throughout. All those whose sins are atoned for by the blood of Jesus are the New Jerusalem.

"Now the wall of the city had twelve foundations, and on them were the names of the twelve apostles of the Lamb." (v14) The church needs to remember its foundations, where it has sprung from. This in no way contradicts the fact that as Paul wrote, "For no other foundation can anyone lay than that which is laid, which is Jesus Christ."(1Corinthians Ch.3v11) The church is built on Christ, He is the author and finisher of our faith, He has brought the church into being as He said "I will build my church, and the gates of Hades shall not prevail against it."(Matthew Ch.16v18) But this is a picture of the bride and so it is appropriate that where the bride sprung from is seen in this picture. The church owes its existence to the obedience of the twelve apostles who were wise master builders of the church, some of whom bequeathed the scriptures to us which are the ground of our faith. The apostles also represent not only Jews but also Gentiles, for in Christ Jesus they are one body, one church and one bride, they are the foundation of the church as a whole.

Next John saw the angel who was talking to him take the golden reed which he had in his hand and measure the city. It was square in shape and as high as it was broad and long. The measurement of the three dimensions was twelve thousand furlongs, which is about 1,380 miles. Here we have again another illustration of the number one thousand representing completeness. Completeness in height, length and width, the church as the bride of Christ which has sprung from the twelve tribes, will be complete in every way. This cannot be a literal measurement, because we are not looking here at a literal city. If it were a literal city why would God create a new earth for Him and His people to dwell on? The angel then measured the wall, and it was one hundred and forty four cubits. The wall also represents the joining of the Jews and Gentiles in one body, hence the measurement being a multiple of the twelve tribes and the twelve apostles. The wall was of jasper stone, which is very often a fiery red color. This city is protected it would seem by walls of fire, in appearance like the One that John saw upon the throne. This is the city of God and He surrounds it, and is I believe also part of it. What a mystery divine that the bride who is one with Christ, is also one with the Father. We are reminded again of the prayer of Jesus in John Ch.17v23, "I in them and You in Me," this is how it will be as the glory of God is revealed in the church throughout eternity.

The city itself was pure gold like clear glass. No such gold exists, but then John is seeing a heavenly representation of the beauty of the bride of Christ. Gold is the most unique of metals and very highly prized. Men have given their lives in search of gold, and indeed have spent their lives panning in rivers, digging in dangerous mines, all in search of that illusive golden metal that could make them rich. Jesus gave His life in order to purchase for Himself a bride that would be more pure than the most refined gold, more precious and costly, more prized and sought after than any large nugget of gold from this old earth. The gold that John sees is the church, is a clear gold like glass, in fact this whole city is clear and transparent just as you would expect, because as God's new creation in Christ Jesus it is pure and holy.

The foundations of the city are adorned with twelve different kinds of precious stone. What an amazing sight, these twelve foundations set with jewels of different colors and hues, each individual stone being beautiful and unique set in its own place. I say this because the word adorn in the Greek means basically to set in order. How simply breathtaking the sight of this city must have been to John, how he must have wondered at its glory. The church may seem at the moment to be insignificant and despised, but then in eternity she will shine, Oh how she will shine with the glory of God! This wonderful description of the church, no doubt, was given to John to send to the churches so that they would get the message, this is what you are going to be so shape up now and begin by the grace and power of the Holy Spirit to overcome. Have your glorious future in mind and don't get caught up with the evil, sordid, filthy things that belong to a world that is going to pass away.

John sees that the twelve gates are twelve individual pearls. How fantastic, how out of this world, gates as least as tall as the walls, which were one hundred and forty four cubits tall. The church is fantastic, she is the dwelling place of God and perfect in beauty. Pearls are also sought after and sometimes very dangerous to obtain. They are created because of irritation inside the shell of a mollusk caused by a piece of grit or some such thing. The mollusk then begins to cover the irritant with a substance that as it builds up over the grit, becomes a pearl. The gates of the city therefore also speak to us of the pain that Jesus has had to go through in order to bring the church into being. We were those who caused Him pain, but He has taken us and transformed us into that which is beautiful in His sight.

The city has only one street, and John saw it was pure gold, like transparent glass. The one street in this city, the bride, is the unity of the Spirit that will be perfect throughout eternity. All earthly cities have many streets, all going in different directions and to different places. In the church, Jesus is the way, the truth and the life and that will never change, and as Paul wrote in Ephesians Ch.4v4-6, "There is one body and one Spirit, just as you were called in one hope of your calling; one Lord, one faith, one baptism; one God and Father of all, who is above all, and through all, and in you all." There is and will be forever an essential unity in the bride that is precious like gold, a unity where Father, Son and Holy Spirit have brought the church into perfect unity with themselves, and they will live forever in harmony. This does not mean in any sense that the bride is equal to God, for the bride will serve and honor the Father, Son, and Holy Spirit and worship them forever.

The city has no temple, unlike the temples that were built in the former earthly Jerusalem. The Lord God Almighty and the Lamb are the temple in the New Jerusalem. This of course is no surprise for the church lives in God, as well as the Spirit of God living in the church. This, among so many other things confirms that we should not think of this city as being a material city in which the church lives. For when John writes that God and the Lamb are the temple, that is exactly what he means. God is not a building and neither is Jesus. This is speaking of the fact that throughout eternity the bride will be constantly praising and worshipping God and serving Him. That was the function of temples on the earth. This also speaks of our nearness to God that he will be living among His people and they will be in his presence in a way that is not possible now.

The city had no need of the light of the sun or the moon, for the glory of God and of the Lamb is its light. There is no darkness in God at all, and everything will be transparent and light in the church. Jesus is the one who makes the church shine. All the adorning of precious stones, all the transparent gold of the city and its street, would not be seen if the Lamb were not the light and it did not shine with the glory of God. O the Lamb is the light, and the church had better not forget it, and the Father is its glory. Without Jesus the church is nothing, just as the most perfect diamond in the world is nothing unless light is shone through it. It has no beauty, only hardness, and the very best diamonds are mined for their potential beauty, not for industrial use. This should have spoken to the seven churches in Asia, that they needed to have Jesus in their midst, for as it will be in eternity, so it is now for the bride of Christ.

The next verse is most interesting and needs careful consideration. "And the nations of those who are saved shall walk in its light, and the kings of the earth bring their glory and honor into it."(Revelation Ch.21v24) The nations refers to the Gentile nations and emphasizes the fact that although the church has Jewish roots and it was through Israel that the gospel came to the Gentiles, yet from every kindred, tongue, tribe and nation, men and women will be saved. They will walk in the light of the city which is the Lamb. We are not of course thinking here of a literal light, but of the light of life that the Lamb gives to all His people. There will be no more spiritual darkness and everyone will walk in the perfect light of God. John talks about walking in the light in his first epistle. Walking in the light is walking in love and obedience to God. Paul indicates that many things will vanish away in eternity, but faith hope and love will abide, and so they will as the bride lives forever with the Lamb in perfect harmony. As the city is the bride, that the kings of the earth will bring their glory and honor into it is stating the obvious. The city, the bride, will be filled with glory and honor, as we have seen those that make up the city are those who have been glorified and honored and rewarded by God for their faithfulness to Him on earth. They are the kings of the new earth who will reign with God and the Lamb forever.(Revelation Ch.22v5) The beauty and glory and brilliance of the city comes from the glory of God and the Lamb being reflected through the beauty of the gold and precious stones that God has made his people to be. Daniel describes the saved in similar terms when he wrote, "And many of those who sleep in the dust of the earth shall awake, some to everlasting life, some to shame and everlasting contempt. Those who are wise shall shine like the brightness of the firmament, and those who turn many to righteousness like the stars forever and ever."(Daniel Ch.12v2-3) The prophet Malachi writes in a similar vein in Ch.3v16-17, "Then those who feared the Lord spoke to one another, and the Lord listened and heard them; So a book of remembrance was written before Him for those who fear the Lord and who meditate on His name. "They shall be Mine," says the Lord of hosts, "On the day that I make them my jewels. And I will spare them as a man spares his own son who serves him" Then you shall again discern between the righteous and the wicked." The word translated jewels means special treasure, and on that day when the Lamb marries the bride of His choice, she will be His special treasure and will be as beautiful as John sees the New Jerusalem to be.

The gates of the city are never shut, because there is no night there, John says in v25. This speaks to us of the perfect freedom that the bride will enjoy as she lives forever with her Husband the Lamb. Darkness will be a thing of the past, because darkness belongs to the kingdom of Satan, so all the darkness is confined to the lake of fire. There is perfect freedom in walking in the perfect light of God. The children of God enjoy only a measure of the freedom now that they will enjoy then. But not only does this speak of freedom, but also of the fact that there will be no need to fear attack from any enemies. The bride in eternity will be without any enemies at all, unlike the time that she spent on earth. So much of Revelation has been taken up with the story of God's people and their struggle against God's enemies and theirs. The gates of earthly cities were always shut at night in order to offer protection to those who lived in the city, but now that all things are new there are no enemies to be protected from. Not only is the bride safe from former enemies, but also from infiltration by those whose part is in the lake of fire. It will be impossible for the bride to be contaminated by any one who would defile her. This has always been a problem for the church on earth as the messages to the churches in Asia make clear. Nothing that defiles, or causes an abomination or a lie can enter the city, and again John states the obvious when he writes that only those whose names are in the Lamb's book of Life can enter and be part of the bride.

The angel further shows John a river that is absolutely pure, flowing with the water of life. It is clear as crystal and it flows from the throne of God and of the Lamb. This is not a literal river on the new earth, but it is the eternal life that flows from the throne of God. The new earth will be full of God's life that will flow on and on forever. It is life at its absolute eternal best, there is nothing in it that is in anyway impure or unholy, and it is clear as crystal. We will not need to drink any kind of physical water on God's new earth, we will all be living in immortal bodies that have no need of food or drink. This life is already in every child of God, it is the water that Jesus promised to the Samaritan woman that He met at Jacob's well, that would be in those who believed on Him. Jesus said it would spring up unto eternal life. (John Ch.6) But on the new earth as the bride of the Lamb, we shall enjoy the life of God without any restrictions or the limitations of mortal bodies that still have a sinful nature.

On the new earth there is the tree of life. As John saw it the tree was in the middle of the street of the city and on either side of the river. The tree of life has always held out the possibility that whoever ate of it would live forever. There is mystery surrounding the tree of life in the garden of Eden, but we read in Genesis Ch.3v22, Then the Lord God said, "Behold the man has become like one of Us, to know good and evil. And now, lest he put out his hand and take also of the tree of life, and eat, and live forever" The tree of life for all who have believed on the Lord Jesus Christ, is Jesus Himself. Jesus said, "I am the way, the truth and the life," John wrote in his first epistle Ch.5v11-12, "And this is the testimony; that God has given us eternal life, and this life is in His Son. He who has the Son has life; he who does not have the Son of God does not have life." It is obvious that a literal river, street and tree are not in view here, but that what the picture that John saw is portraying to us is the truth that is stated again and again, that Jesus the life of the church is in the midst of the city in every way. He is the life at the very centre of the city and is all encompassing. There is a suggestion from some Bible commentators that the leaves being for the healing of the nations, is expressing the thought that the leaves are health giving. From this we could conclude that there will be no sickness or disease in the bride, and this is the truth that is being conveyed. The life of Christ is expressed in many and varied ways, as John sees that the tree of life bears twelve different fruits, on a monthly basis. Again it is easy to see that these are not literal fruits, because in eternity there is no time. But the bride will enjoy throughout eternity the endless pleasures of the life that she finds in her husband, the Lamb.

John then goes on to say that there will be no more curse. God cursed the earth, man and the serpent along with the rest of creation, because of Adam's sin, but now on the new earth there is no more curse. How could there be? The One who sits on the throne has made ALL THINGS NEW! Instead of death there is an endless flow of life from the throne of God. Instead of endless hard labor and sorrow there are endless pleasures at Gods right hand. Instead of sickness and disease there is immortality and life, with no possibility of pain and decay in the new bodies that the redeemed have. The throne of God and of the Lamb will be in the city, and His servants shall serve Him. At the beginning of Ch.21 John records that he heard a voice from heaven saying that the tabernacle of God is with men and He will live with them, and now we have it restated.

At the end of Revelation Ch.7 John is given a preview of how things will be for the servants of God on the new earth. In v15 John says that God will live with His people and that they will serve him. We are not given any details as to what this service will involve, but it does indicate the relationship between the church and her heavenly Father. Although God has now made His home on the new earth with His people, and they are in Christ Jesus and Jesus is in them being perfectly joined as husband and wife, yet there is a clear distinction in status between the men that God is living with and Himself. As well as being the beautiful bride, the bride is His servant. But one thing I am sure of is that although our service to God on this present earth is so inadequate and imperfect, yet then it will be entirely pleasing to God and totally satisfying to us who will be there.

The bride will see the face of the bridegroom. Not only do we not see Jesus physically now, but also we have such an imperfect understanding of who He is. The Holy Spirit has come to reveal Jesus to us and there is nothing imperfect in the work of the Holy Spirit, but our ability to see and perceive the things the Holy Spirit wants to reveal is very limited. As Paul wrote in 1Corinthians Ch13v12, "For now we see in a mirror, dimly, but then face to face. Now I know in part, but then I shall know just as I also am known." There will also not only be a full recognition of who Jesus is, but there will also be a full understanding of those things that out limited intellect and insight could not grasp here and now. When we see the face of Jesus He will communicate to us the things that are now hidden from our view, as we shall talk face to face. Husbands and wives on earth share intimate secrets, and open up their minds and thoughts to each other, when we see Jesus face to face, things that have been mysteries and things that we have not been able to reconcile in our minds now, will become plain. So let us not burden ourselves now with things that cannot become plain until we see Him face to face.

Those who are His servants and His bride will have His name on their foreheads. This was one of the things that was promised to those who overcome, and it denotes the fact that we belong to the Lord. Just as those who worshipped the beast had the number of his name on their foreheads or hands to show their allegiance, so the wife of the Lamb bears his name. This really means that she bears His nature, for the names of the Lord reveal who He is. This is true for all of God's children now as Peter makes clear in 2Peter Ch.1v4, "By which have been given to us exceeding great and precious promises, that through these you may become partakers of the divine nature, having escaped the corruption that is in the world through lust." The divine nature within the children of God at the moment is in conflict with the sinful nature in our mortal bodies. But then in eternity, seeing the Lamb of God face to face, the divine nature will have its full and perfect expression in us. We will be able to bear His name without any imperfection or sin.

Once again John records that there will be no night there. I believe the new earth will be surrounded by supernatural light, for God will be everywhere on the new earth and where the immediate presence of God is there is glory and light. But the predominant thought is that there will be no sin, or evil, nothing that could possibly spoil what we have normally called heaven. Actually heaven for the children of

God will be the new earth in which only righteousness dwells and God and the Lamb live with their people forever.

John concluded with, and they shall reign forever and ever. All through the scriptures there are references to the kingdom of God that shall never pass away. Daniel saw the rock that struck the kingdoms of the earth and demolished them completely and they were blown away like chaff. But then the stone became a mountain that filled the whole earth, which represented the kingdom of God that would never end. That kingdom is coming and will not delay. God has His timetable that is already set in stone and if you are not part of His kingdom in this life, you can never become part of it at all. Those who are part of His kingdom will reign with Him forever, those who are not will be in torment with the devil and his angels forever and ever.

CHAPTER 28

"BEHOLD I AM COMING QUICKLY

We have now come to the section in the book of Revelation that could be called the summing up of all that John has seen and heard. Like a great orchestral piece of music that clearly defines in the opening stanzas the tunes that will be the main themes of the different movements and then ends with a great finale bringing together all the musical themes, so this revelation of Jesus Christ laid out in the opening chapter the main themes of the book and now at the end reiterates them to complete the work. These final verses of Ch.22 are indeed a fitting end to such a great drama.

The angel that has been talking to John now says to him, "These words are faithful and true."(Revelation Ch22v6) This book is not a concoction of visions borrowed from other writings, nor the ramblings of an old man who is in exile on the island of Patmos who is loosing his mind. These words are the Words of God, and they came to John as a revelation while he was in the Spirit on the Lord's Day. They accord with all the other scriptures, as I have done my best to show, by quoting frequently from both the Old and New Testaments. The God of the prophets, who prophesied of these things in the Old Testament, had sent His angel to show the servants of God in John's day the things that must shortly take place. The same God who spoke to Isaiah, Jeremiah, Ezekiel and Daniel is the God that has spoken to John also. The things that John has seen will begin to unfold in his day and continue to unfold, until the bride is safely in eternity with God and the Lamb. God wants the church to know these things because they all concern the church. Jesus said to the disciples that they were not only servants but friends, and as friends they would know what He was doing. No other book in the New Testament reveals so much of what Jesus is doing as this book does.

Then Jesus Himself speaks saying, "BEHOLD, I AM COMING QUICKLY! BLESSED IS HE WHO KEEPS THE WORDS OF THE PROPHECY OF THIS BOOK"(Revelation Ch.22v7) Jesus Himself is authenticating the words of the prophecy of this book. Blessing from the Lord Himself will come to all who treasure this book. Look carefully and steadfastly for my coming and be alert for I am coming quickly, I am coming suddenly and all those who are children of the night will be caught out. My desire in writing this book, whether or not you agree with how I have interpreted it, is that you will be blessed by reading, studying and keeping in your heart the words of this testimony of Jesus Christ. For the time is always at hand for the return of the Lord, in the respect that He has always wanted His people to be looking for Him to come.

John emphasizes that he saw and heard all these things. Not only are these words faithful and true and words that bring blessing from the Lord, but the testimony of the man who wrote this book is that he actually saw and heard these things. So impressed was John with all these things that he instinctively fell down to worship at the feet of the angel who was revealing them to him. I am sure that John was not intending to do anything wrong, but was just so overwhelmed by this whole experience of the revelation of Jesus and God on His throne and their ultimate victory. But his action did bring the same rebuke as it did before when he had reacted in the same way in worshiping the angel. The angel repeated that he was a fellow servant who kept the words of this book. How important this book is for the church, but sadly rather neglected.

John is writing again many of the things that he wrote in the introduction to emphasize how important this prophecy is. The angel tells John not to seal up the book, for the time is at hand. In v3 of Ch.1 he wrote that the time is near for the things in this book to come to pass. This is confirmation that it is right to interpret the events spoken about as spanning the history of the church, and not just things that are in the future. The seven churches in Asia to which this book was sent would have quite rightly and understandably understood Revelation in this way. John repeating this right at the end of the book clearly shows that all that is in between is relevant to the churches, and to the church from then till now.

The next verse, v11 seems to be rather curious, as it seams to be saying that evil and filthy men should continue in their evil way, although the next half of the verse is more understandable as it is saying that righteous and holy men should persevere in the way of holiness. I believe however that it is referring to the time when after the rapture of the church, only those who have received the mark of the beast will be on earth, and those who are left behind are without hope. There is also the suddenness of the Lord's return that will catch evil men entirely by surprise, so they may as well continue in the way they are going.

Again Jesus repeats the phrase, "Behold I am coming quickly and my reward is with me to give every one according to his work." Jesus is coming to reward His people and those who are going to be separated from Him forever. This is an echo of the verses we looked at in Ch11. v18, where the twenty four elders are saying that the time has come for the dead to be judged, these are those consigned to the lake of fire, but also for the prophets and saints to be rewarded. Jesus is coming to give to every man according to his works.

It is fitting that Jesus should also repeat the statement that He is the Alpha and Omega, the Beginning and the End, the First and the Last. He was there at the beginning of the book, He is there at the end of the book. The devil, who is Satan, that serpent of old, is no more along with the beast and false prophet. All the riders who went out at the Lamb's command are not in the picture, the demons who played their part, the nations who rebelled and fought against God are in the lake of fire, but Jesus remains forever, He is the same.

Blessed are those who are obedient to the Lamb, because they have the right to eat of the tree of life, who is Jesus, and enter the city, the bride of the Lamb. In other words those who obey the Lamb will be His bride and enter into all the goodness of eternal life that is in Jesus.

But those who practiced sorcery and sexual immorality, murder and idolatry and those who loved to lie and practiced deceit, will never be a part of the pure and holy bride that the church will be in eternity. They will be forever outside and excluded from the holy city. Once again this truth is reiterated, just in case anyone should think that there will be some kind of second or third or fourth chance to change sides after all and escape the punishment of the lake of fire. No! He who is filthy let him be filthy still, that is the Lords decree concerning those whose names are not in the book of life, and have practiced the evil things catalogued in this book.

The next verse, v16 is in my view almost the most important verse in the whole of this book, as it has coloured very strongly my interpretation of Revelation as a whole. One interpretation of the book of Revelation says that the church is not in view after the end of Ch.3, until halfway through Ch.19 when the Lord returns. This means in effect that the bulk of the book does not have any real relevance to the church, and although it is interesting to see what the rest of the book is saying, it has no bearing on the church. After all, if the church is not on the earth from the beginning of Ch.4, why should the Lord have bothered writing to the churches and the church about it at all? But Jesus specifically says, "I, Jesus have sent My angel to testify to you these things in the churches." It could not be more plain, this entire book is for the churches in Asia and the church universal because all of it concerns the church and is relevant to the church.

Jesus then says that He is the root and the offspring of David. David is the most significant king in the long line of Israel's kings. He was the king that God said was the king after His own heart. He was the king that God promised to establish his royal line forever, and this promise is fulfilled in Jesus. Jesus is great David's greater son, but also as the Son of God who is eternal with the Father and Holy Spirit, Jesus is also the root of David and his kingdom. This is the deity and humanity of Jesus expressed in terms of Him being the King of Kings and Lord of Lords, which is the great theme of this book. Jesus says that He is also the Bright and Morning Star. His coming heralds the dawning of a new day, new in every way. There have been many false dawns in the history of the world. Great men have risen up promising great things that have come to nothing. In the end the antichrist will come and set himself up as god, promising great things, speaking boastfully, but he will be defeated at the coming of the Bright and Morning Star from heaven, and the righteous will enter into the kingdom prepared for them since the foundation of the world, but the unrighteous into everlasting torment.

The climax of this book is the coming of Jesus in power and great glory to establish His eternal kingdom on the new earth. We have looked at all the wonderful changes that God is going to make, but if they were to be summarized, those wonderful new things could all be said to be in the eternal life that is in Jesus the Lamb. Those who believe on the Lord Jesus Christ do not have to wait until the new heavens and earth to begin to experience eternal life, but can enter into that life here and now. So John writes that the Spirit and the bride say, "Come!" and let all those who hear the message of this book say, "Come!" In fact let everyone who is thirsty for God, for the eternal life found only in Jesus, let them come and drink of the water of life freely. "For God so loved the world that He gave His only begotten Son, that whoever believes in Him should not perish but have everlasting life."(John Ch.3v16) "But the water that I shall give him will become in him a fountain of water springing up into everlasting life."(John Ch.4v14) "Most assuredly, I say to you, he who believes in Me has everlasting life. I am the bread of life."(John Ch.6v47&48) "If anyone thirsts, let him come to me and drink. He who believes in Me, as the Scripture has said, out of his heart will flow rivers of living water." (John Ch.7v37&38) "I am the light of the world, he who follows Me shall not walk in darkness, but have the light of life."(John Ch.8v12) "My sheep hear my voice, and I know them, and they follow Me. And I give them eternal life, and they shall never perish; neither shall anyone snatch them out of my hand."(John Ch.10v27-28) "I am the resurrection and the life. He who believes in Me, though he may die, he shall live. And whoever lives and believes in Me shall never die. Do you believe this?"(John Ch.11v25&26) "He who loves his life will lose it, and he who hates his life in this world will keep it for eternal life. If anyone serves Me, let him follow Me; and where I am, there will My servant be also. If anyone serves Me, him will My Father honor."(John Ch.12v25-26) "I am the way, the truth, and the life. No one comes to the Father except through Me."(John Ch.14v6) "As You have given Him authority over all flesh, that He should give eternal life to as many as You have given Him. And this is eternal life, that they may know You, the only true God, and Jesus Christ whom You have sent."(John Ch. 17v2-3) "But these things are written that YOU may believe that Jesus is the Christ, the Son of God, and that believing you may have life in His name."(John Ch.20v31) These are a selection of verses from John's gospel, from which it is plain to see that eternal life, the life that is in Jesus, is a constant theme throughout the book. It is one of John's favorite themes. In his first epistle John writes in Ch.5v13, "These things I have written to you who believe in the name of the Son of God, that you may know that you have eternal life, and that you may continue to believe in the name of the Son of God." So here right at the end of this wonderful revelation of Jesus Christ John writes, COME and drink of the water of life FREELY. This water of life is only found in Jesus so if you are thirsty for life as God intended you to have it, COME TO JESUS before it is too late. Jesus is coming quickly so treasure the words of this book and obey His commandments.

There follows a stern warning that if anyone adds to the things that have been written God will add to him the plagues that are written in this book. The church has always had to beware of adding to the scriptures, and still needs to be. The Roman Catholic Church has down through the centuries added to the scriptures their own traditions, most of which are in conflict with the scriptures. There are some cults and religions in the world that have taken some scripture and some of their own ideas and formulated their own set of beliefs. But beware for God will bring all such into judgment, and they will be severely punished for their sin, for they have led millions of people astray from the truth as it is in the scriptures. A similar punishment awaits those who take away from the words of the prophecy of this book. Error comes just as much from deletion as it does from addition. There have been many down through the time since the scriptures were compiled that have rejected the things in the scriptures that they found inconvenient or unpleasant to them. Many have deleted the lake of fire from their theology because they have a mixed up view of the love of God. Some have also deleted the actual physical return of Jesus Christ from their faith. In the light of all the Old and New Testament scriptures that speak of this event, this deletion by some is reprehensible. Their part in the book of life will be taken away, for God will not have His word tampered with for it is settled in heaven it is set in stone.

John who is testifying to the things that he has seen and heard records once again for us to hear loud and clear, "Surely I am coming quickly." If you have not got the message yet through the study of this book, you are either ignoring it or refuse to believe it. In the special messages to each of the churches in Asia, there is something promised to those who overcome, and every one of those promises relates to the time after which Jesus has come for His church. This is a message that Jesus wants the churches and the church today to grasp, I am coming quickly and my reward is with me. I am coming as King to reign and My kingdom will not pass away. From John there is a loud AMEN, EVEN SO COME LORD JESUS! Let that sentiment also echo in our hearts, come Lord Jesus.

John ends this revelation of Jesus Christ with the benediction that is so treasured by the Lord's people for they know that they owe all that they have and all that they are to the grace of the Lord Jesus Christ. "The grace of our Lord Jesus Christ be with you all. Amen."(Revelation Ch.22v21) For to the church in Ephesus that had left the primary love, the agape love of God, to the church in Smyna that would endure tribulation ten days, they would overcome by the grace of the Lord Jesus. The church at Pergamos that was infiltrated by sexually immoral and greedy people, and the church at Thyatira that was similarly contaminated with idolatry as well, would only walk in white on the new earth by the grace that flows from God and the Lamb. The church at Sardis whose works were incomplete and at Philadelphia where the saints were weak and insignificant, but were battling through and persevering, they all would drink of the crystal clear water flowing from the throne of God, because of the grace that ever flows to the people of God. The lukewarm church at Laodicea, even they by the grace of our Lord Jesus Christ would make it to stand before the throne of God and see Jesus face to face. By the grace of our Lord Jesus, all those who are God's children will stand with them, all the saints, prophets, martyrs, overcomers all, who comprise the holy city, the bride of the Lamb.

Printed in the United Kingdom
by Lightning Source UK Ltd.
115491UKS00001B/16